Sustainable Automobile Transport

ESRI STUDIES SERIES ON THE ENVIRONMENT

In April 2000 the Japanese government launched a series of comprehensive, interdisciplinary and international research projects called the 'Millennium Projects' and as part of this initiative the Economic and Social Research Institute (ESRI) of the Cabinet Office of Japan initiated a two-year project entitled 'A study on Sustainable Economic and Social Structures in the 21st Century', which focuses on ageing and environmental problems in the Japanese and international context.

The *ESRI Studies Series on the Environment* provides a forum for the publication of a limited number of books, which are the result of this international collaboration, on four main issues: research on solid waste management; the analysis of waste recycling and the conservation of resources and energy; research on the compatibility of environmental protection and macroeconomic policy and the analysis of problems related to climate change. The series is invaluable to students and scholars of environment and ecology as well as consultants and practitioners involved in environmental policymaking.

Titles in the series include:

Sustainable Automobile Transport

Shaping Climate Change Policy

Lisa Ryan

School of Geography, Planning and Environmental Policy, University College Dublin and Comhar – Sustainable Development Council, Dublin, Ireland

Hal Turton

Energy Economics Group, Paul Scherrer Institute, Switzerland and formerly at the International Institute for Applied Systems Analysis (IIASA), Austria

With contributions from Frank Convery, Asami Miketa and Leo Schrattenholzer

ESRI STUDIES SERIES ON THE ENVIRONMENT

Edward Elgar
Cheltenham, UK • Northampton, MA, USA

Published by
Edward Elgar Publishing Limited
Glensanda House
Montpellier Parade
Cheltenham
Glos GL50 1UA
UK

Edward Elgar Publishing, Inc.
William Pratt House
9 Dewey Court
Northampton
Massachusetts 01060
USA

A catalogue record for this book
is available from the British Library

Library of Congress Cataloguing in Publication Data

Ryan, L. (Lisa B.)
    Sustainable automobile transport : shaping climate change policy / by Lisa Ryan and Hal Turton.
        p. cm. — (ESRI studies series on the environment)
    Includes bibliographical references and index.
    1. Transportation, Automotive—Environmental aspects. 2. Automobiles—Environmental aspects. 3. Transportation—Passenger traffic.
I. Turton, Hal. II. Title
    HE5611.R93 2007
    629.2′31—dc22

2007011642

ISBN 978 1 84720 451 6

Printed and bound in Great Britain by MPG Books Ltd, Bodmin, Cornwall

Contents

Abbreviations

ACEA	Association des Constructeurs Européens d'Automobiles (European Automobile Manufacturers Association)
ACT	annual motor or circulation tax
AEEI	autonomous energy efficiency improvement
AFC	alcohol fuel cell vehicle
AFR	Sub-Saharan Africa
AFV	advanced fuel and vehicle
AIAMC	Association of International Automobile Manufacturers of Canada
am	ante meridiem
AT–PZEV(s)	advanced technology – partial zero emission vehicle(s)
ATR	auto-thermal reformer
avg.	average
BMW	Bayerische Motoren Werke AG
C	carbon
CAFC	company average fuel consumption
CAFE	Corporate Average Fuel Economy
CARB	California Air Resources Board
CCAP	Climate Change Action Plan (USA)
CCGT	combined cycle gas turbine
CCS	carbon capture and storage
CCTI	Climate Change Technology Initiative (USA)
CDM	Clean Development Mechanism
CD-ROM	compact disc – read only memory
C-e	carbon-equivalent
CEV	clean energy vehicle
CH_4	methane
CHP	combined heat and power
CIVITAS	EU project CIVITAS – cleaner and better transport in cities – stands for CIty-VITAlity-Sustainability
CNG	compressed natural gas
CO	carbon monoxide
CO_2	carbon dioxide
CPA	Centrally Planned Asia, including China

CVMA	Canadian Vehicle Manufacturers' Association
CVT	continuously variable transmission
DOE	Department of Energy (USA)
DRA-forestation	deforestation, reforestation and afforestation
DVD	digital video disk
E3	energy–economy–environment
ECS	Environmentally Compatible Energy Strategies Program (IIASA)
ECTOS	Icelandic New Energy organisation and EU project
EEU	Central and Eastern Europe
EITs	economies in transition
EPA	Environmental Protection Agency (USA)
ERC(s)	early reduction credit(s)
ERIS	Energy Research and Investment Strategy model
ERP	electronic road pricing
ETBE	ethyl-*tert*-butyl-ether
ETS	emissions trading scheme
ETSAP	Energy Technology Systems Analysis Programme
EU	European Union
EU ETS	European Union Emissions Trading Scheme
EU15	European Union 15
EU25	European Union 25
EV(s)	electric vehicle(s)
FC	fuel cell
FCV(s)	fuel-cell vehicle(s)
FSU	Former Soviet Union
FT	Fischer–Tropsch
g	gram
GBP	Great Britain pounds
GDP	gross domestic product
GHG(s)	greenhouse gas(es)
GIMVEC	Government Industry Motor Vehicle Energy Committee (Canada)
GPS	global positioning system
H_2	hydrogen (molecular)
HC	hydrocarbon
HCCI	homogeneous charged compression ignition
HEV(s)	hybrid-electric vehicle(s)
HFC	H_2 fuel cell vehicle
IAH	alcohol hybrid electric-ICE vehicle
IAT	Clinton Administration's Interagency Analytic Team (USA)

ICA	alcohol ICE vehicle
ICAO	International Civil Aviation Organisation
ICC	petroleum ICE vehicle
ICE	internal combustion engine
ICEV(s)	internal combustion engine vehicle(s)
ICG	natural gas ICE vehicle
ICH	petroleum hybrid electric-ICE vehicle
IEA	International Energy Agency
IGH	natural gas hybrid electric-ICE vehicle
IHH	H_2 hybrid electric-ICE vehicle
IIASA	International Institute for Applied Systems Analysis
I–O	input–output
IPAT	Impact = Population x Affluence x Technology
IPCC	Intergovernmental Panel on Climate Change
ISO	International Organization for Standardization
J	joule
JAF	Japan Automobile Federation
JAMA	Japan Automobile Manufacturers Association
JI	Joint Implementation
J-VETS	Japan Voluntary Emissions Trading Scheme
KAMA	Korean Automobile Manufacturers Association
l (and L)	litre
LAM	Latin America and the Caribbean
LDT1/LDT2	light duty trucks classified in the US as LDT1 if gross vehicle weight registered (GVWR) is less than 3750lb and as LDT2 if GVWR is less than 6000lb.
LEV(s)	low-emission vehicle(s)
LNG	liquid natural gas
LPG	liquid petroleum gas
m	metre
M85	methanol:gasoline 85:15 mix
MARKAL	MARKet ALlocation Model
MEA	Middle East and North Africa
MEPS	Minimum Energy Performance Standard
MOU	memorandum of understanding
mpg	miles per gallon
MTBE	methyl-*tert*-butyl-ether
N_2O	nitrous oxide
NACE	National Average CO_2 Emissions (Australia)
NAM	North America
NEA(s)	negotiated environmental agreement(s)

NEDO	New Agency and Industrial Technology Development Organisation (Japan)
NGO(s)	non-governmental organization(s)
NHTSA	National Highway Traffic Safety Administration (USA)
NO_x	oxides of nitrogen
NRC	National Academies' National Research Council (USA)
NRCan	Natural Resources Canada
OECD	Organisation for Economic Cooperation and Development
p.a.	per annum
PAO	Pacific OECD
PAS	Other Pacific Asia
PATH	Partnership for Advancing Technology in Housing – US programme
PAYD	pay-as-you-drive
PC	passenger car
PCAs	Pollution Control Agreements (Japan)
PEM	polymer electrolyte membrane
PFC	petroleum fuel cell vehicle
p-km (and pkm)	passenger-kilometres
PM	particulate matter
pm	post meridiem
PMV(s)	passenger motor vehicle(s)
PNR	private non residential
pop	population
ppmv	parts per million volume
PPP	purchasing power parity
PZEV(s)	partial zero emission vehicle(s)
R&D	research and development
R/P	reserves-to-production ratio
RD&D	research, development and demonstration
RE	renewable energy
ROW	rest of the world
SAS	South Asia
SO_2	sulphur dioxide
SR	steam reformer
SRES	IPCC's Special Report on Emissions Scenarios
SUV(s)	sports-utility vehicle(s)
t	metric tonne
TDM	transport demand management

TERM	transport and environment reporting mechanism (EU)
TTW	tank-to-wheels
UK	United Kingdom of Great Britain and Northern Ireland
UNFCCC	United Nations Framework Convention on Climate Change
US (and USA)	United States of America
VA(s)	voluntary approach(es)
VAT	value added tax
W	watt
WEC	World Energy Council
WEU	Western Europe and Turkey
Wh	watt-hour
WTT	well-to-tank
WTW	well-to-wheels
ZEV(s)	zero emission vehicle(s)

The following prefixes are used with m, t, g, l (and L), J, W and Wh to indicate different orders of magnitude:

c	centi-	10^{-2}
k	kilo-	10^{3}
M	mega-	10^{6}
G	giga-	10^{9}
T	tera-	10^{12}
P	peta-	10^{15}
E	exa-	10^{18}
Z	zeta-	10^{21}

Foreword

The growth in global greenhouse gas emissions and the ensuing climate change have become amongst the most pressing of global environmental problems. The key overarching challenge is how to address this problem successfully and maintain competitiveness; that is, how to integrate environment and economy so as to achieve sustainability and a vibrant economy. The Economic and Social Research Institute of the Cabinet Office, Government of Japan, has engaged in a rolling series of International Collaboration projects, with the objective of bringing together some of the best thinking and research internationally and nationally to inform the choices which Japan faces in this area. Some of the key insights and findings are being published by Edward Elgar in a series of books.

Road transport represents a fast-growing source of greenhouse gas emissions and changing this emissions trajectory is proving difficult. This comprises both a threat and an opportunity. For those in the industry who succeed in developing commercially viable cars that are attractive to consumers and reduced emissions of greenhouse gases, there are great market-expanding opportunities. For those who fail to meet this challenge, market opportunities are likely to shrink, as the world becomes increasingly carbon-constrained. Therefore, I welcome this book, which is the product of the research undertaken as part of the International Collaboration projects. It attempts to provide technology and policy-based solutions to the mitigation of greenhouse gas emissions from passenger cars. The book looks forward and not only presents the technologies in the automobile sector that will be necessary to make automobile transport sustainable, but also discusses an array of policies that can achieve this objective. As such, I hope and expect that it will help improve the quality of the debate as we consider how to move forward in this area, one which is of particular interest for Japan.

Masahiro Kuroda, President
Economic and Social Research Institute,
Cabinet Office, Government of Japan

Acknowledgements

This book is the result of work that was begun as one of the international Collaboration projects by the Japanese Economic and Social Research Institute (ESRI), Cabinet Office, Government of Japan in 2003–2004, entitled 'Sustainable Economic Growth and the Challenges of Global Warming'. We would like to thank the staff of the Economic and Social Research Institute for their support throughout the project and especially for their assistance at the meetings in Tokyo. We are particularly grateful to Koichi Hamada and Hiromi Kato of ESRI for initiating this project and providing this opportunity to work with Japanese researchers on such an important and global topic. We are grateful for the continued support of ESRI by successive presidents. We would also like to thank the Mitsubishi Research Institute and Nomura Research Institute for coordinating the project so efficiently.

Many thanks to Leonardo Barreto from the Paul Scherrer Institute (Switzerland) for collaborating on earlier developments with the ERIS model. We would also like to thank Professor Andreas Schafer, from the Department of Architecture of the Cambridge University (UK), for permitting use of his passenger transportation demand model, and to Maria Argiri from the International Energy Agency (IEA) and Keywan Riahi from IIASA for their generous help in providing relevant data.

L.R.
H.T.

1. Introduction

The concept of sustainable development has evolved into a guiding principle for a liveable future world in which human needs are met without compromising the ability of future generations to meet their own needs (UN, 1987). One of the implications of the pursuit of sustainable development is that the natural systems that support present and future needs must be maintained. However, addressing the challenge of sustainability encompasses other social, economic and environmental dimensions, and requires a long-term systematic perspective and the integration of many different elements. Energy and transport are two such elements, and directing the global energy system and transport systems onto a sustainable path is becoming an increasingly important concern and policy objective (Schrattenholzer et al., 2004; IEA, 2001; Riahi et al., 2001; Barreto et al., 2003).

Among other factors, climate change constitutes one of the most serious threats to achieving the goals of sustainable development, and for energy sustainability in the long term. There is mounting evidence of human interference with the Earth's climate system and increasing concern about possible serious adverse impacts resulting from future global climate change (IPCC, 2001a). Realizing sustainable energy and transport systems with a low impact on the global climate, but that still achieve other long-term development goals, such as poverty alleviation and maintaining a secure energy supply, may require profound and wide-reaching changes.

The objective of this book is to analyse these changes in terms of the potential to establish a sustainable global transport system as part of the realization of a sustainable global energy system. Envisioning and understanding how long-term future global energy and transport systems can meet increasingly stringent requirements in a sustainable way is an important element for designing policy responses that will promote the transition towards a future in which economic development, energy security and climate change mitigation are simultaneously realized. However, there are significant social, economic, environmental, technological and political uncertainties that may influence energy system development, meaning that many alternative sustainable energy pathways may emerge.

Accordingly, we examine the technologies and energy carriers that could play a role in these pathways to sustainable development, including their potential, market opportunities and the barriers they could face as well as the conditions and policy actions necessary for their successful diffusion (Williams et al., 2000). Since the evolution of transport and energy systems is slow and may span decades or sometimes even centuries, the emergence of a sustainable global energy and transport system is likely to be a gradual long-term process requiring profound transformations from the current infrastructure to new systems and structures. This highlights the need to take a very long-term perspective both in terms of studying the potential to realize a sustainable transport system and also when formulating policy responses aimed at securing the benefits of sustainable development.

In this book we seek to take such a long-term perspective and investigate how a possible transition to a transport and energy system compatible with the broader goals of sustainable development could unfold, with the aim of identifying potential technology targets for government policy support and intervention. Importantly, energy and transport systems are faced with unique and substantial challenges in realizing the goals of sustainable development, particularly in terms of avoiding serious consequences of climate change and reducing greenhouse gas emissions. The enormity of this challenge is best illustrated by looking at historical and current trends.

1.1   CLIMATE CHANGE AND SUSTAINABLE DEVELOPMENT

Emissions of greenhouse gases from human activities are leading to changes in the composition of the global atmosphere. This is illustrated in Figure 1.1 for emissions of carbon dioxide (CO_2) – one of the most important greenhouse gases – from combustion of fossil fuels,[1] which have been increasing almost continuously since the industrial revolution. The changes in atmospheric composition from these and other emissions are already leading to changes in climate (IPCC, 2001a) and, depending on future emissions and other uncertain factors, may result in significant changes to global climate (for an illustration of the range of possible impacts on temperature, see Figure 1.2). This is likely to result in a range of impacts on many physical, biological and ultimately human systems, including agricultural productivity, health, biodiversity, precipitation, and flood risk, to name but a few (see IPCC, 2001a, for a more comprehensive description of possible impacts). The impact of climate change on these systems will be wide-scale, long-term and in many cases irreversible, with the possibility of very dramatic and unpredictable changes (ibid.). Anthropogenic climate change affects many of the systems upon which human welfare depends and this represents one of the most serious challenges to achieving sustainable development.

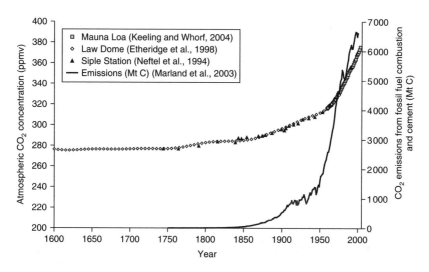

Figure 1.1   Historical atmospheric CO₂ concentrations and emissions from fossil fuel combustion

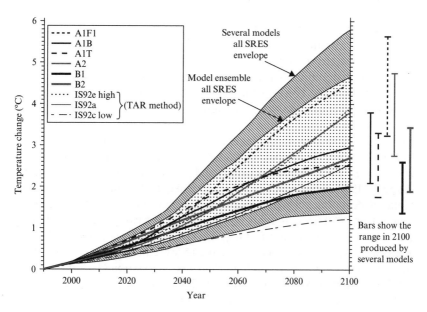

Source: IPCC (2001a).

Figure 1.2   Range of future temperature scenarios from IPCC, relative to 1990

The historical increase in emissions of greenhouse gases (GHGs) is the result of a number of demographic, economic, technological, resource and policy driving forces. This can be understood by decomposing emissions into some of the key variables representing these forces, based on the IPAT identity (where Impact = Population × Affluence × Technology) (Ehrlich and Holdren, 1971). For instance, carbon dioxide (CO_2) emissions from energy use can be represented by the following decomposition formula:

$$CO_2 = Pop \cdot \frac{GDP}{Pop} \cdot \frac{Energy}{GDP} \cdot \frac{CO_2}{Energy}. \qquad (1.1)$$

Here, the impact on CO_2 emissions is a function of population (*Pop*), per capita incomes (or affluence) (*GDP/Pop*), and two factors representing technology: the amount of energy required to produce a unit of GDP (*Energy/GDP*), which depends on economic structure and end-use and con- version technologies, and the carbon intensity of the energy source (*CO_2/Energy*), which depends largely on energy production technology and fuel choice. All other things being equal, an increase in population or affluence will lead to an increase in emissions. Of course, the relationship presented in the decomposition equation is highly aggregated and one needs to remember that changes in consumption and production structure are likely to accompany changes in incomes (Hamilton and Turton, 2002), among others. However, it provides a useful guide to the core driving forces. One additional and critical driving force is policy, which influences all of the elements in the IPAT formula. Accordingly, policy can play a poten- tially major role in curtailing greenhouse gas emissions.

Looking at historical data, it is clear that the growth in greenhouse gas emissions has usually accompanied economic development and expansion (that is, the combined impact of population and per capita income growth), and Figure 1.3 shows how emissions and global GDP have developed since the early 1970s. However, Figure 1.3 also partly illustrates a slow 'decou- pling' of economic growth and greenhouse gas emissions, with the global economy in 2000 being roughly 35–40 per cent less carbon-intensive than in the early 1970s, largely as a result of technological development and a shift from emissions-intensive manufacturing to less emissions-intensive services (that is, changes in the technology elements in equation (1.1) above). This development offers some hope for achieving the goals of sustainability, and highlights the potentially important role of technology. Nevertheless, Figure 1.3 also implies that a continuation of historical trends alone is unlikely to be compatible with realizing the goals of sustainable development.

Figure 1.3 partly shows how developed countries (OECD[2] and economies in transition (EITs)) have historically been responsible for most emissions of

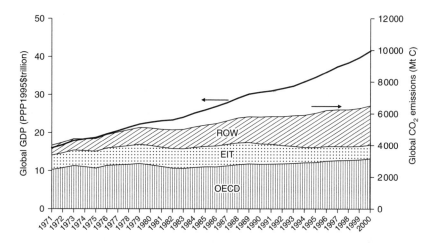

Source: IEA, 2003a; IEA, 2003b; IEA, 2003c; IEA, 2003d.

Figure 1.3   Global CO$_2$ emissions from energy, 1971–2000

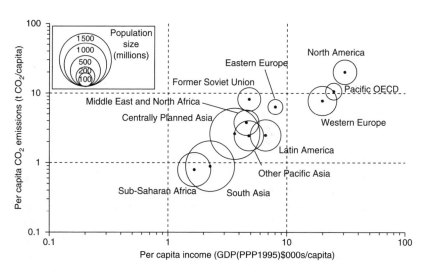

Source: IEA, 2003a; IEA, 2003b; IEA, 2003c; IEA, 2003d; UN, 2004.

Figure 1.4   Per capita emissions, per capita income and population, 2000

CO_2, and developing regions (ROW) are only just now beginning to achieve comparable aggregate emissions (while their per capita emissions remain much lower). Looking more closely at the contribution of different world regions, Figure 1.4 plots regional per capita income against per capita CO_2 emissions from fossil fuel combustion for 11 major world regions. The relative population of each world region is represented in Figure 1.4 by the area of the circle surrounding each data point. On this regional level there is a relatively strong correlation between per capita income and per capita emissions (as predicted by the IPAT identity), although some regions are slightly more or less carbon-intensive. On the other hand, population and greenhouse gas emissions are relatively unrelated, and around 15 per cent of the world's population is responsible for almost half of global emissions. One of the most significant challenges facing the global energy system and climate is the potential impact on energy use and greenhouse gas emissions of economic development in developing countries, and the economically and socially desirable goal that they achieve levels of prosperity similar to those existing in developed countries today.

To better appreciate which activities are responsible for global emissions of CO_2, the principal GHG, and may pose the greatest threat to sustainability, Figure 1.5 shows global emissions according to the broad sector directly responsible for those emissions for the 30 years ending in 2000. The direct emissions from manufacturing, services and the residential sector have been roughly steady for 30 years, and most of the growth is apparently from electricity generation. This reflects the fact that the end-use sectors have shifted away from direct fuel combustion to greater use of electricity, because it is a flexible, convenient and clean fuel for the end user.[3] The other source of emissions that is growing rapidly is transport, and in the last 30 years this sector accounted for almost all of the growth in energy emissions outside the electricity sector. Increasing emissions from road transport have driven much of this growth, and this mode accounted for close to 18 per cent of global CO_2 emissions from fossil fuel combustion in 2000, up from around 12 per cent in the early 1970s. Figure 1.5 shows that total annual CO_2 emissions from road transport increased from roughly 475 million tonnes of carbon (Mt C) in 1971 to almost 1130 Mt C in 2000. A continuation of these trends in emissions implies that transport, in particular road transport and private automobile use, may become one of the most substantial sources of greenhouse gas emissions in the future. This represents a potential challenge to long-term sustainable development, and identifies transport as an increasingly important target for mitigation policy intervention and technology deployment.

In the last 30 years over half of the growth in global road transport emissions occurred in OECD countries, and emissions originating from this

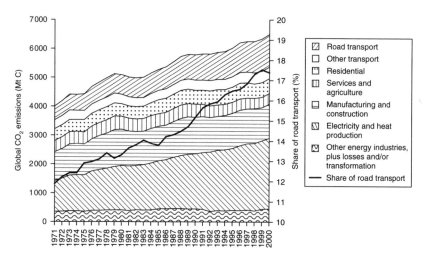

Source: IEA, 2003a; IEA, 2003b; IEA, 2003c; IEA, 2003d.

Figure 1.5   Global carbon emissions from fossil fuel combustion (1971–2000)

region represent an important existing threat to sustainable development. However, emissions from road transport have been growing much faster in many developing regions, as illustrated in Table 1.1, which shows that growth in non-OECD Asia outpaced that in the rest of the world, although even after three decades of rapid growth this region was still responsible for only 13.8 per cent of global emissions from road transport in 2000. These growth trends have important implications for medium- to long-term greenhouse gas emission abatement, and imply that the biggest future threats from transport to the goals of sustainable development are likely to emerge in today's developing regions. Accordingly, realizing sustainable transport systems is a challenge confronting policy makers throughout the world.

1.2   RECENT TRENDS AND THE CURRENT STATE OF GLOBAL TRANSPORT ENERGY DEMAND

To assess the threats to sustainable development from future growth in greenhouse gas emissions from transport, it is necessary to identify the activities responsible for emissions in the transport sector. The latter is relatively straightforward, because almost all of the emissions from transport are

Sustainable automobile transport

Table 1.1   *Road transport CO_2 emissions, historical regional shares and growth rates*

	Annual growth in emissions			Share of emissions				Share of global population
	1971–1980 (%)	1980–1990 (%)	1990–2000 (%)	1971 (%)	1980 (%)	1990 (%)	2000 (%)	2000 (%)
OECD	2.9	2.0	2.1	78.9	71.7	67.3	64.6	15.3
Economies in transition	5.8	2.8	−2.4	7.5	8.8	8.9	5.4	6.8
Asia (non-OECD)	10.4	8.0	7.1	3.1	5.4	8.9	13.8	53.5
Africa and Middle East	10.4	3.4	3.8	3.5	6.0	6.5	7.3	16.0
Latin America	5.9	2.8	3.3	6.9	8.1	8.3	8.8	8.5
World total	4.0	2.6	2.6	100.0	100.0	100.0	100.0	100.0

Source: IEA, 2003a; IEA, 2003b; IEA, 2003c; IEA, 2003d.

produced from the combustion of fossil fuels. Accordingly, the emission growth presented in Table 1.1 has been accompanied by a corresponding increase in transport energy use, which is illustrated in Figure 1.6. Figure 1.6 shows that road and air transport energy demand more than doubled between the early 1970s and 2000, consistent with the emissions growth shown in Table 1.1, whereas the combined energy use of rail, marine, pipeline and other transport barely changed (IEA, 2003a; IEA, 2003b). Private automobile travel volume during the same period increased to over 2.5 times the level in the early 1970s (based on Schafer and Victor, 2000; Schafer, 2003).

By 2000, global final consumption of energy in the transportation sector had risen to just above 80 exajoules (EJ, 10^{18} joules), accounting for approximately 28 per cent of global final-energy consumption. Figure 1.7 illustrates regional differences in per capita transport energy demand, which is highest in developed regions such as North America (NAM), Western Europe (WEU) and the Pacific OECD (PAO). On the other hand, it is much lower in the least developed regions, including Centrally Planned Asia (CPA), South Asia (SAS) and Sub-Saharan Africa (AFR). This is important to bear in mind when exploring the possible impact of future economic development on transport activity and greenhouse gas emissions. Figure 1.7 also shows transport's share of final-energy demand in different world

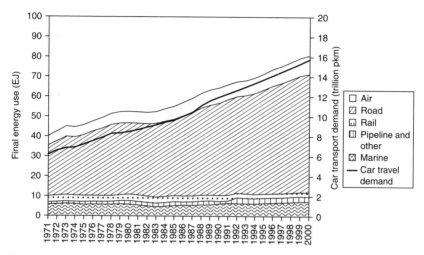

Source: IEA, 2003a; IEA, 2003b; Schafer, 1995; Schafer, 1998; Schafer and Victor, 2000.

Figure 1.6 Historical energy use in transport and car travel demand, 1971–2000

regions, which ranges between roughly 11 and 38 per cent, although it should be recognized that this share is an indicator, of not only the importance of the transport sector in a given region, but also the size and energy intensity of other sectors, particularly manufacturing.[4] Variation is also explained by regional geographic and infrastructure features, such as the organization of human settlements.

Of the 80 EJ of energy used by transport globally in 2000, almost 96 per cent comprised petroleum products, such as motor gasoline, diesel oil, kerosene jet fuel and so on, with the remaining fuel supplied by gas, biofuels (mainly ethanol), electricity and a small amount of coal (see Figure 1.8). Globally, the transportation sector consumed 60 per cent of all the petroleum products used by end-use sectors,[5] and road vehicles accounted for 77 per cent of this petroleum consumption in 2000. Figure 1.8 shows that the remaining 23 per cent is divided mainly between air transport (12 per cent), mostly jet kerosene, and marine transport (10 per cent), primarily heavy diesel oil. Most of the small remainder is heavy diesel oil used in rail transport.

In developed regions, private automobile travel is estimated to account for around two-thirds of total road transport energy use (based on Landwehr and Marie-Lilliu, 2002; FHA, 1996; Davis and Diegel, 2004; IRF, 2000; EIA, 1999). Importantly, demand for private automobile travel is growing faster than total road transport energy demand, which itself

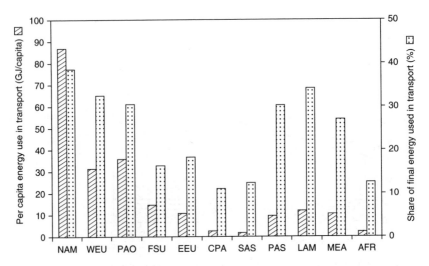

Notes: NAM: North America, WEU: Western Europe and Turkey, PAO: Pacific OECD,
FSU: Former Soviet Union, EEU: Eastern and Central Europe, CPA: Centrally Planned
Asia, SAS: South Asia, PAS: Pacific and Other Asia, LAM: Latin America, MEA: Middle
East and North Africa, AFR: Sub-Saharan Africa.

Source: IEA, 2003a; IEA, 2003b.

Figure 1.7   *Per capita energy consumption in the transportation sector in
each world region, and percentage share of total final energy
used in transportation, 2000*

accounted for most of the historical increase in energy demand (and greenhouse gas emissions) from transport as a whole (see Figure 1.8).
Accordingly, we pay special attention to passenger road vehicle transportation in Section 1.2.1.

Before doing so, we briefly discuss global consumption of non-
petroleum fuels in the transport sector, which is summarized in Figure 1.9
(IEA, 2003a; IEA, 2003b). Apart from synthetic liquid fuels (mainly
ethanol) derived from biomass feedstocks, these other fuels are used mainly
in non-road transport. Bioethanol, in contrast, is used almost entirely in
road transport where it is often blended – to various percentages – with
gasoline to increase octane rating; the improved oxygenation also reduces
emissions of some harmful pollutants. The second most important transport fuel after petroleum in the year 2000 was natural gas, which is used
predominantly in pipeline transport (mainly for transportation of natural
gas). Natural gas supplied less than 1 per cent of road transport demands
in 2000. The remaining transportation sector demands were met by coal

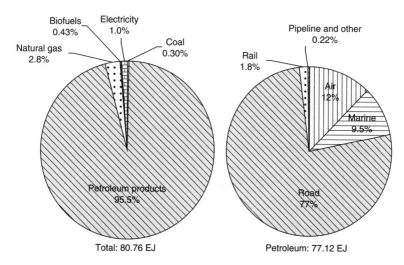

Source: IEA, 2003a; IEA, 2003b.

Figure 1.8 *Mix of fuels used in global transportation, and consumption of petroleum by different transport modes, 2000*

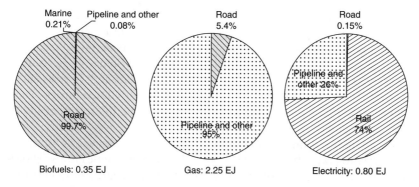

Source: IEA, 2003a, IEA, 2003b.

Figure 1.9 *Global biofuel, gas and electricity consumption and use in the transportation sector, in 2000*

and electricity, both of which are used mainly in rail transport, although use of coal is declining and in 2000 it accounted for only 11 per cent of energy use in rail transport.

This broad historical snapshot of the transport sector highlights a number of key elements. Firstly, road transport dominates fuel consumption in the transport sector, and in developed regions around two-thirds of the energy used in road transport is consumed in private motor vehicle transport. Moreover, most of the growth in transport energy demand can also be attributed to road transport, and demand for passenger automobile transport is growing at a faster rate than overall road transport energy demand (Figure 1.6). Given the significance of private passenger transport, the rest of this chapter (and much of this book) focuses on this activity, particularly the implications for future car transport demand in a scenario of economic and social development outlined in Section 1.2.1.

1.2.1 Global Private Passenger Transport

As discussed, our focus on global private passenger transport is warranted because car travel demand is growing rapidly, contributing to the increasing overall road transport energy demand, which itself is responsible for an increasing share of energy consumption, and hence greenhouse gas emissions.

In 2000, most private passenger transport activity occurred in developed regions of the world. Table 1.2 presents the number of private passenger vehicles[6] in this year for 11 world regions, estimated from a number of sources (AAMA, 1996; AAMA, 1997; FHA, 1996; Davis and Diegel, 2004; IRF, 2000; EIA, 1999; EIA, 2002). Globally, it is estimated that there were close to 600 million passenger vehicles (cars and light trucks used ostensibly as cars) in 2000, although there is some uncertainty regarding these figures, particularly for developing regions.[7] Some 35 per cent of these vehicles could be found in North America, around 31 per cent in Western Europe and 10 per cent in the Pacific OECD countries. Thus, almost 77 per cent of all passenger vehicles are found in these three industrialized regions.

This concentration of vehicle ownership is also reflected in estimated 'motorization rates' (that is, vehicles per 1000 people). These are also shown in Table 1.2 and appear to correlate with per capita incomes, although other factors appear also to influence this relationship.[8] Regional vehicle ownership rates vary from 660 per 1000 people in North America down to around five per 1000 people in South and Centrally Planned Asia (based on population figures from UN, 2004). For these regions it is important to note that the motorization rate estimates exclude two-wheeled vehicles, which are a relatively significant transport mode in many Asian countries; for example, in India and Indonesia two-wheelers outnumber cars by up to 5:1 (and the figure may be around 3:1 in China) (IRF, 2000). The global average motorization rate was estimated to be around 100 cars per thousand people in 2000.

Table 1.2   Estimated number of passenger vehicles (cars and light trucks used as cars), and number per 1000 persons in 2000

World Region	Passenger vehicle numbers (millions)	Motorization rates (PMV/1000 people)
North America	211.1	660
Western Europe	188.3	410
Pacific OECD	60.5	403
Former Soviet Union	18.1	62
Eastern Europe	18.0	148
Centrally-Planned Asia	6.9	4.9[a]
South Asia	7.4	5.4[a]
Other Pacific Asia	26.3	55[a]
Latin America	41.8	81
Middle East and North Africa	11.8	34
Sub-Saharan Africa	9.5	15
World	599.7	99 (avg.)

[a] Note that in these regions two-wheelers represent a very substantial part of the private vehicle fleet. For example, in China, India and Indonesia, it is estimated that there are 3 to 5 times as many motorized two-wheelers as there are cars. Accordingly, the level of private mobility is underestimated if one considers car numbers alone.

Source: Estimates based on AAMA, 1996; AAMA, 1997; FHA, 1996; Davis and Diegel, 2004; IRF, 2000; EIA, 1999; UN, 2004.

One key question for exploring the possible emergence of a future sustainable transport system is whether economic development in today's developing countries will lead to demands for the same levels of personal mobility that exist in today's industrialized regions. The values in Table 1.2 provide some indication of how high future levels of global car ownership could rise, which in turn has implications for energy demand and greenhouse gas emissions. We explore this more concretely in later chapters.

1.3   THE ROLE OF TRANSPORT IN SUSTAINABLE DEVELOPMENT

Transforming global social and economic systems, including global energy and transport systems, from their current structure to one that is compatible with the goals of sustainable development is a long-term process involving continual change to a range of physical, technological and institutional systems. However, understanding how this long-term process might unfold can help guide policy responses aimed at achieving the long-term strategic goals of sustainable development. One way to explore a possible trajectory for the transformation of the global energy and transport system is with long-term (until 2100) energy–economy–environment (E3) scenarios. Such scenarios are useful for enhancing our understanding of highly complex systems, of which energy and transport are prime examples. Importantly, scenarios are not intended to be predictions, but enable us to explore plausible questions of 'what if' related to key future uncertainties. They can also illustrate some of the possible impacts of today's policy and technology decisions, and are therefore an essential tool for policy makers confronting long-term challenges.

In this book an E3 scenario is used to explore a number of issues related to the role of private transport and personal mobility in sustainable development. Importantly, a single E3 scenario can only represent one configuration of the future, while significant social, economic, environmental, technological and political uncertainties mean that many pathways are possible. An extensive sensitivity analysis of the impact of these uncertainties on possible transformations of the global energy system would provide useful insights for designing robust strategies for realizing sustainable development. However, a single scenario that is carefully defined, internally consistent and intuitively plausible can provide important additional insights about technological developments and possible targets for policy support. With this in mind, this analysis focuses on carefully describing a single 'core' scenario of sustainable development, while also examining some of the elements that contribute to the significant levels of uncertainty – particularly social and political – by also exploring some alternative pathways in which decision makers place a lower priority on sustainable development.

One of the specific questions we will attempt to address with these E3 scenarios is whether the level of personal mobility in developed regions, and achieving the mobility aspirations of the developing world, is inconsistent with sustainable development. Moreover, we will explore the technology pathways for transport that are most compatible with sustainable development. Importantly, however, we do not intend to explore all aspects of sustainable development, which covers a very broad range of activities and goals, but rather focus on those most relevant to energy and transport systems, such as climate change mitigation, as discussed above. Accordingly, we examine here in detail only a limited set of necessary conditions for achieving sustainable development based on four key principles that can be applied to E3 scenarios (see Box 1.1).

BOX 1.1 THE IIASA–ECS DEFINITION OF SUSTAINABLE DEVELOPMENT SCENARIOS

Sustainable development is a widely accepted principle in the design of long-term energy–economy–environment (E3) strategies. Despite a broad consensus on the general idea of sustainability, varying degrees of agreement exist on specifics, in particular on trade-offs between incommensurable objectives.

In an effort to perhaps contribute one step to a possible future consensus in the field of sustainable development, IIASA–ECS has proposed a working definition of sustainable-development E3 scenarios. This working definition consists of quantitative criteria, which can be used to classify long-term E3 scenarios, covering economic and environmental sustainability as well as inter- and intra-generational equity (Klaassen et al., 2002).

More specifically, we define sustainable development scenarios as those that meet the following four criteria.

(1) Economic growth (GDP/capita) is sustained throughout the time horizon of the scenario.

(2) Socioeconomic inequity among world regions, expressed as the world-regional differences of GDP (gross domestic product) per capita, is reduced significantly over the 21st century, in the sense that, by 2100, the per capita income ratios between all world regions are reduced to ratios close to those prevailing between OECD countries today.

(3) Long-term environmental stress is mitigated significantly. In particular, carbon emissions at the end of the century are approximately at or below today's emissions. Other GHG emissions may increase, but total radiative forcing, which determines global warming, is on a path to long-term stabilization. Other long-term environmental stress to be mitigated includes impacts on land use, for example desertification. Short- to medium-term environmental stress (for example, acidification) may not exceed critical loads that threaten long-term habitat well-being.

(4) The reserves-to-production (R/P) ratios of exhaustible primary energy carriers do not decrease substantially from today's levels.

However, it must be emphasized that these criteria cover only a part of the full spectrum of sustainable development, and are of limited applicability for assessing some elements of and challenges to sustainability, such as biodiversity, desertification, ozone layer depletion and others.

This analysis will then seek to determine whether establishing a sustainable transport system based on the four fundamental principles in Box 1.1 will, for instance, require restrictions on mobility or access to particular transport modes, or if technological development can overcome the negative effects of transportation.

The future choice of technologies will clearly be one critical element for achieving a gradual transformation to an environmentally sustainable world. New technologies have a substantial potential and can play an essential role in any transition to a sustainable future, and deserve particular attention. Accordingly, in subsequent chapters of this book we investigate in detail the transport sector technologies and energy carriers most characteristic of sustainable development (see Ausubel et al., 1998; Nakićenović, 1991). These can include, on the one hand, technologies that represent a significant departure from today's fossil-based systems, and which may be well-suited for the very long term. On the other hand, there are also 'bridging' technologies, which, while compatible with the dominant structure of the global energy system, pave the way for the transition towards sustainable energy futures. The early identification of those technologies with the potential to accelerate or help overcome potential barriers to the transition to a sustainable energy system is essential for providing guidance to policy makers about the most appropriate forms of policy support needed to achieve long-term sustainability strategies (Klaassen et al., 2002).

Within this context there has been a substantial debate on the role of hydrogen (H_2) fuel and fuel cell (FC) cars in a strategy to mitigate GHG emissions, particularly on the timing of this option (see for example Keith and Farrell, 2003; Azar et al., 2003). It has been argued that climate change mitigation, among others, could be a reason to support the early introduction of these technologies. However, these are very immature and expensive technologies and much of the necessary supporting infrastructure does not yet exist, making it difficult to see how a so-called 'hydrogen economy' could emerge. This is one of the many questions that the analysis in subsequent chapters will seek to explore.

Moreover, energy systems based on alternative fuels, including hydrogen (to use the example above) are not necessarily more sustainable in terms of greenhouse gas emissions, since they are often energy-intensive and may rely on other fossil fuels. This highlights the fact that the transport sector cannot be examined in isolation of the rest of the energy system, so in the following chapters we will also explore the broader energy system developments, particularly in terms of fuel production, required for the emergence of a sustainable passenger transport sector. This analysis will provide some insights regarding the technologies that should be the target of increased R&D and commercialization support. The results aim to provide a 'technological road map to sustainable development', focusing specifically on the transportation sector.

Given this overall plan, the remainder of this book is organized as follows. After this introductory chapter, Part I of this book comprises two chapters exploring future transport demands and technology prospects. In the first half of Chapter 2 we describe the basic economic, demographic and other features that form the basis for developing a sustainable transport scenario. The remainder describes the construction and features of an accompanying, consistent travel demand scenario, and vehicle market characteristics. Chapter 3 then examines the characteristics, current status and future prospects for a range of vehicle and fuel technologies, compatible with sustainable development and otherwise. In Part II we combine the elements presented in this introduction and Part I to present a selection of detailed transport technology scenarios. We start in Chapter 4 by first presenting the analytical framework applied to assess long-term technology potential in a sustainable energy and transport scenario. Chapter 5 then describes such a scenario, and examines the role of different vehicle technologies and the impact on greenhouse gas emissions. In Chapter 6 we investigate alternative scenarios of future transport technology deployment, including one where sustainable development is largely ignored and commercial potential alone (under current institutions and incentives) determines technology choice. This complements Chapter 5, which describes a possible technological roadmap to sustainable development, by identifying those technologies likely to require support to achieve commercialization.

Since policy initiatives are likely to be of critical importance in achieving the goals of sustainable development in the transport sector, including greenhouse gas abatement, in Part III we look in detail at the suite of policy instruments, measures and other agreements in place or under consideration to mitigate greenhouse gas emissions from transport. We focus especially on initiatives in Europe and Japan, since these regions are relatively advanced in incorporating environmental assessment and objectives into policy design and implementation. Chapter 7 presents a general overview of the range of policy instruments suitable for GHG abatement in the automobile sector, while Chapter 8 explores in detail market-based demand-side instruments, which are attracting increasing attention among policy makers. Complementing this demand-side policy analysis, we also examine supply-side initiatives, focusing in Chapter 9 on voluntary or nego-tiated agreements. Chapter 10 then discusses the role of supply-side support related to R&D support and investment leading to technological development, which is another important element of any strategy to address the long-term challenges emerging in the global transport sector.

Part IV presents a 'road map' to achieve a sustainable transport scenario by synthesizing, in Chapter 11, the findings of the analysis from Part II on technology developments in transport with the review of transport policy instruments in Part III. Chapter 12 and Chapter 13 explore the role of a variety of policy instruments in implementation of the technological roadmap described in earlier sections, and derive critical policy insights for achieving sustainable automobility and reducing GHG emissions.

NOTES

1. We use the term 'fossil fuels' throughout to refer to carbon fuels of geological origin, including coal, gas and oil. However, this term may not be entirely correct since there is some evidence that some geological stores of carbon fuels are of abiogenic origin (see summary in Odell, 2004, ch. 6).
2. The definition of OECD used here includes only those countries who were members of the Organisation in 1990, and therefore excludes newer entrants such as Mexico, South Korea, Poland, the Czech Republic, Hungary and Slovakia.
3. Electricity's share of final-energy consumption increased from 10 to almost 16 per cent between 1971 and 2000.
4. So, although the shares are high in developed regions (NAM, WEU and PAO) and low in the least-developed regions (SAS and AFR), transport's share of final energy use in mod-erately developed regions, such as the economies in transition (FSU and EEU) is low partly because of the higher energy intensity of other end-use sectors. Conversely, regions such as Latin America (LAM), the Middle East (MEA) and Other Pacific Asia (PAS) have a share almost as high as the developed regions because energy use in other sectors is rel-atively small, even though per capita energy demand in transport is much lower in these regions.
5. Note that this includes also fuels used for international air and marine transport.
6. Private passenger transport can normally be thought of as car transport. However, in North America a majority of the light vehicles sold in recent years have been light-duty trucks instead of cars (with light trucks accounting for 52.8 per cent of light vehicle sales in 2003, according to Davis and Diegel (2004, Table 4.9)). Since most of these are used for personal transport (75 per cent in 1997, based on Davis and Diegel (2004, Table 5.7)), it is more accurate to use the broader term 'private passenger vehicle'. For convenience, however, we will use this term and the term 'car' interchangeably to cover private passen-ger vehicles.
7. And probably around 800 million of all types of road vehicles with four wheels or more (based on the same sources). In developing regions, commercial vehicles represent a much larger share of total vehicle fleet than in developed regions (AAMA, 1997; IRF, 2000).

8. For example, region-specific factors are apparent for North America, where vehicle ownership rates are more than 50 per cent above those in other industrialized regions, and in sub-Saharan Africa, which has a higher vehicle ownership rate than the relatively richer South Asian and CPA regions, although lower numbers of two-wheelers.

PART I

Future transport demand and technology prospects

2. Future drivers and projections of transport demand

2.1 A SUSTAINABLE DEVELOPMENT SCENARIO TO EXPLORE FUTURE TRANSPORT

Greenhouse gas emissions from transport are growing rapidly, and this sector is accounting for an ever-increasing share of total anthropogenic emissions, driven mainly by increasing incomes. The key question arises as to whether future transport activity, propelled by continued economic growth, will necessarily undermine the achievement of environmental sustainability, or whether technological and structural changes will enable the transport sector to develop in ways that are compatible with the principles of sustainable development, without necessarily restricting mobility. Although restricting access to particular modes of transport could achieve some aspects of environmental sustainability, it may undermine other aspects of development, including economic activity, social development and human welfare.

It is the purpose of the following chapters to investigate the role of transport, particularly the role of the private automobile and personal mobility, in sustainable development. To explore these issues we start by describing a scenario of future demographic, economic and energy-intensity trends that will later be used to investigate global transport in more detail. As discussed, scenarios can help to enhance our understanding of highly complex systems, such as the future development of the global energy and transport system. In this study, we seek to use scenario analysis to better understand the technology transitions, and the potential role for policy support, required to realize a more sustainable transport system.

Importantly, for this exercise it is not necessary to develop all elements of a scenario from scratch since many scenarios are available already, such as the 40 scenarios presented in the Special Report on Emissions Scenarios from the Intergovernmental Panel on Climate Change (Nakićenović and Swart, 2000).[1] These scenarios of overall demographic, economic and technological development were used by the Intergovernmental Panel on Climate Change (IPCC) to assess the impact of a range of uncertainties on future GHG emissions in the absence of climate policies. All of these

Table 2.1   Storyline features from the SRES

	Storylines			
	A1	A2	B1	B2
Population (2100)	Low	High	Low	Median
Economic growth	Very high	Median	High	Median
Global income equality	High	Low	High	Median
Technological change	High	Low	Median	Median
Energy demand	High	High	Low	Median

Source: Kram et al., 2000.

scenarios were constructed from four main 'storylines', and some of the key features of these storylines are presented in Table 2.1.

A number of the storylines presented in Table 2.1 describe future worlds in which basic economic and social drivers are consistent with some key elements of sustainable development (including economic and social sustainability), and which therefore may be suitable for exploring the potential emergence of a sustainable energy and transport system. However, for our analysis some of these storylines are unsuitable: in particular, we want to avoid using a scenario which relies on heroic or utopian assumptions, since these are less likely to provide useful policy insights, and are inconsistent with current institutions and driving forces. For instance, very rapid economic growth and technological change, or rapid convergence between incomes in the developed and developing worlds, although perhaps desirable from a sustainable development perspective, are divergent from historical experience and many current trends, which may take a long time to change.

For this reason, as a starting point we select the B2 storyline from the IPCC's Special Report on Emissions Scenarios (SRES) (Nakićenović and Swart, 2000; Riahi and Roehrl, 2000). In Table 2.1 we can see that the B2 storyline describes a world in which demographic, economic and technological drivers are in the centre of the range of all the storylines. B2 also presents a world where there is a strong emphasis on local solutions to economic, social and environmental sustainability, which makes it well-suited to examining sustainable development (Nakićenović and Swart, 2000). However, it should be noted at the outset that the B2 scenario published in the IPCC SRES is not itself a scenario of sustainable development, nor are

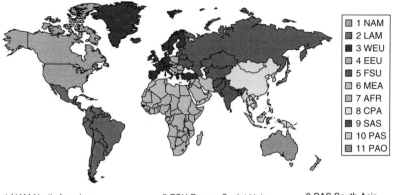

1 NAM North America
2 LAM Latin America & The Caribbean
3 WEU Western Europe
4 EEU Central & Eastern Europe

5 FSU Former Soviet Union
6 MEA Middle East & North Africa
7 AFR Sub-Saharan Africa
8 CPA Centrally Planned Asia & China

9 SAS South Asia
10 PAS Other Pacific Asia
11 PAO Pacific OECD

Note: Five regions portray the so-called industrialized regions and the economies in transition (NAM, WEU, PAO, FSU, EEU). Six additional regions represent the developing world (CPA, SAS, PAS, LAM, AFR, MEA).

Figure 2.1   World regions used in this analysis

we using the SRES B2 quantification for the analysis in the following chapters. Instead, we are using some elements of the B2 storyline and scenario which are compatible with sustainable development as the basis for constructing a new scenario. Below we describe in more detail, and quantify, some of the key B2 scenario variables for 11 major world regions, presented in Figure 2.1. In later chapters we use these key variables representing the basic drivers to develop a full E3 scenario to study the role of passenger transport in the possible development of a sustainable global transport system.

The B2 scenario closely follows the median population and economic growth trajectories of a large number of scenario studies (see Nakićenović and Swart, 2000, ch. 2). In other words, the economic and demographic trend assumptions in the B2 scenario are plausible and uncontroversial, and are based on current institutional frameworks. The economic and demographic trends in the B2 scenario also reflect some of the elements of a sustainable development scenario, based on the criteria described in Box 1.1. In particular, under the B2 scenario 'education and welfare programs are widely pursued, resulting in reductions in mortality and, to a lesser extent, fertility' leading to a long-term population of 10.4 billion by 2100 (UN, 1998). Figure 2.2 shows the population in each world region over the period 2000–2100 under this scenario.

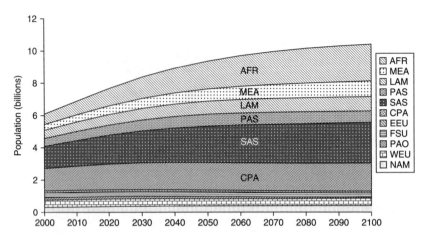

Figure 2.2   Scenario of global population growth

Further, in this scenario differences in economic growth across world regions are gradually reduced, and high priority is given to human welfare and equality within regions. Growth in regional per capita GDPs is presented in Figure 2.3, which shows that, by the end of the 21st century, all but three world regions achieve levels of material prosperity at least equal to the levels prevailing in today's developed regions. Even the more slowly developing regions (Africa, the Middle East and South Asia) undergo substantial improvements in their absolute and relative material well-being. Overall, there is a 'considerable improvement in interregional equity' in this development scenario, and this is reflected in the world regional Gini index[2] presented in Figure 2.4 (Gini, 1921). Importantly, this regional Gini index cannot be interpreted in the same way as a conventional Gini index because it is based on world regional averages and is highly aggregated.[3] However, it provides an indication of inequality between regions. Global inequality in 2000 (with a Gini index of 71.8 from Figure 2.4) is worse, for example, than the level of national inequality in Namibia (70.7), Sierra Leone (62.9) and Colombia (57.6) in 2004 (UNDP, 2004). By 2050, global inequality is comparable to the 2004 national level of inequality in Russia (45.6) or China (44.7). In 2100, it is around the level in the United Kingdom (36) or Australia (35.2), but worse than in Sweden (25.0). Importantly, this scenario does not rely on heroic assumptions about a rapid convergence in global per capita incomes, so regional differences in income, and hence inequality, persist at the end of the century. However, the distribution of income in the world in 2100 under this scenario is much more even than in 2000, and the divergence in incomes in 2100

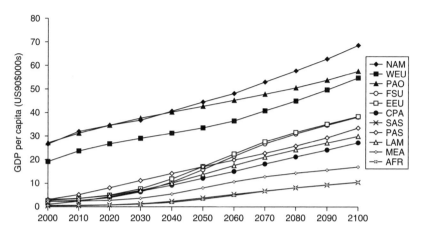

Figure 2.3   Scenario of economic growth

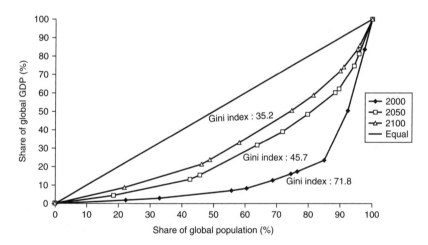

Figure 2.4   Increasing equality between world regions

between different regions is similar to the current divergence among OECD countries.[4]

Technological development and diffusion under the B2 scenario is moderate, and innovations are regionally heterogeneous, with uneven technological change across the globe. On average, energy efficiency under the B2 scenario improves at about 1 per cent per year, the same rate that 'has prevailed over the past 100 years in countries for which long-term . . . data are

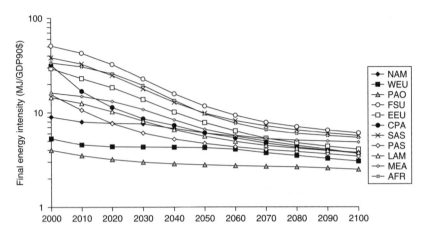

Figure 2.5   Scenario of developments in energy intensity

available' (Nakićenović and Swart, 2000, Section 4.4.5.7). The regional improvements in energy intensity are presented in Figure 2.5, and these rates are used in this analysis to define improvements for all activities other than passenger transport.

Accordingly, as mentioned earlier, B2 represents a scenario which is consistent with the central elements of economic and social sustainability. In addition, the B2 storyline encompasses continuing concern for environmental protection, addressed through technical and community-based social solutions. In other words, this scenario forms a good basis for exploring sustainable transport. However, it should be underlined that this scenario is only one of many possibilities that are consistent with these particular principles of sustainable development. We have chosen a B2 scenario because it is not significantly divergent from historical and prevailing trends, and relies on existing institutions, and is therefore intuitively plausible to the reader. However, this does not necessarily mean that this future is more likely than any other scenario. Importantly, by using a scenario based on many current trends and institutions, we can make an assessment of whether these structures are incompatible with a sustainable energy system, and hence whether it may be necessary to break from existing paradigms.

The basic scenario features described in this chapter can now be used for formulating other scenario elements in a consistent way. Some of these elements are discussed in later chapters and many are ultimately formulated with an engineering ('bottom-up') model called ERIS, developed by IIASA–ECS and the Paul Scherrer Institute (see Kypreos et al., 2000;

Turton and Barreto, 2004), and described in detail in Chapter 4. ERIS has previously been used to formulate possible technological choices for a global energy system under different assumptions on possible geopolitical, economic and technological developments (see Barreto and Turton, 2005; Turton and Barreto, 2006; Turton and Barreto, 2007).

First, however, we examine the implications of the scenario of economic and social development described so far in this chapter for future transport demand. This is necessary to determine the full extent of the challenge posed by transport to sustainable development.

2.2 FUTURE PASSENGER TRANSPORT DEMAND AND CHALLENGES TO SUSTAINABLE DEVELOPMENT

The contribution of the transport sector to global greenhouse gas emissions has been increasing over the last thirty years, both in absolute terms and relative to other sources (see Chapter 1). Future transport demand is uncertain, but there is an expectation that transport activity will experience rapid growth over the 21st century as incomes in developing countries rise, with a concomitant increase in energy consumption. For example, some of the nearer-term projections suggest that global transport energy demand could increase to 120–135 EJ by 2020 (EIA, 2002; IEA, 2004a), with the lower estimate consistent with consumption of 145 EJ by 2030 (IEA, 2004a), compared to around 80 EJ in 2000. In passenger transport, without either a substantial reduction in demand for mobility or a shift towards public transportation (mass transit), both of which run counter to current global trends, curtailing this growth in energy demand is a significant challenge. In fact, on the basis of historical experience, transport is an area that presents potentially the greatest challenge in terms of achieving environmental and social sustainability.

However, a proper analysis of the future threat to sustainability posed by transport requires an assessment that incorporates the drivers of demand, and possible limits to continued growth. On our way to conducting such an analysis, earlier in this chapter we began constructing a long-term E3 scenario of many of the variables that ultimately influence long-term demand for passenger transportation. The next step is to apply the broad socioeconomic drivers described in Section 2.1 to construct a future long-term transport scenario.

Before we do, however, it is important to note that we have varied one element of the B2 storyline that relates specifically to passenger transportation. Under the B2 storyline used in the SRES '[u]rban and transport infrastructure is a particular focus of community innovation, contributing to a low level of car dependence and less urban sprawl' (Nakićenović and Swart, 2000, Section 4.3.4). However, given other elements of the B2 storyline, this represents a somewhat courageous assumption. In particular, the gradual changes in demographics, geopolitics, productivity, technology and other 'salient scenario characteristics' in the B2 scenario (ibid., Section 4.4.2.4), do not appear to be consistent with rapid changes in systems with high inertia, such as transport infrastructure and urban form. Moreover, the B2 storyline envisages a continued reliance on current institutional frameworks (Nakićenović and Swart, 2000, Section 4.3.4) which have generally shown themselves unable to shift trends in personal mobility towards lower car dependence.

Accordingly, we present here a passenger transport demand scenario that reflects a continuation of current trends, many of which appear unlikely to change in the medium term.

2.2.1 Transport Demand Scenario

Using the demographic and economic scenario described above, we developed a consistent scenario of passenger transportation demand to 2100, using the work of Turton and Barreto (2007), which is based on an enhanced version of the passenger transportation demand model of Schafer and Victor (2000).[5] In this scenario, demand grows according to passenger travel time and money share budgets, which are historically and cross-regionally stable (Zahavi and Talvitie, 1980). As mentioned, this scenario of transport demand is consistent with the main elements of the B2 scenario, including GDP growth rates (which determine money budgets, and were presented in Figure 2.3), and the total volume of transport is driven also by B2 population projections. Importantly, this transport scenario does not envisage a major shift to more public transport (mass transit), a redesign of urban areas, or any significant attenuation of demand growth arising from information or communications technology. It can be argued that this development in transport is consistent with other aspects of the B2 storyline presented above.

Global passenger car travel demand under this scenario is presented in Figure 2.6, which also presents an estimate of historical demand. In this scenario, global demand grows from roughly 16 trillion passenger-km in 2000 to 41 trillion pkm in 2050, and 53 trillion pkm in 2100.[6] Clearly, the trajectory of future travel demand shown in Figure 2.6 has major social (in terms of urban planning, mobility, access) economic (infrastructure, investment, congestion) and environmental (emissions, resource extraction) implications. Figure 2.6 also shows that in this scenario most of the

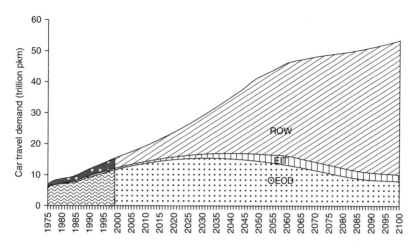

Figure 2.6   Scenario of global passenger demand

growth occurs in developing regions (ROW), with total travel demand in industrialized regions (OECD and economies in transition (EIT)) falling below year 2000 levels before the end of the century. It is also worth noting that, in this travel demand scenario, aggregate car transportation in developing regions surpasses that in the industrialized world in around 2040–50. In subsequent chapters we combine this travel demand scenario with an energy system model to elucidate possible energy supply and technology scenarios, and to explore the implications for sustainable development.

The long-term stabilization and decline of transport demand in industrialized regions is one of the key features of the scenario presented in Figure 2.6, and can be attributed partly to stabilization and decline of population, but mostly to a shift to faster and more expensive modes of transportation as incomes rise, which itself has significant implications, in terms of resource consumption, pollution and infrastructure needs (and these are incorporated in the analysis in subsequent chapters). Over a longer time horizon, the developing regions would also be expected to exhibit such a stabilization and decline. However, under the scenario assumptions used here, this does not occur this century. One important trend that is assumed to occur in developing countries as a result of increasing incomes is a decline in the relative contribution of two-wheelers (which are not included in Figure 2.6). However, in those regions where two-wheelers are important, ownership rates are still assumed to increase over the long term up to levels in the OECD Pacific, where they are highest today (WBCSD, 2004).

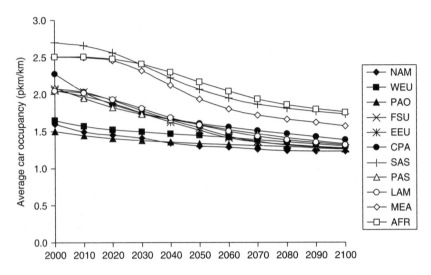

Figure 2.7   Scenario of future average car occupancy rates

To better understand the implications of this scenario for vehicle travel and energy demand, the passenger transport demand projection in Figure 2.6 (in passenger-km) was converted into a scenario of demand for passenger vehicle travel (in km), based on a scenario of future vehicle occupancies (Schafer and Victor, 2000; Turton and Barreto, 2007). In developed regions, average vehicle (car) occupancy rates have been declining (EEA, 2002; Davis and Diegel, 2004) and this trend is expected to continue with further increases in incomes, although the average occupancy is not expected to decline much below 1.25 people per vehicle. In developing regions, developments in vehicle occupancy are expected to follow roughly the historical path of developed regions.[7] This occupancy scenario is quantified in Figure 2.7. When combined with the passenger travel demand scenario presented above, these occupancies imply the passenger car travel demand scenario presented in Figure 2.8, where car transportation grows from roughly nine trillion kilometres of travel in 2000 to around 37 trillion kilometres in 2100.

This increase in car travel represents one of the principal challenges to sustainable development arising in the transport sector. It is worth restating that this is the level of vehicle use that is consistent with the population and economic development described in Section 2.1, which itself is needed to realize other aspects of sustainable development, including poverty alleviation and greater global equality.[8] Moreover, the assumptions described above, upon which this travel scenario is based, are consistent with the

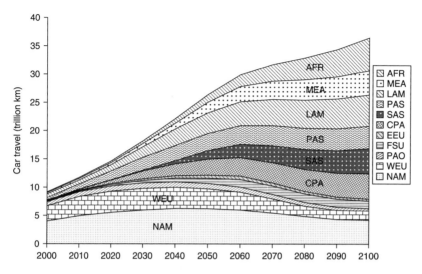

Figure 2.8   Scenario of future global car travel

current institutional framework, gradual changes in economic and social factors, and the application of many of the historical trends experienced by today's developed countries to the developing world. We now look at the implications of this demand growth for the global passenger vehicle market.

2.2.2   Vehicle Numbers and Ownership

To determine what the vehicle travel scenario above means for global vehicle ownership, and as a reality check on the overall scenario, vehicle numbers were estimated based on utilization rates (or annual vehicle driving distances). Estimates of 1990–2000 vehicle utilization rates were derived from data on vehicle numbers (AAMA, 1996; AAMA, 1997; FHA, 1996; Davis and Diegel, 2004; IRF, 2000; EIA, 1999) and Schafer and Victor's (2000) models of occupancy and travel demand. These trends were extrapolated based on convergence around 10–16000 km p.a. (Schafer, 1995; Schafer, 1998) for all world regions except North America, where average vehicle travel distances are assumed to converge to around 22000 km p.a. The choice of these values is based on historical trends and analysis done by Schafer (1995).

It must be stressed, however, that estimating future average vehicle driving distances is highly uncertain. Economic development, on the one hand, results in higher incomes and improved road transport infrastructure,

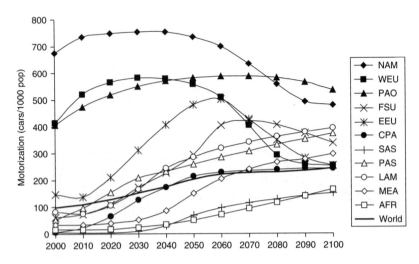

Figure 2.9   Future passenger vehicle ownership rates

which may encourage a shift to private transportation and longer average vehicle driving distances. On the other hand, economic development also results in improvements in public transportation infrastructure, higher car ownership (if one household owns more than one car, for example, average travel per vehicle may decrease), and higher levels of congestion. Looking at estimates for 1990–2000 it is difficult to find a clear pattern across different regions between average driving distance and economic development alone. Developing regions may exhibit high average driving distances, and this is the case for Latin America (LAM) and the Middle East (MEA), but North America also exhibits high average driving distances. In addition to the factors mentioned above, we can speculate that geophysical characteristics, urban form and population density may also be highly influential. Accordingly, the average vehicle driving distance estimates applied here are uncertain, and are heavily guided by trends in today's developed regions.

Figure 2.9 presents the implied levels of vehicle ownership in the scenario developed here, based on the estimated vehicle driving distances described above. Figure 2.9 shows three main trends: (1) car ownership in developed regions peaks and begins to decline as higher incomes (and larger travel money budgets) make faster modes more attractive; (2) a catching-up of Eastern Europe (EEU) and the Former Soviet Union (FSU); and (3) rapid growth in some developing regions, notably Other Pacific Asia (PAS) and Latin America (LAM).

By 2050 in this scenario, global average vehicle ownership is projected to double compared to 2000. Between 2050 and 2100, however, private automobile ownership rates are expected to increase by only roughly 25 per cent, largely because the large increase in today's developing regions is partly offset by a decline in ownership levels in developed regions and regions in transition. It should be mentioned that this scenario anticipates that an initially rapid growth in ownership in population-dense regions (for example, CPA) will give way to a slower increase as the impact of congestion (from the high vehicle density) is felt at lower motorization rates than in today's developed countries.

2.2.3 Vehicle Sales

The estimated levels of vehicle ownership can be used to estimate the size of the global car market (new car sales) that is consistent with the passenger transport future described above. The size of this market has important implications for the rate at which new technologies can penetrate, including the prevalence of niche applications which provide a foothold for new competitor technologies. Two illustrative estimates of the global car market were developed by applying a simplified vehicle stock model, based on an average service life of either ten or 15 years (weighted according to utilization). These lifespans correspond roughly to the average automobile age and the median vehicle scrappage age, respectively, in the USA in 2000 (Davis and Diegel, 2004).[9] One might assume that in poorer regions the average automobile is used for a longer period before it is scrapped. However, poorer road conditions and limited maintenance services may reduce the effective service life in these regions. Ultimately, increasing incomes are expected to increase vehicle turnover in all regions, resulting in a lower average age, although this may be offset by refinements in vehicle technology that continue to increase the lifespan of the average vehicle.

Figure 2.10 shows the development of the global passenger car market under the transport scenario described here, using the two different estimates of average vehicle lifespan (including an estimate for 2000). These two estimates provide an indication of the impact of the uncertainty associated with alternative future vehicle turnover rates on the estimated output of the global passenger vehicle market. Figure 2.10 shows the market increasing from the 2000 estimate of just below 50 million to around 170 or 250 million vehicles per year at the end of the 21st century, depending on the assumed vehicle lifespan. The relative importance of the regions also changes substantially. In 2000, more than 75 per cent of passenger vehicles were sold in industrialized regions, but this is projected in this scenario to decline to around one-third by 2050 and less than 15 per cent by 2100. Even given the relatively conservative nature of the projection for CPA, the size of this region's vehicle market is expected to exceed

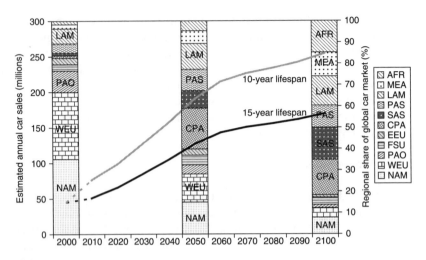

Figure 2.10   Development of the global passenger vehicle market

that of NAM by 2040, and surpass the aggregate size of today's industrialized regions in the second half of the century. All of today's developing regions will also have large passenger vehicle markets by this stage under this scenario.

2.3   SUMMARY

In this chapter we have presented a consistent scenario of economic, social and technological development and applied this scenario to construct a projection of future passenger transport demand, in terms of vehicle travel and the global vehicle market. The scenario of future transport demand described here anticipates that achieving other goals of sustainable development, including economic development and more income equality between world regions, in the context of existing institutions and only relatively gradual changes in socioeconomic variables, will lead today's developing regions to follow a path of transport system development roughly similar to the historical trajectory followed by today's developed regions. As a consequence, the private motor vehicle will continue to be a very important technology throughout the 21st century. This presents not only challenges, but also opportunities for sustainable development, since there are already a number of well understood, technically viable alternative motor vehicle technologies that have the potential to alleviate some of the potential environmental impacts concomitant with the increase in road transport envisaged in this scenario. We explore the characteristics of these technologies in the following chapter.

NOTES

1. Which also reviewed over 400 global and regional scenarios of greenhouse gas emissions (Nakićenović and Swart, 2000, section 2).
2. The Gini index is generally used to measure the degree of income inequality within a country. For example, a Gini index for household income is calculated by first constructing a Lorenz curve, in which the cumulative share of household income is plotted against the cumulative share of households arranged from poorest to richest. The index is then calculated as one (1) minus twice the area under the Lorenz curve (with the result usually multiplied by 100). Perfect equality results in a Gini of zero, and a perfect inequality in a Gini of 100.
3. For instance, within each region there is likely to be inequality which would also be expected to affect the Gini index, although under this scenario intraregional equality also improves, perhaps more than global equality (Nakićenović and Swart, 2000, Section 4.3.4).
4. The ratio of GDP per capita (in purchasing power parity terms) between the richest and poorest region declines from close to 18 in 2000 to 6.5 in 2100. For comparison, the ratio between the OECD members Luxembourg and Turkey in 2000 was approximately 9, and between Norway and Turkey around 5.6 (IBRD, 2004).
5. The original model of Schafer and Victor (2000) projects total demand for passenger travel (in passenger-km), shares of various modes and vehicle occupancy rates to 2050 for the IS92a/e scenario (Leggett et al., 1992) based on stable time and money share budgets. It was necessary to modify the original model to extrapolate these projections beyond the original income range to cope with a different income scenario and timeframe.
6. This can be compared to 36–37 trillion p-km of car travel estimated by WBCSD (2004) for 2050, although this study relied on a very different set of assumptions. For example, WBCSD (2004) assumed higher economic growth in some regions, but a weaker link between income and travel demand in a number of regions. Schafer and Victor (2000) estimated total car travel demand in 2050 at around 45 trillion p-km, but again this was also based on a different scenario (IS92a; see Leggett et al., 1992) which included, among other features, higher growth in developed regions than B2. However, not all scenarios concur closely with the one presented here. For example, Azar et al. (2003) project total car travel in 2100 to reach 113 p-km (compared to 53 p-km here), mainly because of an assumption that there is only a limited shift to faster modes, which implies that increasing incomes lead to a declining share of expenditure on transport at higher incomes and implicitly a willingness to devote more time to travel – a trend yet to be observed (Schafer and Victor, 2000).
7. Occupancies in 2000 were estimated using EEA (2004), Davis and Diegel (2004) and Michaelis et al. (1996).
8. Although it is obviously not the only possible path for achieving these goals.
9. The average age accounting for utilization is lower than the median scrapping age because new vehicles have much higher utilization rates (for example, in the USA, vehicles less than five years old travel around twice the distance of vehicles more than ten years old (Davis and Diegel, 2004)).

3. Transport technology and fuel characteristics and future prospects

Future population growth and increasing incomes throughout the world are expected to drive increasing demands for private mobility, particularly automobile transport over the 21st century. Satisfying this emerging demand for global automobile transport is likely to pose many challenges to long-term sustainable development. In particular, the need to reduce greenhouse gas emissions to avoid the worst impacts of climate change, and to manage non-renewable energy resources, are two challenges that appear incompatible with a large expansion in automobile use.

However, as briefly discussed in Chapter 1, the application of new technologies has the potential to alleviate some of the impacts. For instance, vehicle technologies able to achieve high fuel efficiencies, or to utilize alternative renewable energy sources, represent promising possibilities for satisfying mobility demands while avoiding some of the negative impacts of transport on sustainability. The potential far-reaching impact of technology is perhaps best appreciated by considering the role of the internal combustion engine (ICE) in the 20th century. The ICE was one of the most important technologies of the century, transforming personal mobility in the developed world and in doing so strongly influencing the development of human settlements, trade, tourism and communication. Moreover, the ICE also transformed global energy production, and has indirectly influenced historical and current global geopolitics. One key question is whether this technology will maintain its position in the 21st century, or be replaced by one of a number of emerging alternatives.

With this in mind, in this chapter we explore some of the more promising transport technologies and their future prospects. This forms an essential input to Part II of this book, where we combine information on technology performance and prospects with the basic socioeconomic drivers and transport scenario described in Chapter 2 to investigate the possible emergence of a sustainable transport system, along with some of the key policy uncertainties. Even though this present chapter discusses current characteristics and performance of different technologies, it should be remembered that our interest is in long-term sustainable development.

As in the rest of this book, the focus here is on technologies that are applicable to private passenger transport, although many described below can be used in other transport applications, particularly road, rail, marine and some types of air transport.[1] The emphasis here is on those engine technologies that are technically proven, although they may still face a number of challenges to achieve commercial viability. Accordingly, we do not consider every possible innovation in engine technology. Below we describe engine technologies and fuels in conjunction, since in many cases it is characteristics of the fuel, such as production costs or distribution, that have a major bearing on the competitiveness of particular vehicle technology–fuel combinations.

3.1   INTERNAL COMBUSTION ENGINE (ICE) VEHICLES

The ICE is a mature technology that has undergone a massive amount of technological development, and continues to receive enormous R&D support, which is likely to sustain its dominance of the automobile and truck market for at least the medium term. Almost all of today's road vehicles are powered by internal combustion engines (ICEs), in which combustion is induced by a spark or by compression. At present, the spark ignition engine (usually petrol-fuelled) is cheaper, smaller, lighter and quieter than the diesel compression engine and offers reasonable performance, although with relatively lower fuel efficiency. However, progress in conventional engines research and development is leading towards convergence of spark and compression ignition engines, exemplified by petrol-fuelled direct homogeneous charged compression ignition (HCCI) systems. This technology involves premixing the fuel with air, as in a spark-ignition engine, and igniting it through compression, as in a diesel engine. As a consequence, HCCI and similar technologies are able to combine the high efficiencies of compression combustion systems with the lower NO_x and particulate emissions of spark-ignition vehicles. Nonetheless, important challenges remain, and these combustion systems are not expected to be widely available for another decade (Steiger, 2002).

Improvements to combustion systems, as discussed above, exhaust treatment and faster warm-up are estimated to have the potential to improve ICE efficiency by up to 20 per cent (IEA, 1997). Other potential efficiency improvements are discussed in more detail in Section 3.4.

The petroleum fuels upon which almost all of today's road vehicles rely are obtained almost exclusively from refined crude oil, although a very small amount is synthesized from coal and natural gas, mainly in South

Africa and Malaysia. This synthesis uses the Fischer–Tropsch (FT) process and involves reacting coal or gas with oxygen and steam to produce a synthesis gas that is then converted into a range of hydrocarbons, including synthetic petroleum products (called FT liquids) (for example, see SFA Pacific, 2000; SASOL, 2005). These fuels can be handled in much the same way as conventional petroleum fuels,[2] unlike the coal and gas feedstocks from which they are produced, which may be difficult to store and transport, or inconvenient to use in a vehicle. One drawback, however, is that the FT process relies on another fossil fuel and is quite energy-intensive, and therefore has a relatively poor performance in terms of greenhouse gas emissions, although synthetic petroleum fuels produced from natural gas may be similar to diesel in terms of emissions (Clark et al., 2002). However, other feedstocks can be used to produce FT liquids, including biomass which is potentially more sustainable (Hamelinck et al., 2003). One attraction of FT liquids is that coal or biomass feedstocks are relatively abundant around the world, and so these fuels have the potential to improve security of energy supply, and to extend the life of oil reserves.

ICE vehicles using non-petroleum fuel configurations are also available, and these are briefly described below.

3.1.1   Natural-gas Vehicles with ICEs

Natural gas is a relatively well-tested alternative to petroleum in transport applications, with around half a million compressed natural gas (CNG) vehicles in use in OECD countries (IEA, 1997). Although, as discussed in Chapter 1, only a relatively small amount of natural gas is used in road transport, this fuel appears to have many advantages. These include gas's clean-burning properties, the availability of existing distribution infrastructure in many regions, and its potential to reduce dependence on imported oil (although CNG vehicles will clearly increase dependence on gas). From a sustainable development perspective, it is estimated that CNG engines produce around 30 per cent fewer CO_2 emissions on a tank-to-wheels basis, and significantly fewer harmful emissions, such as benzene, smoke or sulphur oxides, than reformulated petrol or diesel engines (IEA, 1997). In addition, commercially available medium- and heavy-duty natural-gas engines are able to achieve reductions in emissions of carbon monoxide (CO) and particulate matter of over 90 per cent, and reduction in nitrous oxide (NO_x) emissions of over 50 per cent relative to commercial diesel engines (AFDC, 2003). However, there is some concern that emissions from CNG vehicles of methane (a potent greenhouse gas) may undermine some of these benefits.

The principal drawback of natural gas vehicles relates to fuel storage, and natural gas must be stored in cylinders either compressed (as CNG) or as a liquid (that is, liquefied natural gas (LNG)). In practice, however, CNG vehicles are generally much more attractive, owing mainly to the cost and relative difficulty of, handling LNG.[3] Natural gas vehicles may also emit similar or possibly higher levels of NO_x than petrol or methanol vehicles (IEA, 1997). Another barrier to use of natural gas relates to the need for an alternative infrastructure for delivery to and distribution at filling stations.

Liquid petroleum gas (LPG), a by-product of crude-oil refining consisting mainly of butane and propane, is another well-known transport-fuel alternative to petrol and diesel. LPG technology is popular with some because of its practical storage capability, and is the most widely used alternative transportation fuel in the United States (Greene and Schafer, 2003; IEA, 1997). However, the application of LPG is likely to remain limited owing to the relatively small scale of reserves compared with natural gas and crude oil.

3.1.2   Alcohol and Biofuel Vehicles with ICEs

Alcohol fuels, typically methanol and ethanol, are also proven alternatives to petroleum-based fuels. For example, methanol has been used in North America as an alternative fuel in flexible-fuel vehicles that are able to run on M85 (a blend of 85 per cent methanol and 15 per cent petrol). However, usage is decreasing in this region because of the limited number of refuelling stations, and because car-makers are no longer supplying methanol-powered vehicles.

Nonetheless, in the long run, methanol has the potential to play a role in a possible transition to a hydrogen economy, where hydrogen replaces fossil fuels as the most important energy carrier, because it can be readily used as a feedstock for hydrogen production. The methanol industry is working on technologies that would allow methanol to be used as a source of hydrogen for fuel cell vehicle applications (AFDC, 2003), which are discussed in Section 3.2.2.

In terms of production, today most of the world's methanol is synthesized by steam reforming of natural gas. This involves reacting natural gas with steam to produce a mixture of CO and hydrogen (called 'synthesis gas'), which is then placed under high pressures and temperatures in the presence of a catalyst to produce methanol (AFDC, 2003). However, there is also interest in the possibility of producing large amounts of methanol from other non-petroleum feedstocks such as coal or biomass (including organic wastes).

Bioethanol is another alcohol fuel, similar to methanol although less toxic and corrosive. Brazil, the USA,[4] Sweden and Canada are among the countries that have commercially introduced bioethanol in blends with gasoline (called gasohol), or are using it in higher concentrations (85–100 per cent) on a large scale, distributed through existing retail systems and with only minor vehicle modifications (AFDC, 2003; IEA, 1997).

Blending bioethanol with gasoline increases the fuel octane rating and results in better oxygenation, thereby improving combustion and emissions quality – in particular, reducing ozone pollution (AFDC, 2003). However, both bioethanol and methanol have different combustion characteristics from petroleum, and fuel quality in petroleum–alcohol blends needs to be maintained when used in conjunction with sophisticated exhaust after-treatment systems (Faucon and Leport, 2002). Accordingly, bioethanol is often converted to ETBE (ethyl-*tert*-butyl-ether) that can be easily blended with conventional gasoline. A further area of possible concern with both bioethanol and methanol vehicles is the emission of toxic formaldehyde (IEA, 1997).

Today, the majority of the world's bioethanol is produced by fermenting starch crops that have been converted into simple sugars. Viable starch and sugar feedstocks for this fuel include corn, barley, wheat and sugarcane, but ethanol can also be produced from 'cellulose biomass' such as trees, grasses and other agricultural wastes. However, production of bioethanol is currently expensive in some parts of the world (for Europe, see Ryan et al., 2005),[5] requires large harvests of suitable crops and potentially large inputs of energy (see Jungmeier et al., 2005), which leads to other environmental problems, in particular soil degradation (IEA, 1997).[6]

It is appropriate here to emphasize that, when evaluating the possible contribution to sustainable development of alternative transport fuels, it is important to consider not only the characteristics associated with final use of the fuels, but also fuel production and synthesis. For example, although the combustion of biofuels, such as biomethanol and bioethanol, produces CO_2 emissions, an equivalent amount of CO_2 is absorbed during the growth of the biomass used to produce these fuels. On the other hand, there are also additional energy inputs to the production of this biomass and the synthesis of the biofuels. This has been analysed in detail by others (for example, see Jungmeier et al., 2005; Henke et al., 2003; Shapouri et al., 2002), and the net GHG emissions of different fuels varies considerably depending on the synthesis pathways and sources of feedstock employed; moreover, this applies to all of the fuels discussed in this chapter. We return to this issue in subsequent chapters, where we incorporate into our analysis detailed representation of an extensive range of synthesis pathways and regional differences (see Section 4.3).

Alcohol fuels are not the only biofuels showing promise.[7] For example, biodiesel is a proven alternative to conventional diesel fuels, although there has been relatively less market experience with this fuel.[8] One advantage of biodiesel is that it can be blended with petroleum diesel fuels in almost any proportion, and used in conventional compression engines with only minor modifications. Biodiesel can achieve superior emissions performance to petroleum diesel because it contains very little sulphur and few aromatic compounds.

Most biodiesel is produced by reacting oils and fats with methanol in the presence of a strong base such as sodium hydroxide. Accordingly, biodiesel is usually synthesized from waste oil from the food industry, or directly from oil crops. However, because of the limited quantities of waste oil, larger-scale production of biodiesel would rely principally on oil crops, which are generally lower yielding than the cellulosic crops that can be used or alcohol production. This lower yield, combined with competing demands for land (food, fibre, biodiversity), are likely to make alcohol fuels more attractive if large-scale production of biofuels is used to improve energy sustainability.

3.1.3   Other Possibilities: ICEs Powered by Hydrogen

One further ICE–fuel option is hydrogen. This alternative is receiving attention because ICE hydrogen-fuelled vehicles produce no direct greenhouse gas emissions, although they still produce some pollutants such as emissions of NO_x.[9] Moreover, hydrogen can be produced from a variety of primary-energy sources, reducing dependence on conventional transport fuels such as oil.

For these reasons there is much interest in the concept of a 'hydrogen economy' in the future that will solve greenhouse gas and energy supply problems.[10] Nonetheless, there are many technological issues that remain to be solved in both fuel production and utilization, before hydrogen's potential can be realized.

The use of hydrogen as a transport fuel, including important barriers, is discussed in much more detail in Section 3.2.2, in the context of fuel cell vehicles.

3.2   ELECTRIC VEHICLES (EVs)

The preceding section examined a number of alternative fuel options for the conventional ICE, many of which may be suited to a sustainable transport system. However, all of the options canvassed above rely on a single technology for generating motive power, the ICE. In this section we examine the potential of radically different engine systems, specifically those relying on electric motors.

The main attraction of electric vehicles is the complete absence of tail-pipe emissions, and consequently the promise of improved urban air quality. A further advantage is that using electricity to power vehicles affords much greater primary fuel flexibility, reducing dependence on petroleum products, but importantly also enabling vehicles to be powered ultimately by renewable energy sources like solar, wind or hydroelectric power. Consequently, electric vehicles have the potential to be essentially pollution-free on both a well-to-tank and tank-to-wheels basis (IEA, 1997).

Electric vehicles are also able to achieve very high levels of efficiency compared to ICE vehicles. This is because they avoid the large thermodynamic energy losses associated with the conversion of the chemical energy stored in fuel into mechanical power in ICEs (via a series of controlled explosions). In comparison, electricity can be converted directly into motive power through an electric motor. The critical issue for electric vehicles, however, is how to store and supply the electric power for the electric motor, and this is discussed below.

3.2.1 Battery Electric Vehicles

As the name suggests, battery electric vehicles store the electricity used to power the vehicle in on-board batteries, and these batteries are recharged by connecting the vehicle to the electric grid (AFDC, 2003). The potential impact of battery electric vehicles on long-term sustainability is therefore highly dependent on the fuels and technologies used for electricity production. However, depending on electricity prices and gasoline taxes, fuel costs for electric vehicles may be lower than for gasoline ICE vehicles. In addition, EVs generally have lower fuel and maintenance costs because they have fewer moving parts requiring servicing or replacement, although in current models the batteries must be replaced every three to six years (AFDC, 2003).

The cost and performance of battery EVs, and hence their attractiveness, is ultimately determined, however, by the cost and performance of the energy storage batteries. Currently several types of automotive batteries are available and/or under development,[11] although even the best of these has an energy density well below that of petrol. This is partly offset by the greater efficiency of electric motors, but the driving range of EVs is still very limited and, without major technological breakthroughs, electric vehicles are considered unlikely to be accepted by consumers as a practical alternative to ICE vehicles, consistent with historical experience with these vehicles (USDOE and USEPA, 2003a).

Between 2000 and 2003, five main battery electric vehicle models were introduced to the US market, with fuel consumption rates between 1.9 and

4.3 litres of petrol equivalent per 100 kilometres (l/100km), and driving ranges between 68km and 219km (USDOE and USEPA, 2003a).[12]

3.2.2 Fuel Cell Vehicles

One way to overcome the problems associated with batteries in electric vehicles is instead to generate electricity on board using another energy carrier. The main problem with this approach is that it may undermine the efficiency benefits of using an electric motor, unless an extremely efficient electricity generation technology is available. Fuel cells represent such a technology.

Fuel cell vehicles (FCVs) represent a radical departure from vehicles with conventional internal combustion engines. Like electric vehicles with batteries, FCVs are propelled by electric motors, and are also able to achieve high system efficiencies: up to 60 per cent, compared to around 20 per cent for petrol ICEs (IEA, 1997). But while battery electric vehicles use electricity from an external source (and store it in a battery), FCVs generate their own electric power on board through an electrochemical process using hydrogen fuel (pure hydrogen or hydrogen-rich fuel such as methanol, natural gas or even petrol) and oxygen from the air.

The fuel cell technology receiving the most attention for transport applications is polymer electrolyte membrane (PEM) technology. This technology is relatively low-weight and compact compared to other types of fuel cell, and operates at lower temperatures, meaning faster start-up, less wear and better durability. This makes it particularly well-suited to transport applications. However, current PEM fuel cells require an expensive catalyst (usually platinum) to separate the protons and electrons in the hydrogen fuel; the protons then travel through the electrolyte, whilst the electrons must travel through an electric circuit, thereby generating power (EERE, 2005).

A number of additional technical challenges must be overcome before fuel cells can be widely adopted for transportation, including the need to increase durability and dependability.[13] Also, all fuel cells are prone, in varying degrees, to 'catalyst poisoning' by carbon monoxide impurities (which arise when fuels other than pure hydrogen are used), which decreases fuel cell performance and longevity. Research into these areas is continuing and the US DOE among others is sponsoring and participating in demonstration programmes to test the durability of new components and designs (EERE, 2005).

There are a number of ways of supplying hydrogen to the PEM fuel cell, and these are examined below.

Hydrogen fuel cell vehicles

The most obvious ways of powering the PEM fuel cell is to fuel vehicles directly with pure hydrogen. FCVs fuelled with pure hydrogen emit no pollutants, only water and heat. Moreover, hydrogen FCVs achieve very high fuel efficiencies, as evidenced even in today's prototypes, which are estimated to be 1.50–1.74 times more fuel-efficient than near-identical conventional vehicles (Bevilacqua Knight Inc., 2001).[14] However, the biggest challenge confronting FCVs fuelled directly with hydrogen is fuel storage. Hydrogen can be stored on board in a number of ways, but among those receiving the most attention is storage in high-pressure tanks. This storage option still faces a number technical challenges, given that hydrogen has a high energy density per unit weight but a low energy density per unit volume, so it is difficult to store the volume of hydrogen needed to generate the same amount of energy stored in a small volume of conventional fuels such as petrol. This is a significant problem for fuel cell vehicles (and hydrogen ICE vehicles), which need to achieve a driving range of 500 to 600 kilometres between refuelling in order to be attractive to customers and competitive with petrol vehicles. Research is also being conducted into the use of other storage technologies such as metal hydrides, carbon nano-structures (materials that can absorb and retain high concentrations of hydrogen) and liquid hydrogen (EERE, 2005; Doyle, 1998).

Besides these technical difficulties of storing hydrogen on board a vehicle, the distribution of hydrogen may represent another major barrier to its widespread use. The cost of cryogenic or pipeline transport to retail fuelling stations, as well as of storage (infrastructure, refrigeration costs), could be relatively high (IEA, 1997). To circumvent these difficulties, alternatives such as using a fuel that is a more conveniently handled (methanol or petrol) and from which hydrogen can be produced on board the vehicle, are being tested and show technical potential (see the next section, 'Alcohol or petroleum FCV with on-board reformer').

When considering the prospects of a hydrogen-based economy, it is important to remember that hydrogen is an energy carrier rather than an energy source. Accordingly, hydrogen must be produced using another energy source, although a variety of primary-energy options are available, including fossil fuels, renewable sources, and nuclear energy. This flexibility means that hydrogen fuel cells have the potential to improve security of the energy supply by reducing dependence on imported fuels such as oil. Even today, hydrogen is produced from a range of alternative feedstocks, with steam reforming of natural gas accounting for around 50 per cent of production, followed by oil with around 30 per cent, 18 per cent from coal and around 4 per cent by electrolysis of water (EERE, 2005). Production is also possible from biomass which, like coal, can be gasified and used in a steam-reforming process to synthesize hydrogen. Hydrogen production with electrolysis, although only accounting for a small share of current production, potentially provides further flexibility, since the electrical energy can come from any generation source, including renewables such as solar and wind (AFDC, 2003).

Given the current challenges to hydrogen FC vehicles, this technology option is not seen as a short-term solution, although FCVs may be attractive in the medium to long term.

Alcohol or petroleum FCV with on-board reformer

Fuel cell vehicles can also be fuelled with hydrogen-rich fuels, such as methanol, ethanol, natural gas or even petroleum fuels. However, these fuels must first be reformed on board the vehicle to produce pure hydrogen for the fuel cell. Because all these fuels contain carbon, the reforming process results in some emissions of CO_2, but the much higher efficiency of the fuel cell means that the level of emissions is much lower than for a comparable ICE vehicle (USDOE and USEPA, 2003b). Moreover, reforming these fuels results in much lower levels of all other air pollutants compared to direct combustion.

Compared to FCVs using pure hydrogen, there are two main advantages of reformer-based fuel cell vehicles. Firstly, reformers allow the use of fuels with higher energy density than that of pure hydrogen gas. Second, and more importantly, reformers allow FCVs to use conventional fuels delivered using existing distribution systems, avoiding the need to develop new and costly infrastructure before FCVs can be adopted on a large scale. Although the fuel efficiency of fuel cell vehicles relying on on-board reforming is below that of direct hydrogen fuel cell vehicles, these vehicles are still relatively efficient compared to ICE vehicles.[15]

The main disadvantage facing this type of FCV, however, is that on-board reformers add to the complexity, cost and maintenance demands of the vehicle (EERE, 2005). Another disadvantage, as mentioned earlier, is that the reforming process emits CO_2, although less than conventional ICE-based vehicles. For these reasons fuel cell vehicles using pure hydrogen may be more desirable in the long term, although fuel cell vehicles using hydrogen-rich alcohol fuels may feature in a potentially long-term transition before the technological barriers related to hydrogen storage and distribution can be overcome.

3.3   HYBRID ELECTRIC VEHICLES

The fuels and technologies discussed so far fall into two largely separate groups: ICE- and electricity-based vehicles. However, it is also possible to combine, or hybridize, mechanical and electrical conversion technologies on board a single vehicle to exploit the advantages of each. In the most general sense, hybrid vehicles combine two or more energy conversion technologies (for example, internal combustion engines, fuel cells, generators or motors) with one or more energy storage technologies (for example, fuel, batteries, ultracapacitors or flywheels). Within this broad classification, one commercial example is hybrid ICE–electric vehicles, which combine elements of battery electric and ICE vehicles, and represent a transition from an existing technology as opposed to a radical departure like FCVs. Hybrid electric vehicles (HEVs) are generally fuelled in the same way as ICEs; that is, all the fuel alternatives discussed in relation to ICEs in Section 3.1 apply to HEVs.

Currently, there is no single definition of a hybrid ICE–electric vehicle, and a number of manufacturers are experimenting with different combinations of technology components. HEV systems can be defined in terms of four main elements. The first is 'stop and go' ICE technology, whereby the ICE is switched off when the vehicle is stationary, instead of idling, and an electric motor is used to restart the vehicle (similar to the starter motor in conventional ICEs). This has the potential to reduce engine wear, fuel consumption and air pollutant emissions. The second feature is regenerative braking, where some of the kinetic energy from the vehicle's motion is captured and stored (in a battery or super-capacitor) during braking, instead of being dissipated in the form of heat on the brake-pads. This improves fuel efficiency because the ICE is not used to charge the battery and, when combined with the two features discussed below, the electric energy can also be used to propel the vehicle. The third and perhaps most important feature of hybrid vehicles is electric-motor assist of the ICE, where the electric motor directly powers the driveshaft. This enables increased power output with a smaller ICE, and avoids the need to operate the ICE outside its optimal power output range. The smaller ICE reduces fuel consumption, and operating the engine in its optimal range greatly improves tailpipe emissions.[16] The fourth element, and the logical extension of electric motor assist, is fully independent electric drive powered either by the battery alone or through an alternator powered by the ICE. This enables the vehicle to operate in completely electric mode, usually at low speeds.

Hybrids may include some or all of these features: the more features that are included the better the energy efficiency (and 'stronger' the hybridization), but the more complex and costly the system. Generally the larger the role played by the electric motor, the larger battery system required. Of the hybrid vehicles already on the market, the Honda Insight, Accord and Civic hybrids have relatively small electric motors (10–12 kW), and are 'mild hybrids' whereas the Toyota Prius (50 kW), Lexus RX400h and Ford

Escape (70 kW)[17] are able to operate in fully electric mode, and electric motor assist contributes more to total power output (CARB, 2005). One current drawback of hybrid vehicles is their cost, which is generally around $3–5000 higher than the equivalent petrol vehicle, and the additional complexity and weight of the battery and electric motor systems. Nonetheless, over 400 000 hybrid vehicles were sold between 2000 and 2005 in the USA alone, and Toyota and Honda have sold over 500 000 and 100 000 hybrid vehicles worldwide, respectively (Toyota, 2005; Honda, 2005).[18]

Fuel cell vehicles can also be hybridized to incorporate regenerative braking and battery assist to the fuel cell. Similar to the ICE–electric hybrids, this means a smaller fuel cell is required, since the battery system is able to supplement the output of the fuel cell during times when peak power is required, for instance during acceleration. Because fuel cell systems themselves are currently very costly, this has the potential to reduce significantly the cost of fuel cell vehicles.[19]

3.4   EFFICIENCY PROSPECTS

Changing from the ICE to other engine technologies, and from petroleum to other fuels, clearly has the potential to reduce the environmental impact of vehicle travel, along with enhancing the diversity of energy supply. However, it is important to recognize that more evolutionary changes to existing engine technology and vehicle design may also go some way towards improving the long-term sustainability of transportation. To examine this potential we briefly review some of the recent literature on potential fuel efficiency improvements.

Most of this literature focuses on the short to medium term, whereas our interest is the long term. Accordingly, we focus below on the more technologically optimistic or aggressive assessments of the short term, which may provide a good indication of long-term potential under more modest assumptions.

Under the National Academy of Science's (NAS, 2002) most aggressive technology path for the next 10–15 years, including the introduction of emerging technologies, the estimated fuel consumption reduction potential ranges from 27.9 to 36.7 per cent for different car types over a period of 15–25 years (see Box 3.1 for a summary of this and other studies discussed in this section).[20] This is similar to the results of the Massachusetts Institute of Technology's (Weiss et al., 2000) simulation of future fuel consumption rates for petrol/diesel cars, where it was estimated that, under an advanced technology case, rates could decline between 45 and 50 per cent by 2020 (after accounting for the longer timeframe). This estimate accounts for the

BOX 3.1 SUMMARY OF PUBLISHED ESTIMATES OF POTENTIAL IMPROVEMENTS OF FUEL CONSUMPTION RATES FOR PASSENGER LIGHT-DUTY VEHICLES (CARS AND LIGHT TRUCKS)

	Fuel efficiency (reference year) (l/100km)	Reference year	Fuel efficiency in the projection year (l/100km)	Projection year	Decrease, fuel consumption rate (%)
EIA (2003a), reference case	9.8	2001	9.0	2025	7.7
Weiss et al. (2000), reference case	8.5	1996	5.5	2020	36
Weiss et al. (2000), advanced technology case	8.5	1996	4.8/4.2 (gasoline/diesel)	2020	45/51 (gasoline/diesel)
NAS (2002), Path 1		2000		2010–15	12 (cars only: 7.4–11.2)
NAS (2002), Path 2		2000		2010–15	27 (cars only: 15.5–28.8)
NAS (2002), Path 3		2000		2010–15	35 (cars only: 27.9–36.7)
OTA (1995), Advanced conventional	8.4	1995	3.7–4.2	2015	50–6
NRC (1992), Shopping cart projections	7.5–9.9/9.3–12.1 (cars/light trucks)	1991	5.8–7.4/7.2–9.3 (cars/light trucks)	2006	22–5/23–6 (cars/light trucks)
Lightfoot and Green (2002)	8.4	1988 (peak year)	4.0	2100	54
Schafer et al. (1999), moderate vehicles	9.5	1995	5.5	2010	42

impact of advanced body designs, lightweight materials and improvements to the ICE.[21] Assuming a slightly less aggressive technology path, such improvements are likely to occur instead over a longer timeframe. For example, the US National Research Council (NRC, 1992) made a more modest projection of the potential impact of the uptake of specific, well-established and proven technologies that could be implemented by car makers as part of the normal replacement cycle for manufacturing equipment in 15 years or less. They estimated improvements for cars and light trucks ranging from 22 to 26 per cent.

The US Office of Technology Assessment (OTA, 1995) has also assessed the possible fuel efficiency performance of advanced vehicles to be introduced during the next ten to 20 years. Based on a survey of car manufacturers, the maximum fuel consumption improvement that could be achieved by an advanced ICE vehicle was estimated at 56 per cent compared to the current *average* new car, while maintaining interior space and performance constant at 1995 levels. To achieve this fuel economy, vehicles would need to combine an optimized aluminium body, continuously variable transmission, advanced low-rolling resistance tyres and advanced ICE technology. As mentioned earlier, the IEA (1997) roughly estimates that ICE efficiency could be improved by a maximum of 20 per cent with improved exhaust treatment, improved combustion and fast warm-up.

Clearly, the consensus among these and other sources (such as Schafer et al., 1999; Lightfoot and Green, 2002) is that there is considerable technological potential to improve the efficiency of the automobile. It would probably not be unreasonable to assume that average fuel consumption rates could be reduced by 50 per cent over the 21st century, ignoring the impact of hybrid systems or fuel cells. Moreover, many of the technology developments leading to improved efficiency will benefit all passenger vehicles regardless of engine technology, including improvements resulting from lightweight materials, reduced-rolling resistance tyres and better aerodynamics. On the other hand, improvements to engine features, such as variable value timing and direct fuel injection, are specific to ICEs. Considering that fuel cells are a relatively less mature technology, significant efficiency improvement possibilities can also be expected for FCVs.

However, one must be cautious when considering the overall impact of these efficiency technologies on the vehicle fleet. In particular, the impact of other likely developments in the vehicle market should also be considered. This is illustrated by a US Energy Information Administration (EIA, 2003a) study which examined not only the impact of technologies, but also that of structural changes in the automobile market. They forecast for the USA that advanced technologies such as variable valve timing and direct fuel injection, as well as electric hybrids for both gasoline and diesel

engines, would decrease average fuel consumption of new light duty vehicles by only 8 per cent by 2025. Importantly, this study assumed that fuel efficiency standards remained at current levels, fuel prices stayed low and *higher personal income increased the demand for larger and more powerful cars.*[22]

This analysis by the EIA (2003a) captures the impact of current trends in the USA, where a shift from cars to light trucks is largely responsible for average private passenger vehicle fuel efficiency having increased by only 8 per cent between 1980 and 2003,[23] even though tighter standards resulted in an average car efficiency improvement of roughly 21 per cent over the same period (Davis and Diegel, 2004, Table 4.18). Moreover, such trends towards larger vehicles are not confined to the USA, with average new-car weight in the European Union increasing by 25 per cent between 1980 and 1999, and average new vehicle power increasing by 40 per cent (ECMT, 2000).[24]

The fact that without policies supporting improved efficiency standards, structural changes (such as a shift to larger vehicles) in the automobile market could substantially offset what would otherwise be large improvements in fuel economy, illustrates two important features for further analysis. First, it highlights the importance of increasing incomes and consumer vehicle preference; second, it illustrates a potential need for policy to support deployment of even more efficient new technologies in order to improve fleet fuel economy. We return to both of these issues later.

3.5   SUMMARY

We have seen in this chapter that there exists a wide range of technological options for the transport sector, particularly for private automobile transport, and these technologies have the potential to alleviate some of the environmental impacts of transportation. However, the technological transitions that could take place in the global automobile sector in the course of the 21st century are uncertain. Over the long term, fuel cell and hybrid-electric vehicles could be serious challengers to the currently dominating internal combustion engine vehicle although, as discussed in Section 3.1, their potential is affected not only by characteristics of the technologies themselves, but by the development of the energy system as a whole. Uncertainty over the evolution of the global energy system means, in particular, that it is unclear which energy carriers would play a role in the long term. Several energy carriers could substitute for petroleum products, which have well-known environmental and geopolitical problems, but these alternatives face an array of challenges in terms of production, distribution and storage.

Whether it is possible to realize the potential of the technologies briefly described in this section to achieve some of the environmental goals of sustainable development is a question explored in the following chapters.

NOTES

1. A large amount of air transport relies on the jet engine, which the technologies discussed in this section are unlikely to replace without major unexpected technological breakthroughs.
2. In addition, they can be 'made to order' because the production process can be controlled to yield fuel properties as desired, including ultra-low sulphur, aromatics and olefins, and for advanced combustion powertrains such as HCCI, mentioned in Section 3.1.
3. In the United States, the total number of CNG vehicles (light-duty, medium-duty plus heavy-duty) on the road was 11 000 in 2001 (EIA, 2003b). In comparison, the number of LNG vehicles was only 400, all for heavy duty applications.
4. Where flexible-fuelled ethanol vehicles (using 85 per cent ethanol:15 per cent petrol) account for approximately 1 per cent of the total passenger vehicle stock (Kohler, 2003).
5. Although, as shown in Figure 4.3 in Section 4.2, ethanol is competitive with petroleum fuels in some markets, such as Brazil.
6. Nonetheless, there is stronger policy support for ethanol as an alternative transport fuel. For example, the EU has introduced targets for biofuel use in transport of 2 per cent in 2005 and 5.75 per cent by 2010 (European Directive 2003/30/EC). The IEA is recommending a target of up to 8 per cent by 2020, and China and India are also moving to support the introduction of ethanol (Ministry of Environment (Japan), 2003).
7. For instance, the European Commission's biofuels directive (2003/30/EC) distinguishes between bioethanol, biomethanol, biodiesel, biogas, bio-di-methyl-ether, bio-ETBE (ethyl-tert-butyl-ether), bio-MTBE (methyl-tert-butyl-ether), synthetic biofuels, biohydrogen and pure vegetable oil. Crop yields, production efficiencies, feedstock availabilities, costs and difficulties with consumer acceptance mean that only a few of these are likely to be long-term options for large-scale biofuel production.
8. Nevertheless, over one million tonnes of biodiesel was produced in the EU in 2002 (European Bioenergy Networks, 2003), with a large share of this produced in Germany.
9. Hydrogen ICE vehicles are receiving significant interest from BMW, who intend to begin selling such vehicles in the near future in Europe.
10. Iceland, which produces around 55 TWh of geothermal and hydro electricity annually for only \$0.02/kWh, is aiming to achieve a 'hydrogen economy' within a few decades. Hydrogen produced from Iceland's cheap electricity is competitive with imported petroleum at prices of around US\$60/barrel.
11. To date lead acid batteries have been mainly used in electric vehicles. They are relatively inexpensive but have low energy density and poor performance in cold temperatures. Nickel-metal hydride and lithium-ion batteries achieve significantly higher energy densities, but are relatively expensive.
12. For comparison, the EV version of the RAV4 from Toyota consumes 2.1 litres of gasoline-equivalent per 100 kilometres, whereas the gasoline version of the RAV4 2WD consumes 8.7 l per 100 km.
13. For example, PEM fuel cells require effective water management systems to operate dependably and efficiently.
14. These comparisons were made for prototypes developed by Ford and Daimler–Chrysler. The fuel efficiency for the Ford hydrogen FCV based on city and highway driving cycles was 3.5 l/100km (compared to 5.3 l/100km for the equivalent conventional vehicle),

while the vehicle developed by Daimler–Chrysler achieved 4.4 l/100km (compared to 7.1 l/100km).

15.   In the range 2.9–3.9 litres per 100 kilometres (60–80 mpg), compared to 2.8–3.4 l per 100 km (70–85 mpg) for hydrogen FCVs (Marx, 2000).

16.   Some manufacturers are also experimenting with alternative engine cycles to further improve the efficiency gains from operating the engine under optimal conditions: for example, the Ford Escape and Toyota Prius use the Atkinson cycle (as opposed to the Otto cycle used in most ICE vehicles) which sacrifices power for even greater efficiency by employing different expansion and compression ratios in the engine stroke. The power sacrifice can be compensated by the electric motor in the HEV.

17.   See http://www.fordvehicles.com/suvs/escapehybrid/features/specs/.

18.   See http://www.hybridcars.com/sales-numbers.html.

19.   However, in the longer term, if the costs of fuel cell systems decline substantially, the additional complexity associated with manufacturing hybrid vehicles may favour FCV-only propulsion system. Nevertheless, the experience gained with electric propulsion technology from hybrid systems is likely to be invaluable for future advanced systems such as fuel cell technologies.

20.   The NAS (2002) separately analysed ten weight classes, including not only cars but also SUVs, mini-vans, and pickup trucks.

21.   Including hybrid cars, the fuel consumption rate reduction is of course higher; in that case, it was calculated that the fuel efficiency of a gasoline ICE–electric hybrid could reach 70.8 mpg (3.3 l per 100 km) by 2020, and a diesel electric hybrid could achieve 82.3 mpg (2.9 l per 100 km).

22.   It is also worth restating that this estimate includes the impact of the introduction of hybrid electric vehicles.

23.   The market share of light trucks increased from 19.6 to 52.8 per cent over the same period (Davis and Diegel, 2004, Table 4.9).

24.   Based on eight EU countries from 1980–1994 and 13 countries from 1995–1999.

PART II

Sustainable transport technology scenario analysis

4. Modelling transport technology and fuel choice in a long-term scenario with ERIS

Any possible transition towards a sustainable passenger transport system cannot occur in isolation to developments in the overall energy system. Such a transition requires that both suitable technologies and fuels be available in sufficient quantities and at the right time. Looking at fuel production, a transition away from fossil fuels to cleaner energy carriers, such as hydrogen, may require fundamental changes in fuel production and distribution infrastructure. The emergence of a radically different fuel production and delivery system itself is potentially a more significant development than a shift in the dominant automobile technology. Accordingly, any assessment of the potential of vehicle technologies needs also to account for other developments in the energy system. This is also the case with technology development, where many of the potential new automobile technologies, such as fuel cells, are likely to undergo commercialization initially in other applications, before they achieve significant penetration in the automobile market (for example, see Barreto et al., 2003).

To ensure that these factors are considered in our analysis we employ the detailed energy-systems model ERIS (*E*nergy *R*esearch and *I*nvestment *S*trategies), a 'bottom-up' optimization model that includes representation of technologies and technology dynamics. This model is used to construct and explore energy and transport system developments in the E3 scenario that we began defining in Chapter 2. ERIS is a global multiregional model that endogenizes technological learning curves (see Turton and Barreto, 2004; Kypreos et al., 2000; Barreto and Kypreos, 2000; Barreto and Kypreos, 2004a). It models energy demands and technologies in electric and non-electric sectors, covering transportation and thermal needs, in addition to fuel production technologies, specifically for hydrogen, alcohols and Fischer–Tropsch liquids. ERIS also models other aspects of sustainable development, including resource availability (based on Rogner, 1997) and GHG abatement options for several non-CO_2 greenhouse gases (US EPA, 2003), as well as geological and forest sinks (IPCC, 2001b).

The ERIS model selects technologies from a given menu to describe an energy system that achieves particular objectives while maintaining engineering consistency. Engineering consistency is reflected in the reference energy system (see Figure 4.1), which describes possible combinations of technologies (so-called 'energy chains') from resource extraction, through energy conversion and distribution to end use. The range of feasible energy chains is constrained by resource endowments and energy supply infrastructures, among others.

4.1   MODELLING TRANSPORTATION TECHNOLOGIES

The transportation sector in the ERIS has been disaggregated into three main non-electric[1] sub-sectors: passenger motor vehicles (PMVs, cars), air transportation and all other transportation (primarily freight). For the first two sub-sectors, a relatively detailed technology representation is possible. In the aggregate remaining sector, generic technologies are set up to mimic the final-energy consumption. In total, the model distinguishes 17 technology-fuel combinations across the following categories:

Surface transport:
- Combustion technologies:
  - coal (mainly locomotive trains with steam engines),
  - petroleum products (for both heavy road, rail and sea transport and light vehicle transport),
  - natural gas (heavy and light vehicles),
  - alcohol fuels (heavy and light vehicles),
  - hydrogen (heavy and light vehicles);
- Fuel cell technologies:
  - hydrogen (heavy and light vehicles),
  - alcohol (light vehicles); and
  - petroleum products (light vehicles).

Air transport:
- petroleum combustion technologies (mainly jet and propeller engines);
- hydrogen combustion technologies (although assumed not to be available before 2030; see Airbus, 2003).

Hybrid ICE-electric technology variants are also included for all the light duty vehicles listed above (with all FCVs assumed to incorporate hybrid technology).

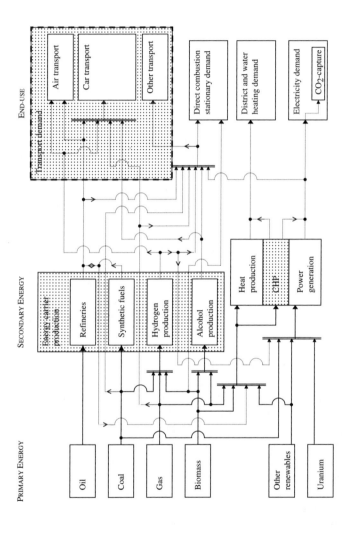

Note: Boxes represent primary fuels, groups of technologies and demand sectors. Lines indicate flows of fuels used for secondary energy production (plain) and for final demand (dashed). Vertical parallel bars are used to group together multiple fuels or energy carriers used by one group of technologies. Patterned areas group together energy carrier production technologies (in the case of secondary energy), and the transportation sector (in the case of final energy).

Figure 4.1   Reference energy system in the ERIS model

As discussed in Chapter 3, some of these new technologies face a range of technical and commercial hurdles before they can achieve performance similar to the conventional ICE at a comparable cost. Within this subset, there are technologies such as light oil fuel cell vehicles that are further disadvantaged by their potential to undermine long-term sustainability – in terms of both their emission of greenhouse gases and reliance on a non-renewable resource – which raises the question of whether they have any place in a sustainable development scenario.[2] However, these technologies may have the potential to act as a bridge between conventional engines and zero-emissions technologies such as hydrogen and alcohol FCVs, before new fuel production and distribution infrastructure is developed.

Overall, ERIS models ten technology–fuel combinations for the private automobile. Estimates of the drivetrain efficiencies (used here to refer to overall efficiency of fuel processing, engine, transmission, system control and power regeneration, in the case of HEVs) of each of these combinations were derived from Weiss et al. (2000, 2003); Thomas et al. (2000); Ogden et al. (2004) and ADL (2002). The technologies, fuels and efficiencies relative to an advanced conventional ICE are presented in Figure 4.2. For most technologies, the efficiency values represent approximate median values from the sources listed above, with the exception of the alcohol and petroleum fuel cell technologies where the distribution of literature efficiency estimates was bimodal, and we selected the more optimistic estimate. Figure 4.2 also presents abbreviated mnemonics for each technology used for convenience later in the next two chapters (for example ICC, IGH, AFC).

It should be noted that efficiencies presented in Figure 4.2 are given as an index relative to the efficiency of the conventional ICE petroleum technology. Some guide to the absolute average global efficiencies of different transport modes is presented in Table 4.1, based on a study by Nakićenović et al. (1996). This table reports estimates of global average conversion efficiencies for end-use transportation technologies. So, for example, around only 6 per cent of the energy in coal used in locomotive engines is converted to useful energy (by the engine). In comparison, in 1990, aircraft engines on average converted 26.3 per cent of the energy in the fuel to useful energy. Although the information in Table 4.1 suggests that there may be significant scope to improve efficiencies, it is important to remember that thermodynamic limits constrain the maximum potential of any technology (Nakićenović et al., 1996). Importantly, the efficiency at which the ultimate energy service (for example, passenger kilometres of travel) is delivered is not reported in Table 4.1, but we discuss this more in Chapter 5.

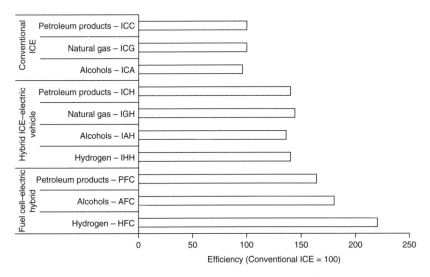

Figure 4.2   Relative drivetrain efficiencies of car technology–fuel combinations

Table 4.1   Global average of end-use efficiencies in 1990, per cent

	Coal	Oil	Gas	Electricity
Bus and truck (diesel)	–	13.8	13.5	–
Car and truck (petrol)	–	11.0	10.4	–
Airplanes	–	26.3	–	–
Ships (internal navigation)	–	31.0	31.8	–
Rail	6.0	25.0	–	75.8

Source: calculated based on Nakićenović et al. (1996).

4.1.1   Other Assumptions in Transport Modelling

In Section 3.4 we discussed the potential for vehicle efficiency improvements aside from those associated with changing drivetrains, and made a moderately conservative assessment that fuel consumption rates could be reduced by 50 per cent over the 21st century. However, we also noted that increasing incomes (which are one aspect of the sustainable-development scenario described in Chapter 2) would in all likelihood continue to shift consumer preferences towards larger vehicles and vehicles with more energy-consuming onboard systems.[3] Based on these two offsetting factors, the average efficiency of the conventional vehicles (ICC) is assumed to improve at 2 per cent per decade over the 21st century, which assumes that roughly 60 per cent of the technical improvement achievable without switching drivetrains is offset by structural changes to the vehicle stock. The relative efficiencies for different vehicle technologies in Figure 4.2 are assumed to remain constant.

Heavy-duty vehicles (including road, sea and rail) are not modelled in the same level of detail as the passenger transport sector, and are covered by five technologies. The efficiencies of these technologies are influenced by a number of factors. Firstly, the higher utilization rates of heavy vehicles mean that adoption of new technologies is generally assumed to be faster. On the other hand, the driving cycle of heavy vehicles (with less stop–start driving and acceleration) means that they benefit less from hybridization. Looking at the application of fuel cell technologies to heavy vehicles, the main drawbacks of using hydrogen FCs, related to fuel storage volume and distribution infrastructure, are less significant for large vehicles that often refuel at a small number of dedicated stations. Given other advantages of hydrogen FC technology, it is assumed that only this type of FC is used in the heavy transport sector. Freight vehicles employing hydrogen FCs are assumed to be 50 per cent more efficient than similar vehicles employing ICE-based drivetrains.

In terms of air transport, it is assumed that commercial hydrogen aircraft are not available before 2030, and even after this date market penetration will remain subdued because it will take time before this technology can achieve the performance of commercial aircraft fuelled with petroleum (see Airbus, 2003). Global air transport energy efficiency was assumed to converge towards 0.9 MJ/pkm – around a 50 per cent improvement in efficiency compared to the estimated average air-transport fuel consumption rate in the most efficient world region (PAO) today, resulting from stock turnover, improvements in aircraft design and higher capacity utilization (from Turton and Barreto, 2007).

4.2   TECHNOLOGY DYNAMICS AND COSTS

Another important methodological feature of the ERIS model is that it incorporates the impact of experience with a new technology on the cost of that technology (also called learning-by-doing) (Argote and Epple, 1990; McDonald and Schrattenholzer, 2001). Across a range of technologies there exists strong evidence of the effect of market experience on technology costs, and an example for the costs of producing bioethanol in Brazil is illustrated in Figure 4.3.

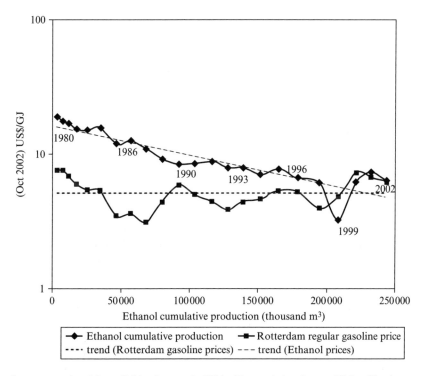

Source: reprinted from Goldemberg et al., 2004 with permission from publisher Elsevier.

Figure 4.3 *Impact of learning-by-doing on Brazilian ethanol production costs*

In the ERIS model, this learning-by-doing is represented by the capital cost of learning technologies being a decreasing function of cumulative installed capacity (which is used as a proxy for experience). The use of experience curves in energy policy assessment is well-established (for example, see Neij et al., 2003), and helps to capture one of the most important features affecting feature technology choice. For our study, this technology representation is critical for examining potential future market deployment of relatively immature transport and other technologies, such as fuel cell or hybrid vehicles.

Another important feature of the ERIS model is that the technology learning process is formulated using a cluster methodology, following the 'key technologies' approach of Seebregts et al. (2000). That is, each energy conversion or end-use technology is made up of a number of components, divided between those that benefit from learning-by-doing and those that are mature. This approach to technological learning allows an energy or end-use technology to benefit from experience gained through the application of another technology that uses a common component.

Looking specifically at passenger transport technologies represented in ERIS, three components used in the ten engine-fuel technology combinations presented in Figure 4.2 are assumed to benefit from learning-by-doing. These comprise the fuel cell system used in all FCVs; the reformer used in the alcohol and petroleum fuel cell vehicles; and the hybrid battery system, used in all vehicles except conventional ICEVs. Non-learning components comprise the internal combustion engine, fuel storage systems, electric motor, generator, transmission and control systems. Accordingly, as an example, experience with developing and manufacturing the battery system used for ICE–electric hybrid vehicles helps all vehicles that use this technology. In addition, more complex interactions are also incorporated. Specifically, we include some limited spillover benefits between stationary FC systems and fuel cells used for transport.

Accordingly, the ERIS model captures some features of technology development, where increasing experience reduces the costs of new technologies. The current and potential future costs of the components used in car transportation technologies may have a major bearing on the relative commercial competitiveness of each technology; however, future technology costs are highly uncertain. Estimates of current and future costs for different car technologies used in the ERIS model are discussed in Box 4.1. Importantly, however, direct costs are only one consideration in the pursuit of a sustainable transport system, and a full accounting of social costs and benefits may favour an alternative set of technologies. Accordingly, given the multiple objectives of realizing sustainable development, and the uncertainty of future technology costs, in the following chapter we focus primarily on the *technical* potential of the technologies discussed here and in Chapter 3 to contribute to sustainable development. That is, we assume a high priority is given to sustainability over necessarily minimizing travel and energy costs. To provide some balance to this approach we look in Chapter 6 at the impact of a scenario where sustainable development is given low priority and technology costs determine deployment. This is helpful for describing the technological road-map to sustainable development while also identifying potential barriers and targets for policy intervention.

BOX 4.1   CAR TECHNOLOGY COMPONENT COSTS

For this study, total drivetrain system costs for mass-produced vehicles are taken from Turton and Barreto (2007), who synthesized results from Ogden et al. (2004); Weiss et al. (2000); Thomas et al. (2000) and ADL (2002). The costs of the various learning components – the fuel cell, reformer and hybrid battery system – used in car transportation technologies are discussed below.

The electric hybrid system (comprising electric motor, generator and battery system) used in both the ICE–electric hybrids and the FC–battery hybrids is assumed to cost $1600 per mass-produced vehicle, based on estimates of battery cost of around $700 and motor, generator and control systems of $900, consistent with a number of estimates (Ogden et al., 2004; Weiss et al., 2000). However, current battery costs are 2.5–4 times the estimated potential (ADL, 2002). This guides the initial and floor costs for the battery system used in HEVs and FCVs. Importantly, HEVs require a smaller ICE (assumed to be $600–700 cheaper), so this partly offsets the additional costs of the hybrid system.

Complete FC system costs for 2001 are estimated to be $324/kW for a 50 kW PEM system (Carlson et al., 2002). The majority of this ($220/kW) is for the FC subsystem and reformer ($76/kW). However, these costs are expected to decline: although various sources present a range of estimates of likely future FC prices from $30 to $60/kW, with complete direct hydrogen FC system cost ranging from $50 to $110/kW (with reformer-based petroleum and alcohol systems likely to cost an additional $20 to $50/kW) (Carlson et al., 2002; ADL, 2002; Ogden et al., 2004; Weiss et al., 2000; Tsuchiya and Kobayashi, 2002).

A power output of 40 kW per PMV was used in this analysis, roughly in line with estimates for a battery-hybrid FC vehicle (ADL, 2002; Ogden et al., 2004; Weiss et al. 2003). At this output slightly higher starting costs for the FC subsystem and reformer unit are assumed ($250/kW and $90/kW, respectively) in line with Carlson et al. (2002). A mid-point in the range of future FC prices is used as the floor costs for this technology.

Methanol-based steam reformers (SR) are expected to remain cheaper than the auto-thermal (ATR) reformers required for gasoline-fuelled FCVs (ADL, 2002; Thomas et al., 2000), and both fuel processing systems will require a more costly FC to cope with the lower fuel quality. Future reformer costs range from $10 to $20/kW for steam, and $20 to $40/kW for auto-thermal (Ogden et al. 2004), which is consistent with Thomas et al., (2000) and Weiss et al. (2000). For this analysis, we have taken a floor cost of $25/kW for the SR and a starting cost of $90/kW (the latter based on Carlson et al. (2000)).Starting and floor costs for auto-thermal reformers are assumed to be $110/kW and $45/kW, respectively.

Table 4.2 shows the starting and floor costs, along with the assumed learning rate (that is, the rate by which costs decline with experience) for each component. Higher learning rates are assumed for the less mature components (FC and B). The rates presented in Table 4.2 are the initial rates defined according to the entire component cost (noting that the inclusion of floor costs changes the effective rate) and are within the ranges suggested by others (for example, see McDonald and Schrattenholzer, 2001).

These costs form an important basis for interpreting the modelling results.

Table 4.2   Starting costs, learning rates and floor costs for car transport technologies

Component	Starting cost ($/kW)	Initial learning rate	Floor cost ($/kW)
Fuel cell (FC)	250 (266 AFC) (275 PFC)	15%	45 (62 AFC) (70 PFC)
Reformer (R)	90 (110 PFC)	5%	25 (45 PFC)
Hybrid battery system (B)	$2500 per vehicle	15%	$700 per vehicle

Note: Currency units are 2000 US dollars.

4.3   MODELLING FUEL PRODUCTION TECHNOLOGIES

Although vehicle technology characteristics are expected to have a major influence on the relative attractiveness of a particular drivetrain technology, the cost and availability of the fuel used by that technology is also critical. As we have seen in Chapter 3, there exists a wide variety of technology and fuel combinations for passenger transport. In addition to the car technology detail discussed in Section 4.1, the ERIS model also includes a detailed representation of energy carrier production technologies, including those for hydrogen (from coal, gas, biomass and electrolysis of water), alcohols (from gas and biomass) and petroleum products (from oil and coal). Estimates of the performance and cost characteristics of these technologies were obtained from a variety of sources (Hamelinck and Faaij, 2001; Simbeck and Chang, 2002; Kreutz et al., 2003; Parsons and Shelton, 2002).

ERIS also accounts for competing demands for fuels and constraints on resource availability. Total global fossil resource availability and extraction costs are derived from Rogner (1997), who classifies each fuel into resource categories comprising conventional, unconventional and enhanced recovery (from conventional sources). Here we use Rogner's (1997) estimates for total conventional resources and enhanced recovery, but assume that only around 2500 billion barrels of unconventional oil and around 16.6 ZJ of unconventional gas are available, and at three to four times the extraction cost of today's conventional fuels. That is, we exclude Rogner's highly speculative and optimistic estimates of 'additional occurrences' of unconventional fuels.

Estimates of biomass resources also potentially have a large bearing on the development of the global energy system, since this feedstock represents an important source of renewable energy. Accordingly, the ERIS model also incorporates biomass resource estimates from Rogner (2000), who identified a global potential in 2050 of between 250 and 400 EJ, after accounting for land requirements for food and fibre. These estimates are based on an estimate that an additional 1.3 billion hectares of land globally could be used for biomass production, mostly in the developing world, particularly in Latin America and Africa. In the ERIS model, we assume that it is not possible to exploit these resources rapidly, and that only 125 EJ of biomass is available in 2020, rising to 235 EJ in 2050 and 320 EJ by 2100.

In addition to modelling fuel extraction and secondary energy carrier production and processing, ERIS also includes transmission and distribution technologies. Transmission and distribution infrastructure development is modelled to account for the fact that it is necessary to build a minimum amount of infrastructure regardless of the quantity of fuel delivered. This means that the marginal cost of delivering small quantities of fuels such as hydrogen is high, but decreases and eventually stabilizes with increasing demand (see Turton and Barreto, 2007).

Accordingly, we now have a framework with which to analyse fully the potential to realize a sustainable transport system. The combination of engine technologies, fuel synthesis pathways, primary resources and abatement technologies in ERIS allows us to explore many energy-chain combinations for supplying demand for transport (and energy). A snapshot of some of the possible fuel and engine technology combinations, and the implications for sustainability, is shown in Figure 4.4. This figure presents different technology–fuel-production combinations and the resulting tank-to-wheels CO_2 emissions (that is, the emissions produced directly from driving the vehicle) and partial well-to-tank emissions, comprising emissions from fuel conversion (synthesis and refining) and distribution, and sequestration. Sequestration includes both terrestrial, via uptake in vegetation used as energy biomass, and geological, via carbon capture and storage (CCS).[4]

It should be noted that Figure 4.4 does not include well-to-tank emissions from sources such as fertilizers used for biomass production, transport of biomass, coal, oil or gas, or non-CO_2 emissions,[5] although the latter are included in the ERIS model. Further, the figure does not include all combinations possible in ERIS, and was constructed on the basis that all fuel requirements for conversion are supplied using the input or output fuel (rather than a third fuel), with the exception of the electricity used for powering CCS – which is assumed to come from conventional coal generation. This explains why, for instance, net emissions for biomass-based fuel options are reported as being close to zero (that is, because all energy requirements for the production of these fuels are assumed to be supplied from biomass, which has net emissions of close to zero). Another important point to mention is that the information in Figure 4.4 is based on ERIS model assumptions for the entire vehicle fleet in North America at the beginning of the 21st century. Technologies and efficiencies vary between regions, and are expected to improve significantly over the century.

Clearly, even with the restricted range of technologies and fuel combinations presented in Figure 4.4, it is apparent that a number of technology options may play a role in a future sustainable transport system, but it is uncertain which will be most attractive, or how the transition may unfold. By using ERIS to develop an E3 scenario of a sustainable energy system we ensure that developments in the passenger car sector are explored within the context of developments in the overall global energy system. This means that we consider not only the characteristics of the transport technologies discussed in Chapter 3, but also the competing demands for transport fuels, which may affect the possible emergence of a sustainable passenger transport system. For example, although Figure 4.4 shows that hydrogen has the potential to play a major role supplying future road transportation energy needs in a sustainable way, it must be considered that hydrogen is a highly flexible energy carrier for which

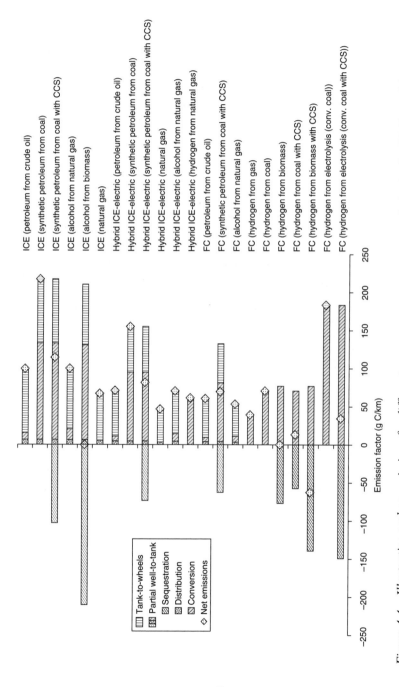

ICE (petroleum from crude oil)
ICE (synthetic petroleum from coal)
ICE (synthetic petroleum from coal with CCS)
ICE (alcohol from natural gas)
ICE (alcohol from biomass)
ICE (natural gas)
Hybrid ICE-electric (petroleum from crude oil)
Hybrid ICE-electric (synthetic petroleum from coal)
Hybrid ICE-electric (synthetic petroleum from coal with CCS)
Hybrid ICE-electric (natural gas)
Hybrid ICE-electric (alcohol from natural gas)
Hybrid ICE-electric (hydrogen from natural gas)
FC (petroleum from crude oil)
FC (synthetic petroleum from coal with CCS)
FC (alcohol from natural gas)
FC (hydrogen from gas)
FC (hydrogen from coal)
FC (hydrogen from biomass)
FC (hydrogen from coal with CCS)
FC (hydrogen from biomass with CCS)
FC (hydrogen from electrolysis (conv. coal))
FC (hydrogen from electrolysis (conv. coal with CCS))

Tank-to-wheels
Partial well-to-tank
Sequestration
Distribution
Conversion
Net emissions

Emission factor (g C/km)

−250   −200   −150   −100   −50   0   50   100   150   200   250

Figure 4.4   Illustrative carbon emissions for different passenger transport energy chains in the ERIS model, North America, 2000–2010

69

non-transport sectors are likely to compete, particularly as fuels such as gas and oil become scarce. Similarly, Figure 4.4 also identifies alcohol fuels from biomass as a promising future transportation fuel compatible with sustainable-development goals; however, the limited availability of biomass may mean that greater economic and environmental benefits can be derived by using biomass in other sectors. The effect of such competing demands, and the many other factors discussed so far, on future transport technology choice is examined in detail in the following chapter.

NOTES

1. Electric rail transportation is treated separately within electric demand.
2. For example, this technology may offer limited efficiency (and environmental) improvements compared to ICEVs (Lovins and Williams, 1999), and the reformers themselves may face a difficult task of removing SO_x (Bevilacqua Knight Inc., 2001).
3. This trend is seen in both the USA and Europe, and in both cases average passenger vehicle fuel economies have improved relatively little, if at all, since 1985 (Davis and Diegel, 2004; ECMT, 2000; IEA, 2003e).
4. In Figure 4.4 net geosequestration emissions are presented on the basis that the additional electricity needed to run the CCS plant is generated in a conventional coal power station.
5. For estimates including these and other factors, such as credits for by-products of biomass production or soil emissions from cultivation, the reader is referred to the review of Jungmeier et al. (2005).

5. Technology development in a sustainable transport scenario

In this chapter we examine whether a sustainable energy and transport system can emerge under the scenario outlined in Chapter 2, and analyse the energy and transport system developments necessary to realize long-term sustainable development. Specifically, we investigate the technical potential over the long term of new technologies and fuels to offset the environmental and resource-depletion impacts of an energy and mobility scenario that incorporates the impact of increasing incomes (with many of the more significant energy and mobility challenges emerging in today's developing world regions). In addition to identifying the features of a sustainable transport system, this allows us to assess whether there is a place for, and explore the implications of, high levels of private mobility in a sustainable-development scenario. This chapter brings together the transport demand scenario described in Chapter 2, the information on technologies described in Chapter 3 and the modelling framework outlined in Chapter 4.

Unlike other studies employing scenario analysis, which often present, first, a baseline or business-as-usual scenario, in this chapter we turn first to the exploration of a sustainable development and transport scenario. The primary reason for this approach is that our main interest is how a sustainable transport system might emerge. However, this approach was chosen also because so-called 'baseline' scenarios assume a certain set of policies (or, more usually, the complete absence of policies), which are no more realistic than an alternative policy scenario (even over relatively short timeframes). More generally, presenting scenarios as 'business-as-usual' may unintentionally imply a higher likelihood than may be warranted.[1]

Accordingly, in this analysis we instead take an alternative approach, and proceed directly to our main area of interest. However, accepting that alternative policy scenarios can provide essential insights into potential barriers to the emergence of a sustainable transport system, in Chapter 6 we examine alternative scenarios, including a 'no-policy' scenario.

It is important to emphasize that in this chapter (Chapter 5) we present an assessment of the technical potential to achieve a sustainable transport system, rather than commercial potential under recent market conditions (which we discuss in Chapter 6). We take this approach because it is logical to examine first whether the technical potential for achieving the desired goals exists, before then focusing in later chapters on the conditions and support measures required to ensure commercial forces are directed towards these goals. If it is not technically possible to develop a sustainable global energy system, based on a set of reasonable assumptions used here, then this would highlight the need for more vigorous policy intervention to encourage lower levels of mobility (at least from emissions-intensive modes) or support for additional technological innovation that could lead to major breakthroughs.

Accordingly, we first attempt to define a concrete scenario of a path towards a sustainable transport system, based on the definition of sustainable development outlined in Box 1.1. To reflect this spirit, we call this B2-based scenario a sustainable development scenario throughout this and subsequent chapters.

5.1 FUTURE TRANSPORT ENERGY CONSUMPTION

As we outlined earlier, particularly in Chapter 1, future passenger travel demand poses a potentially significant challenge to the goal of reducing greenhouse gas emissions. In addition, dependence on oil and the possible long-term depletion of oil resources represents another potential challenge. However, it is possible to describe a long-term transition in the transport sector away from almost complete dependence on fossil fuels consistent with broader energy market developments. Such a transition is presented in Figure 5.1, which we developed using the detailed energy system modelling framework described in Chapter 4, combined with the scenario of socioeconomic development and transport demand described in Chapter 2. Figure 5.1 shows both the transition from petroleum products to a more diverse fuel mix, and broad technological developments. Overall global transport energy demand increases by roughly 200 per cent over the 21st century, although, without improvements in efficiency across all modes of transport, this would be much higher. Part of this increase in efficiency is a consequence of the increasing role of fuel cells in transport applications later in the period.

Figure 5.1 shows that the introduction of fuel cell technologies begins around 2010, although initially in very limited quantities, but their share gradually increases, so that they become one of the most important technologies by the end of the 21st century. Looking at energy carriers, first natural gas, then alcohols and finally hydrogen displace an increasing share of petroleum. Importantly, however, as shown in Figure 5.1, there is scope within a scenario of sustainable development for petroleum products to continue to play a substantial role in the transport system. This level of

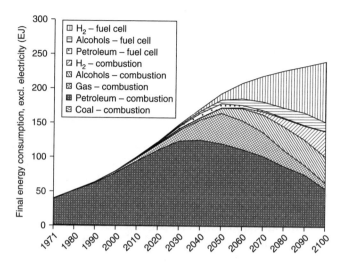

Note: Combustion of coal makes only a very small contribution and is difficult to see on the diagram.

Figure 5.1   Global energy consumption by transportation, historical and sustainability scenario

petroleum consumption is also consistent with the successful maintenance of long-term resources-to-production ratios for non-renewable resources – one of the four sustainability criteria outline in Box 1.1 – even though almost all cheap sources of oil are depleted by the second half of the century. However, there is considerable uncertainty regarding the size of the ultimately recoverable hydrocarbon resource, which we discuss further in Section 5.3.

By 2100, almost all of the petroleum consumed in this scenario is used in high-speed transport, which is assumed to be predominantly air travel.[2] Energy use in air travel increases more than tenfold over the century, although this is less than the increase in demand, with the difference accounted for by improvements in efficiency resulting mainly from a shift to larger aircraft and better load management. The increasing importance of air travel is driven by the significant growth in incomes over the century. There is relatively low penetration of hydrogen into the air travel market (for use in jet aircraft) until late in the century because this fuel can be used much more efficiently in other sectors, thereby displacing greater quantities of fossil fuel. As discussed in Section 4.1, other fuels are assumed to be unsuitable for fuelling jet aircraft.

These aggregate results can be compared to some of the medium-term transport energy demand projections discussed earlier. For example, the

US Energy Information Administration estimates transport energy demand of around 130–135 EJ in 2020 under their reference case (EIA, 2003a), while the International Energy Agency projects demand of 120 EJ in 2020 and 145 EJ in 2030 (IEA, 2004a). In comparison, demand in the scenario presented here is around 123 EJ in 2020 and 148 EJ in 2030.

To look at the same results in a different way, three snapshots of the information in Figure 5.2 (at 2000, 2050 and 2100) are shown in pie-chart form in Figure 5.2. This illustrates the unfolding technological transition towards a sustainable transport system. In 2000, oil-based technologies dominate, satisfying 97 per cent of the total transportation demand.[3] By 2050, this share is reduced by more than one-third, mostly through an increased role for natural gas. Also at this time, a number of fuel cell technologies are competing for a foothold in the transport market, with a combination of world-regional differences, fuel costs and infrastructure availability supporting technology diversity. Alcohol and hydrogen fuels are also beginning to contribute a significant amount of energy to transport applications. However, the transport system in 2050 represented by this snapshot is still dominated by petroleum fuels, and largely conventional technologies. The fact that petroleum still plays such a large role 50 years into a scenario of sustainable development is largely indicative of the inertia in transport systems. Overcoming this inertia requires a long-term commitment to strategic investments in new technologies and infrastructure, but these results show that the results of such a commitment will not be fully realized for many decades. The year 2050 in the scenario presented here appears to represent a point in the long-term transition to an alternative transport system where a critical mass of new infrastructure has been deployed, and major technological hurdles have been overcome, but incumbent technologies are still dominant. The pay-off from the strategic investments and technology support during the first half of the 21st century is only fully realized later.

The impact of the long-term commitment to sustainable development reflected in this scenario becomes apparent in the second half of the 21st century. By 2100, a mixture of new technologies and fuels have usurped petroleum internal combustion engines, and within this group of new technologies a dominant fuel cell technology has emerged (the hydrogen fuel cell) accounting for over one-third of total transport energy use. The length of the transition from petroleum to hydrogen fuel cells again helps illustrate the inertia in the global transport and energy systems, with technology development and diffusion, both in fuel production and vehicle systems, along with infrastructure development and mobilization of new energy sources, requiring a long lead time even under a sustainable-development scenario. The coexistence of H_2- and alcohol-based fuel cell vehicles in 2100

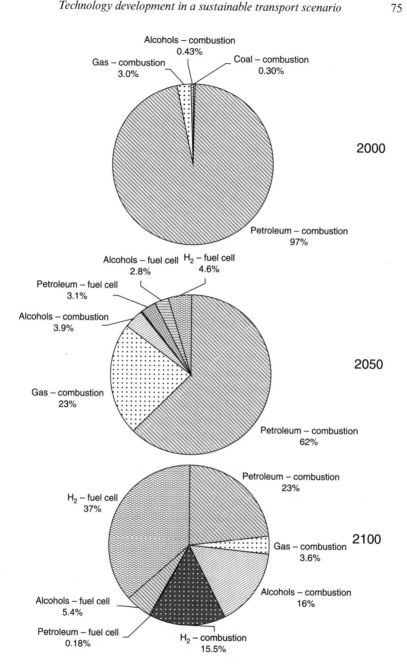

*Figure 5.2   Shares of transportation technologies and fuels (excl.
electricity) in the sustainable scenario in 2000, 2050 and 2100*

partly reflects different resource endowments in different world regions, and the relative levels of hydrogen distribution infrastructure.

Looking at other fuels, petroleum use declines to less than one-quarter of total energy demand by 2100 and, as discussed, most of this is for air transport.[4] Petroleum fuel cell vehicles – one of the promising FC technologies in 2050 – are by 2100 marginalized to a few very small niche markets. This is in contrast to the initial success of this technology earlier in the century (see Figure 5.1), where it played an important role as a 'bridging technology' that enabled experience with fuel cell systems without the need to develop a new fuel distribution infrastructure. A similar development occurs with the use of gas in transport, which plays an important role in reducing transport emissions earlier in the century, before alternative technologies and fuels are sufficiently mature. The remaining energy demand in 2100 is supplied by alcohol fuels and hydrogen used for direct combustion (predominantly in air transport).

5.2   SUSTAINABILITY IN PRIVATE AUTOMOBILE PASSENGER TRANSPORT

Importantly, the pace of the transition towards sustainability under this scenario is different within different transport sub-sectors. As briefly mentioned, air transport remains dependent on a significant quantity of petroleum (roughly equivalent to 70 per cent of today's total transport energy demand). On the other hand, in private automobile transport a rapid shift away from the currently dominating ICE technologies towards alternative technologies is possible. This is illustrated in Figure 5.3, which shows the share of global car travel according to fuel and technology.

In this sector, hybrid ICE–electric technologies are the first to challenge the dominance of the petroleum ICE, and by 2020 account for almost 10 per cent of travel, increasing to more than 20 per cent by 2030 and peaking at almost 60 per cent in 2050. HEVs fuelled with natural gas play the largest role, with smaller shares for petroleum and alcohol HEVs. However, the role of hybrid ICE vehicles is limited to that of a transition technology, albeit for a long transition, towards a transportation system based on fuel cell technologies. In 2050, at the peak in ICE–HEV use, fuel cells account for only one-third of travel but by around 2065 they displace ICE–HEVs as the dominant technology. Importantly, however, hybrid technology continues to be used in FCVs and becomes an integral part of almost all vehicles as the century progresses. By 2100, hybrid fuel cell vehicles account for close to 80 per cent of total travel, leaving only limited markets where alcohol- and gas-based ICE–HEV technologies continue to be attractive

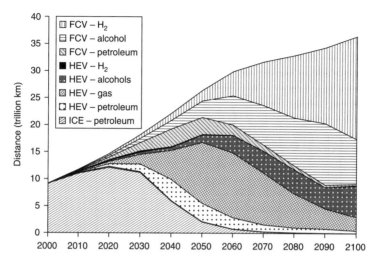

Abbreviations: ICE – conventional internal combustion engine vehicle; HEV – hybrid ICE–electric vehicle; and FCV – hybrid fuel cell–electric vehicle.

Figure 5.3   Technologies and fuels for passenger car travel, sustainability scenario

because of regional circumstances, possibly including limited availability of hydrogen (see Section 5.3).

In the long run, hydrogen- and alcohol-based fuel cell technologies play a very important role, emerging as significant technologies from around 2060 (surpassing petroleum fuel cells). Already by 2070 both technologies represent roughly 27 per cent of the car travel market and, even though in the following decades hydrogen cements its dominance, alcohol FCVs still account for a similar share in 2100. The fact that fuel cell technologies based on different fuels are able to coexist for such a long period mainly reflects feedstock availability for different fuel production technologies, and limits on the speed at which new infrastructure can develop. We shall discuss this issue in Section 5.3.

The penetration of different fuel cell technologies, and the overall timetable of FC introduction in different world regions is presented in Figure 5.4. This figure shows the share of total passenger car travel in each time period accounted for by each fuel cell technology. We can see from Figure 5.4 that, early in the century, almost all regions experiment with a combination of fuel cell technologies, although alcohols and petroleum appear to account for larger shares than hydrogen, reflecting bottlenecks in the roll-out of all the systems and infrastructure required for significant use

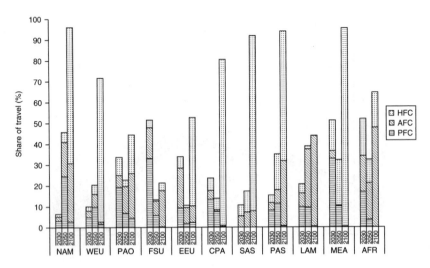

Figure 5.4   Penetration of different fuel cell technologies into the car travel market

of hydrogen in transport. One exception is South Asia (SAS), where the lack of significant indigenous petroleum resources encourages the use of only alcohol and hydrogen fuel cell technologies, with the fuels produced from locally available feedstock, particularly biomass.

Figure 5.4 shows that, by 2050, many regions appear to be favouring particular technologies that are better suited to their circumstances: for example, alcohol fuel cells in Latin America using biomass feedstock for alcohol synthesis, and hydrogen fuel cells in the Middle East using natural gas feedstock. Petroleum fuel cell vehicles play a role primarily as bridging technology, where they help bring about a more rapid introduction and acceptance of fuel cells in transportation before hydrogen and alcohol distribution systems can develop and mature. However, this bridging role is still fairly large, with petroleum fuel cell vehicles accounting for over three trillion km of annual vehicle travel from 2040 to 2050, which is equivalent to more than one-third of global automobile travel in 2000. The drawbacks associated with this technology (namely the need for reforming, lower fuel efficiency and use of a fossil fuel) mean that, once these barriers to other transport technologies are overcome, it largely disappears from the market.

Towards the end of the century some of the technology preferences that were emerging in 2050 become entrenched, and in all regions petroleum fuel cells become less important. By 2100, hydrogen dominates the fuel cell market in Western Europe, CPA, SAS and MEA, whereas alcohol fuel cells dominate in LAM, AFR and FSU.[5] In other regions both fuels coexist. The fuel cell market share ranges from almost 100 per cent down to around 40 per cent in FSU, where alcohol fuels produced from biomass are relatively abundant compared to the size of the transport market, meaning that fuel cells are not required to achieve reductions in greenhouse gas emissions in this region.

5.3   FUEL PRODUCTION FOR SUSTAINABLE TRANSPORT

The attractiveness of alcohol fuel cells is partly related to the fact that, unlike hydrogen, which requires new production and supply infrastructures, methanol and ethanol are liquids at room temperature and pressure and can be handled relatively easily. In addition, these fuels can be distributed utilizing some of the existing fuel delivery infrastructure. However, this advantage comes at a price, since fuel cell cars using methanol or ethanol need an on-board reformer. Still, methanol and ethanol are important for advancing the diffusion of fuel cell technologies in almost all world regions before hydrogen supply infrastructure is fully developed.

Because technologies based on synthetic fuels, including alcohols (methanol and ethanol) and hydrogen, become important substitutes of oil-based technologies in the second half of the 21st century, it is important to look at the source of these energy carriers under this scenario. As mentioned in Chapter 4, ERIS models the entire energy system and ensures engineering and resource consistency are maintained. The ERIS results for this scenario show that supplying the large quantities of hydrogen and alcohols consumed by the transport sector requires a major concomitant structural change in the energy conversion sector. This is illustrated in Figure 5.5, which compares the global output of oil refineries under this scenario to output of hydrogen, alcohols and synthetic Fischer–Tropsch fuels from coal.

As mentioned briefly above, the advantages of alcohol fuels leads to strong growth in synthesis of both ethanol and methanol from biomass feedstocks. Generally methanol is assumed to be produced from either starch- or cellulose-based feedstocks, whereas ethanol is produced primarily from fermentable starch biomass, although synthesis from cellulose feedstocks is also technically viable.[6] Based on the strong growth in alcohol synthesis over the century in Figure 5.5, and the size of the biomass resource required to generate this volume of feedstock, most of the alcohol produced in this sustainable transport scenario can be assumed to be methanol, although ethanol and biodiesel may play an important role

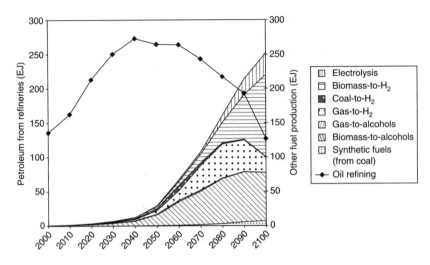

Figure 5.5   Global production of different transport fuels

earlier in the century in fostering the initial market acceptance and penetration of biofuels.

The continuing importance of petroleum throughout the century, as
mentioned earlier, is again illustrated in Figure 5.5, with production in 2100
at roughly the same levels as in 2000. It is not until 2090 that the combined
production of other fuels passes production of petroleum, even though
these fuels are already more important to the transport sector well before
this date.[7] The continuing reliance on petroleum fuels in this scenario
occurs partly because of the barriers to the mobilization of sufficient
resources for large-scale non-fossil synthetic fuel production, particularly
from biomass. It should also be mentioned, however, that there is uncertainty about the size of the ultimately recoverable global petroleum
resources, and in this scenario we have assumed a relatively large oil
resource base (see Section 4.3). If more pessimistic assessments of global
oil resources turn out to be more accurate, achieving the goals of sustainable development, including maintaining energy security, would
require an even faster transition to new fuels and technologies than envisaged in the scenario presented here. Given that the scenario presented here
already involves a number of radical changes to the energy and transport
system, a faster and more extensive transformation poses further challenges and may require additional initiatives aimed at reducing overall
energy demand.

For hydrogen, Figure 5.5 shows that production remains limited for the
first half of the century, and the dominant synthesis route remains reforming

of natural gas until late in the century when biomass becomes the main feed-stock. This complements already extensive use of biomass for alcohol pro-duction. Interestingly, synthesis of hydrogen and petroleum from coal still occurs under this scenario, even though this is an emissions-intensive feed-stock. This is because there remains scope to capture and store some of the carbon in the coal feedstock in both synthesis routes, and this plays an important role in extending the longevity of oil and gas reserves. Synthesis of hydrogen by electrolysis complements the production from other sources, particularly in regions with limited supplies of preferred alternative feed-stocks.

5.4   TRANSPORT FUEL EFFICIENCY AND GREENHOUSE GAS EMISSIONS

The technological change described by this scenario (Section 5.2) includes a major shift to highly efficient technologies as well as the improvement of conventional technologies. It is important to remember that, from a policy perspective, it cannot be assumed that such technological change will arise automatically, but rather is likely to require support in the form of carefully planned investments aimed at specific technologies. However, it is difficult to judge fully the implications of the increasing share of alternative auto-mobile technologies illustrated in Figure 5.3 in terms of fuel consumption. On the one hand the deployment of new technologies has the potential to greatly improve efficiency, whilst on the other the impact of increasing incomes on vehicle choice is likely to offset some of these benefits. Accordingly, to show the overall impact of these factors, in Table 5.1 we present average fuel consumption rates for the entire fleet in each of the 11 world regions analysed in this study. These consumption rates are based on total final energy use in automobile transportation in this scenario, and therefore include both new and old vehicles. Also, although fuels other than gasoline provide most of the energy for car transport in the future under this scenario, the figures in Table 5.1 are given in terms of the equivalent quantity of gasoline.

Table 5.1 shows that overall fuel consumption rates decline by 47–62 per cent over the century, which is modest considering the major technology change the automobile sector undergoes in this scenario. This occurs mainly because a large part of the efficiency gains are offset by changes to the structure of the automobile market, where there is a shift to larger vehi-cles and vehicles with more on-board systems. The significance of this factor is clearly apparent when one considers that there are vehicles in pro-duction in 2005 that achieve the efficiencies presented for 2100,[8] although

Table 5.1 Average in-use fuel consumption rates for all cars under the sustainability scenario (l/100km)

	2000	2010	2020	2030	2040	2050	2060	2070	2080	2090	2100
NAM	11.9[a]	11.6	11.3	10.6	9.3	7.6	6.5	5.9	5.4	5.2	4.9
WEU	7.3[a]	7.1	6.9	6.3	5.1	4.7	4.5	4.3	3.9	3.5	3.2
PAO	9.8[a]	9.4	8.6	6.8	6.3	6.0	5.6	5.2	5.2	5.3	5.0
FSU	9.0[a]	7.5	6.0	5.5	5.6	5.5	5.4	5.2	5.3	5.3	5.0
EEU	9.0[a]	7.0	5.5	5.5	5.5	5.5	5.3	4.9	4.6	4.7	4.3
CPA	10.0[a]	8.7	8.4	7.7	6.4	6.2	5.9	5.5	5.1	4.4	4.1
SAS	10.0[a]	7.5	6.7	6.4	6.2	6.0	5.6	5.2	4.7	4.2	3.9
PAS	10.0[a]	9.6	9.1	8.3	6.6	5.9	5.5	4.9	4.6	4.5	4.1
LAM	10.0[a]	9.5	8.8	7.7	6.4	6.0	6.2	6.0	5.7	5.2	5.4
MEA	10.0[a]	9.1	7.5	6.2	6.0	5.7	5.1	4.5	4.2	4.0	3.8
AFR	10.0[a]	8.7	6.8	5.9	6.0	5.8	5.3	5.0	4.9	4.9	4.9
Global	10.0[a]	9.6	9.1	8.2	7.0	6.2	5.7	5.3	4.9	4.7	4.5

[a] Year 2000 estimates are based on Landwehr and Marie-Lilliu (2002), Davis and Diegel (2004), IRF (2000) and EIA (1999). Because of poor data quality, only rough estimates based on these sources are presented for the developing regions in 2000.

the figures in Table 5.1 are estimated in-use whole-of-fleet averages and the equivalent high-efficiency vehicles in 2100 may achieve fuel economies better than 1 l/100km. These fuel consumption rates resulting from the combination of assumptions applied here can be interpreted as target values for the average fleet vehicle under actual operating conditions (as opposed to the new car performance) consistent with the scenario of sustainable development presented here.

5.4.1   Tank-to-wheels and Well-to-wheels Greenhouse Gas Emissions

One of the most important aspects of this scenario in terms of sustainability is the impact of automobile transport on emissions of greenhouse gases. As discussed in Chapter 1, perhaps the greatest challenge facing car transport if it is to play a role in a sustainable transport system is reducing its contribution to climate change. To explore emissions from car transport under the scenario described here, we present first the tank-to-wheels (TTW) impact on emissions throughout the technology and fuel transitions described above. The concept of tank-to-wheels emissions was mentioned earlier, in Section 4.3, where we presented emissions for a number of illustrative energy chains on this basis in Figure 4.4. To recapitulate, TTW emissions are those arising directly from the use of the vehicle (that is, excluding emissions arising in the extraction, production and delivery of the fuel).

Figure 5.6 presents global TTW emissions and the impact of different factors that improve the emissions intensity, which is also presented. Figure 5.6 shows that, if one considers the volume change in car travel demand alone, annual emissions would quadruple over the century from 650 to 2600 Mt C (the upper curve in Figure 5.6). However, the impact of autonomous energy efficiency improvements (AEEIs, although offset partly by a structural shift to larger vehicles) reduces this to around 2100 Mt C, whilst a shift to HEVs and FCVs reduces this further to 1100 Mt of carbon. The final factor, a shift to low and zero-emissions fuels such as hydrogen reduces TTW emissions from car transport to a little over 500 Mt of carbon by 2100 (the lower curve in Figure 5.6). In other words, the technology transition described above, even with a fourfold increase in global passenger car travel (see Figure 2.8), leads to the emergence of an automobile transport system that has a slightly lower impact on the global climate than do today's automobiles, and therefore goes some way towards sustainability. Moreover, given the nature of these technological transitions, emissions of other airborne pollutants, that is, those responsible primarily for local and regional environmental impacts, are likely to undergo a more rapid and larger decline.

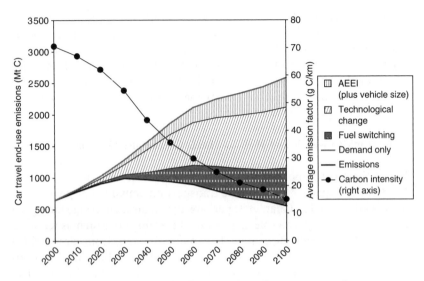

*Figure 5.6   Global tank-to-wheels (TTW) carbon emissions from car
travel, sustainability scenario*

As mentioned, Figure 5.6 shows only the emissions directly from transport, and excludes emissions associated with fuel production or distribution.
Earlier in Section 4.3 we saw, in Figure 4.4, that these 'well-to-tank' emissions
can be substantial for some technology–fuel combinations. Accordingly, to
assess thoroughly the sustainability of passenger transport under this scenario we present in Figure 5.7 the contribution to emission reductions of
technology change and fuel switching on a well-to-wheels (WTW) basis.
Importantly, however, this is only a partial well-to-wheels basis similar to that
presented in Section 4.3, since it excludes non-CO_2 emissions (which arise, for
instance, from fertilizers used for biomass production, or from venting of
gases during oil extraction) and emissions produced in the transport of fuels.[9]

On this partial WTW basis, in Figure 5.7 emissions from car transport
increase to approximately 3500 Mt of carbon by 2100 based solely on demand
increases and an increase in the relative share of synthetic petroleum fuels.[10]
Changes in engine technology and fuel choice greatly reduce emissions, down
to about 180 Mt of carbon in 2100. This is lower than the figure of 500 Mt C
on a TTW basis because the carbon sequestered during the production of biofuels (that is, as a result of photosynthetic CO_2 uptake by growing biomass
feedstocks) is now included in the calculation.[11] Such a large reduction is also
achieved partly because some of the carbon in the biomass used to produce
hydrogen (see Figure 5.5) is also captured and stored (indicated by CCS in
Figure 5.7), leading to net negative emissions from this source of hydrogen.

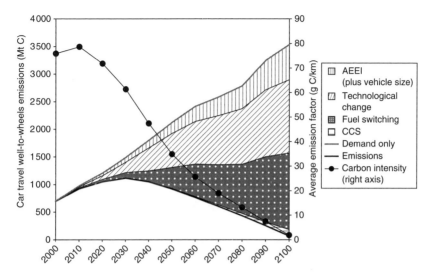

*Figure 5.7   Global well-to-wheels (WTW) carbon emissions from car
travel, sustainability scenario*

A breakdown of global average WTW emissions into well-to-tank
(WTT) and tank-to-wheels (TTW) emissions is presented in Figure 5.8 for
each automobile technology in 2020, 2050 and 2100. Figure 5.8 shows that,
over the century, emissions per kilometre decrease for almost all technologies, and results presented earlier indicate that this can be attributed to
efficiency improvements in both car and fuel production technologies, as
well as a shift to alternative fuel synthesis routes. However, Figure 5.8 shows
that for most technologies the rate at which emissions intensity decreases is
evolutionary rather than revolutionary, with the exception of hydrogen-
based technologies. For these technologies, the emission factors initially
increase because of increasing use of coal in hydrogen production, before
experiencing a large decline as a consequence of a shift to biomass feedstocks and deployment of carbon capture and storage technologies. This
again highlights the potential significance of alternative fuel production
routes to facilitate large-scale abatement. Further, Figure 5.8 also again
illustrates that, under the assumptions used here, stringent abatement goals
may be best achieved by switching to alternative technologies and fuels,
rather than from evolutionary changes in incumbent technologies.

The overall impact of all of the emissions-reducing developments in the
car transport market in the scenario presented in this chapter is to reduce
the average emissions factor continuously over the century to almost zero
by 2100: that is, on this partial WTW basis passenger transport becomes an

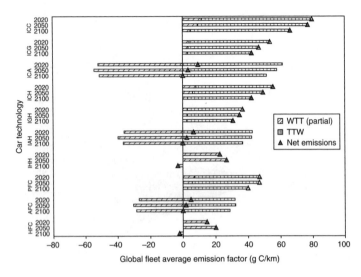

*Figure 5.8   Breakdown of well-to-wheels emissions for car technologies,
              sustainable development scenario*

almost insignificant source of greenhouse gas emissions, although it takes
almost 100 years to achieve this feat. By many indicators car transport
becomes increasingly sustainable as the century unfolds in this scenario.

5.5   A SUSTAINABLE ENERGY SYSTEM

The developments in transport in the sustainable scenario outlined in this
chapter described above represent the transformation of the global energy
system in only one sector. Importantly, in this scenario, emissions reductions are not confined solely to the transport sector. Total emissions under
this sustainability scenario are presented in Figure 5.9, which shows that
global emissions by 2100 from all sources return to roughly the level in 2000
(noting that the emissions from energy presented in Figure 5.9 are reduced
to account for carbon capture and storage and land-use change and forestry,
which are indicated below the horizontal axis in the figure). Emissions peak
in 2070 at just below twice the level in 2000, which differs from the timing of
peak emissions from passenger transport where higher levels of sustainability are achieved much earlier (with WTW emissions peaking at 2030; see
Figure 5.7). Other important results illustrated in Figure 5.9 include substantial carbon sequestration through reforestation and afforestation programmes throughout the world, and an increasingly important role for

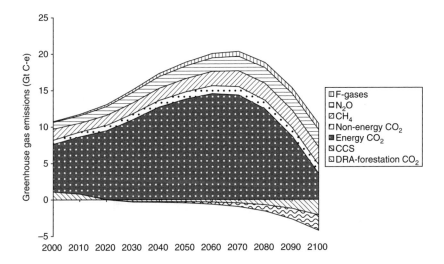

Note: Carbon capture and storage (CCS) from energy emissions is also indicated, as are net emissions or sequestration from deforestation, reforestation and afforestation (DRA-forestation). Emissions of CO_2 from combustion of biomass-based fuels are in balance with sequestration by crops used for energy, and therefore neither appears in this figure.

Figure 5.9   Global emissions and sequestration from all sources, sustainability scenario

carbon capture and geosequestration. By 2100, around 30 per cent of annual global CO_2 emissions from energy are geosequestered.

To explore further some of the main features of the emergence of a sustainable energy system that occur in conjunction with the transport sector developments discussed above, we briefly look at another important sector, electricity production. In this scenario electricity becomes an increasingly important energy carrier, because of its convenience and flexibility, continuing the trend mentioned in Section 1.1. Figure 5.10 shows how total electricity generation and the generation fuel mix change over the 21st century under this sustainable development scenario. The most important trends include initially a shift towards natural gas-fired generation, followed by an increasing role for nuclear energy and a significant expansion in the role of renewables, with these two fuels dominating the generation sector in 2100. The challenge of reducing greenhouse gas emissions, combined with the emergence of inherently safe reactors, spurs this wide-scale acceptance of nuclear energy. Nonetheless, there are a number of significant challenges facing nuclear energy that must be addressed before this technology can be considered suitable for sustainable development.

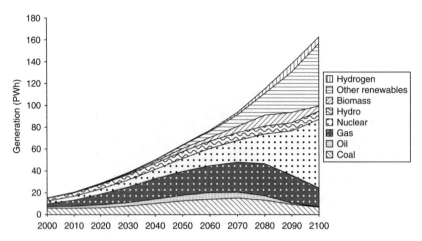

Figure 5.10   Development of a sustainable electricity sector

Under this scenario stationary generation from hydrogen fuel cells supplies some niche markets, but most of the hydrogen is used in other sectors, where there are fewer low-emissions substitutes for fossil fuels. Electricity generation using biomass fuels also remains a relatively small part of the total output, because almost all available biomass is used for synthetic alcohol and hydrogen production.

It is important to mention that the sustainable-development scenario described here does not include large-scale electricity generation using the fuel cells in parked vehicles. Other researchers have suggested that it may be possible to exploit the fleet of fuel cell vehicles when they are not in use as a form of distributed electricity generation at demand centres (including households and places of work), particularly during periods of peak demand or to contribute to system stability (Lipman et al., 2004; Barreto et al., 2003; Letendre and Kempton, 2002; Moura, 2006; Turton and Moura, 2006). However, this scenario already relies on a massive mobilization of resources and the required infrastructure for hydrogen production and distribution and supplying additional hydrogen (or alcohols) for electricity generation poses additional challenges. There are also a number of other potential barriers to the large-scale use of fuel cell vehicles for electricity generation.[12]

Accordingly, the electricity generation system, and the energy system more generally, is based largely on renewable and nuclear energy sources, which are advantageous for delivering high-quality energy services while minimizing a number of environmental impacts, in terms of both consumption of natural resources and pollutant emissions, including greenhouse gases (GHGs). However, although much of nuclear electricity generation in this scenario is from inherently safe third- and fourth-generation reactors, this technology must overcome a number of other major barriers before it can be fully embraced as a contributor to sustainable development, related mainly to waste management and safety, public acceptance and weapons proliferation. In comparison, renewable primary energy sources such as wind and solar power have already found wide acceptance as a means to achieve CO_2 emission reductions as well as to increase energy security by reducing the reliance on the fossil fuels, and these technologies play an increasingly important role in this scenario. These developments are equally important for the emergence of a sustainable transport system, since they ensure that these other sectors do not overly compete with transportation for the fuels (such as hydrogen) required to make the transition to sustainable mobility.

Importantly, the use of hydrogen in transport and other sectors affords similar flexibility to that provided by electricity in the stationary sector. Hydrogen can be produced from a variety of fossil and non-fossil primary energy carriers, and in this scenario the capacity to use initially a mixture of feedstocks, before transitioning through natural gas to biomass for hydrogen production, facilitates faster penetration of efficient hydrogen technologies. In this scenario, the flexibility in hydrogen production and use means that over time the share of renewably produced transport fuels increases further and further, and net sequestration of CO_2 from hydrogen production emerges, fostering the transition to a sustainable energy system. Moreover, like electricity, hydrogen can be used in a variety of applications in an efficient and clean manner, but unlike electricity it has the additional advantage of storability (Barreto et al., 2003).

5.6 SUMMARY

In this chapter we have described one scenario of sustainable development for the transport sector, within a sustainable energy system. This sustainable E3 scenario explores the potential for technological improvements and transitions in both vehicle and fuel production technologies to alleviate the environmental and resource-depletion impacts of future demands for private mobility.

This analysis shows that the passenger car sector has the potential to achieve high levels of sustainability in terms of environmental impact through the adoption of a combination of new engine technologies (including hybrid and fuel cell drivetrains) and zero-emissions fuels such as hydrogen and alcohols from renewable sources. A sustainable transport system emerges despite the impact of structural changes to the passenger vehicle market and increasing demands for car transport, both resulting from growth in personal incomes.

Hydrogen and alcohol fuels play a crucial part in the transition to sustainability. However, petroleum fuels can also play a role in a future sustainable transport system, particularly in air transport, and may also be necessary while barriers to the widespread utilization of hydrogen, such as establishing suitable distribution infrastructure and mobilizing alternative feedstocks on a large scale, are overcome. Renewable and low-emissions resources combined with hydrogen technology have a strategic importance in the pursuit of a low-emission, environmentally benign and sustainable energy system. In the more distant future, these resources and hydrogen could become important energy commodities at the global level.

Accordingly, from a technical perspective, the barriers to the emergence of a sustainable energy and transport system are surmountable, under the assumptions applied here. However, we have not explored the commercial barriers, or the possible trade-offs that are necessary to achieve such an energy system. In a world where sustainability considerations are incorporated into all decision making, both macro and micro, such a system would evolve of its own accord. However, the existence of market failures, such as negative externalities and a failure to incorporate preferences of future generations, renders the optimal allocation of society's scarce resources by market forces alone extremely unlikely. The best way to overcome such market failures may be through policy intervention and support to promote sustainable technologies and systems. To illustrate this need, we show in the following chapter the kind of energy system more likely to develop in a world where markets are driven primarily by economic, rather than social, costs and benefits.

NOTES

1. For example, baseline and business-as-usual scenarios have to date generally excluded greenhouse gas abatement measures, but this approach is becoming harder to sustain given the entry into force of the Kyoto Protocol in March 2005, and the adoption of policies throughout much of the world to mitigate climate change.
2. The modified models of Schafer and Victor (2000) were also used to develop estimates of future passenger air transport that were consistent with trends in car travel.
3. Note that the pie chart for 2000 is identical to that presented in Figure 1.8, except for the exclusion of electricity and rounding differences.
4. Under this scenario, the share of transport energy demand supplied by petroleum drops below 50 per cent soon after 2060.
5. The preference for alcohol fuels in LAM and AFR is not particularly surprising because of the abundance of biomass in these regions. However, for the former Soviet Union (FSU) it is somewhat unexpected that large reserves of gas do not favour the production

of hydrogen from steam methane reforming. This occurs because in this scenario it is more effective to export this natural gas – already a flexible and relatively clean fuel – and use less convenient sources of primary energy for synthesis of transportation fuels. Under this sustainable development scenario, biomass-to-alcohol production is favoured over biomass-to-hydrogen production because it avoids the need to develop a more expensive fuel distribution system in what is a large and sparsely populated world region.

6. Biodiesel produced from oil-based crops and other biomass is another important biofuel, although its production is not modelled explicitly in the framework applied here.
7. The higher efficiency at which these fuels are used, mainly in FCVs, means that they supply a much greater share of travel than petroleum well before 2090.
8. For example, the Toyota Prius 2004 model achieves an efficiency of 4.3 l/100km under European and USA test conditions (*personal communication*, Toyota).
9. Although both of these sources are included in the estimates of total greenhouse gas emissions in the next section.
10. The kink in total emissions in Figure 5.7 between 2080 and 2090 occurs mainly because of a shift towards greater use in synthetic petroleum fuels in some world regions. The impact is exaggerated in Figure 5.7 by the fact that conventional petroleum production is very small in some regions by this stage, so a small change in synthetic fuel production results in a large change in the average emissions factor for petroleum fuels.
11. Although this is slightly offset by the inclusion of emissions produced in hydrogen and synthetic fuel production. However, both of these fuel production activities are amenable to carbon capture and storage (CCS), and application of this technology in this scenario reduces partial WTW emissions to close to 65 Mt C in 2100.
12. See Moura (2006) and Turton and Moura (2006) for further discussion.

6. Alternative scenarios of a future transport system

Adopting new technologies and mobilizing alternative resources has the potential to facilitate the development of a sustainable energy system. Chapter 5 examined and demonstrated the potential of new technologies and fuels to deliver a sustainable transport system, along with a low-emissions global energy system. However, this was only an assessment of technical potential, rather than commercial potential. In this current chapter we examine whether current market drivers alone are sufficient to achieve such a sustainable energy system and, where they fall short, identify possible key targets for policy support to promote sustainable development in the transport sector.

6.1 ENERGY AND TRANSPORT SYSTEM DEVELOPMENT IN THE ABSENCE OF SUSTAINABLE DEVELOPMENT OBJECTIVES

We present here another scenario of the transport sector, again based on the economic, social and transport demand developments described in Chapter 2. The main point of divergence, however, is that we assume that some aspects of sustainability – in particular greenhouse gas emission abatement and strategic management of resource depletion – are not pursued. This assumption means that many key current policy drivers of energy system development are excluded, including current (and future) climate change mitigation policies, efforts to promote energy security and some aspects of technology development (such as R&D). Accordingly, it is not appropriate to refer to this as a 'business-as-usual' scenario, and it is more correctly described as a 'no-policy' scenario. This scenario helps us to understand the type of energy and transport system that may emerge in the absence of policy intervention, thereby illustrating the importance of policy and other measures in achieving a sustainable energy system similar to that described in Chapter 5.

Following the same format as in the previous sector, Figure 6.1 shows the growth in transport energy demand from the early 1970s to the end of the

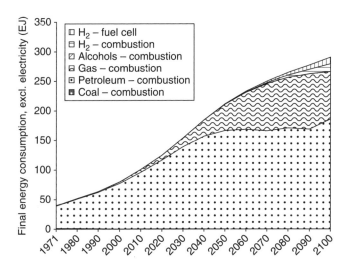

Note: Combustion of coal and alcohols makes only a very small contribution and is difficult to see on the diagram.

Figure 6.1 Global energy consumption by transportation, historical and no-policy scenario

21st century under this no-policy scenario. From the year 2000 to 2100, demand increases from around 80 EJ to almost 300 EJ. In comparison, under the sustainable transport scenario described in Chapter 5, demand grew to less than 250 EJ, and the higher demand in the no-policy scenario can be attributed to a lower uptake of efficient engine technologies. Furthermore, fossil fuels continue to provide almost all the energy required for transportation, although depletion of cheap oil resources promotes greater use of natural gas. Even with this additional use of gas, petroleum product consumption in transport is almost 2.5 times the 2000 level at the end of the century (compared to returning to 2000 levels in the sustainable transport scenario).

The slower adoption of new vehicle technologies is perhaps best illustrated in Figure 6.2, which shows that in the passenger vehicle market the transition from ICEVs to hybrid-electric vehicles occurs later in the century and there is much lower adoption of fuel cell vehicles. Accordingly, prevailing market conditions are sufficient to support the introduction of HEVs, but there are still a number of barriers to fuel cell vehicles. In addition to a reluctance to utilize new technologies, the passenger travel market continues to rely almost exclusively on fossil fuels, although, as was mentioned above, gas is particularly attractive because of declining availability of cheap oil.[1]

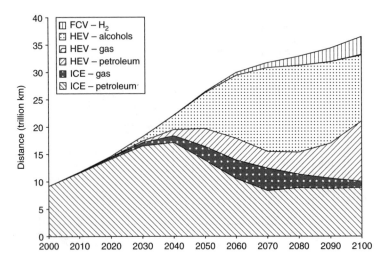

*Figure 6.2   Technologies and fuels for passenger car travel, no-policy
              scenario*

Under this scenario the most efficient engine technologies – the fuel
cells – are not particularly attractive during the 21st century. This can
be attributed largely to the lesser importance given to mitigating climate
change and maintaining oil and gas resources. The small contribution
made by fuel cells towards the end of the century occurs because of declining oil and gas availability, although unlike the sustainable transport scenario described in Chapter 5, this is driven by necessity rather than active
management of the resource base. In some ways this could be viewed as the
first phase in a slow transition to sustainable resource consumption, since
consumption of an exhaustible resource must ultimately decline regardless
of whether sustainable development is a social and political goal (Turton
and Barreto, 2006).

The impact of the technology transition shown in Figure 6.2 on average
fleet fuel consumption rates, using the same assumptions as in Chapter 5,
is presented in Table 6.1. Fuel consumption rates decline only slowly over
the century, and the impact of HEV technologies and other efficiency
improvements (as described in Chapter 5, Section 5.4) is partly offset by
changes to the size and type of vehicles chosen by consumers over the
century. This explains why these average fleet fuel efficiencies in Table 6.1
do not appear ambitious compared to the efficiencies achieved by current
new hybrid vehicles, such as the Toyota Prius, which achieves a fuel consumption rate of 4.3 l/100km under test conditions. Given changing consumer preferences towards larger vehicles, a more appropriate comparison

Table 6.1 Average in-use fuel consumption rates for all cars under the no-policy scenario (l/100km)

	2000	2010	2020	2030	2040	2050	2060	2070	2080	2090	2100
NAM	11.9[a]	11.7	11.4	11.0	10.3	8.9	7.7	7.0	6.3	5.6	5.1
WEU	7.3[a]	7.2	7.0	6.9	6.8	6.6	6.5	6.4	6.2	6.1	6.0
PAO	9.8[a]	9.6	9.4	9.2	9.1	8.8	8.6	8.5	8.3	8.1	8.0
FSU	9.0[a]	8.8	8.6	8.4	8.2	8.0	7.8	7.5	7.0	6.4	6.1
EEU	9.0[a]	8.8	8.6	8.4	8.3	8.1	7.9	7.8	7.6	7.4	7.1
CPA	10.0[a]	9.8	9.6	9.4	9.2	9.0	8.9	8.7	8.5	8.3	8.2
SAS	10.0[a]	9.8	9.6	9.4	9.1	8.9	8.7	8.4	8.1	7.7	7.2
PAS	10.0[a]	9.8	9.5	9.1	8.5	7.3	6.6	6.2	6.0	5.9	5.8
LAM	10.0[a]	9.8	9.5	9.1	8.6	7.8	6.7	6.2	6.0	5.9	5.8
MEA	10.0[a]	9.7	9.3	8.5	7.6	6.8	6.3	6.1	6.0	5.9	5.8
AFR	10.0[a]	9.6	9.2	8.4	7.4	6.9	6.4	6.1	6.0	5.8	5.7
Global	10.0[a]	9.8	9.5	9.2	8.7	8.0	7.3	7.0	6.7	6.4	6.2

[a] Year 2000 estimates are based on Landwehr and Marie-Lilliu (2002), Davis and Diegel (2004), IRF (2000) and EIA (1999). Because of poor data quality, only rough estimates based on these sources are presented for the developing regions in 2000.

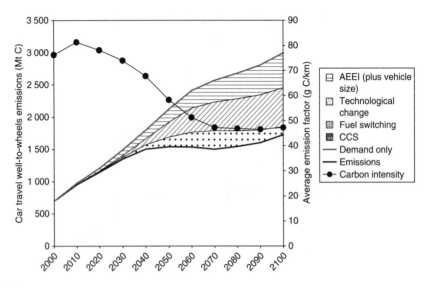

*Figure 6.3   Global well-to-wheels (WTW) carbon emissions from car
travel, no-policy scenario*

would be to the Ford Escape 4WD hybrid, which achieves efficiencies
under test conditions of between 7.1 (city) and 8.1 (hwy) 1/100km,
although these figures are still not directly comparable.[2]

To examine the extent to which the shift from ICEs to HEVs and from
petroleum to gas is able to reduce the impact on greenhouse gas emissions
of transportation, we present partial well-to-wheels (WTW) emissions
under this no-policy scenario in Figure 6.3. Similar to Figure 5.7, Figure
6.3 shows the impact on emissions of the increase in travel demand and
also the impact of efficiency, technology and fuel switching under this scenario. Simply looking at the increase in travel volume in isolation, we see
that total emissions increase to roughly 3000 Mt of carbon by 2100.[3]
However, as discussed in Chapter 5, improved fuel economy from improvements to vehicle weight, aerodynamics, rolling resistance and some engine
features, offset by changes to the type of vehicle purchased, reduce this to
below 2500 Mt C. The impact of major engine technology changes, and
changes to less emissions-intensive fuels reduces emissions to around
1700 Mt of carbon at the end of the century. This is close to three times
the level in 2000. The average WTW emissions intensity reduces by 35 per
cent to around 45–50 grams of carbon per kilometre. In comparison,
under the sustainable transport scenario presented in Chapter 5, WTW

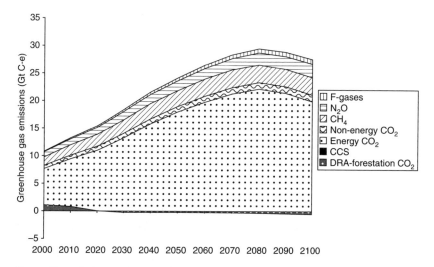

Note: Net emissions or sequestration from deforestation, reforestation and afforestation (DRA-forestation) are indicated. Emissions of CO_2 from combustion of biomass-based fuels are in balance with sequestration by crops used for energy, and therefore neither appears in this figure.

Figure 6.4   Global emissions and sequestration from all sources, no-policy scenario

emissions were reduced to almost zero at the end of the century. The overall trajectory for global greenhouse gas emissions under this scenario is illustrated in Figure 6.4, which shows that emissions continue to rise throughout most of the century.

Accordingly, although the scenarios presented in this and the previous chapter are based on the same economic and social developments, the no-policy scenario cannot be classified as a sustainable development scenario because it fails to achieve environmental and resource sustainability. The sustainability and no-policy scenarios can perhaps be seen as representing two ends of a wide spectrum of possible transport and energy futures, based on a single socioeconomic development scenario. This spectrum covers the significant policy and social uncertainty associated with the extent to which environmental sustainability will be incorporated into future decision making. To explore some of this uncertainty, we will briefly examine the impact on the passenger car technology transition, shown in Figure 6.2, of two additional alternative levels of concern for environmental sustainability.

6.2   THE IMPACT OF CLIMATE CHANGE POLICIES ON PASSENGER TRANSPORT TECHNOLOGY CHOICE

Investigating the impact of changes in the policy environment helps to identify which passenger transport technology and fuel strategies are promising across a range of policies, and hence may be worth pursuing despite policy or scientific uncertainty regarding what will be necessary to realize sustainable development. Moreover, exploring scenarios where sustainable development is of only intermediate social concern helps to identify and reinforce where additional measures will be necessary should policy and scientific uncertainty be resolved in a way that dictates a requirement for a more stringent response. In other words, the uncertainty analysis presented in this section can also highlight where technology hedging strategies may be appropriate.

To assess the impact of alternative sustainable development policy scenarios on the deployment of new passenger transport technologies we have constructed two additional scenarios where the extent of concern for environmental sustainability is represented by the level of tax on greenhouse gas emissions that is tolerated by society. In reality, different countries and world regions are likely to adopt an array of abatement measures, and the use of a GHG tax merely seeks to represent the effective stringency of all of these measures in a single instrument (taxes and other policy instruments are discussed more in Part III). The two tax levels applied in these additional scenarios were designed to represent a moderate and a stringent climate change mitigation policy. The path of passenger transport technology adoption under these scenarios is presented in Figure 6.5 and Figure 6.6, respectively. Under a tax of $150 per tonne of carbon equivalent[4] applied globally throughout the century (Figure 6.5), there is more rapid penetration of hybrid technologies into the vehicle market, and faster transition from petroleum to gas, than under the no-policy scenario. Moreover, this tax level provides sufficient stimulus to the development of a substantial synthetic alcohol industry, and alcohol-fuelled hybrid vehicles account for a significant and increasing share of travel by the end of the century. Hydrogen FC vehicles, on the other hand, continue to play only a small role towards the end of the century under this scenario. Clearly, a number of elements of the technology transition that occurred under the sustainable development scenario are also taking place under this $150/ton C-e tax scenario: a rapid transition to hybrids, an initial shift to natural gas and eventually the mobilization of resources and investment to develop an alcohol fuel production and distribution infrastructure.

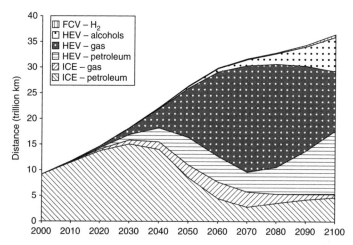

Figure 6.5 Technologies and fuels for passenger car travel, with $150/t
C-e tax

Under a scenario where concern for environmental sustainability is
significantly higher, represented by a willingness to adopt measures equivalent to a tax of $500 per tonne C-e[5] throughout the 21st century, the tech-
nological transition is faster and includes additional elements, as shown in
Figure 6.6. This level of environmental concern not only promotes an even
faster adoption of hybrid technologies, but provides sufficient impetus
for earlier penetration into the vehicle market of hydrogen fuel cell technologies. Under this scenario these technologies achieve levels of adoption
comparable to those under the $150/t C-e scenario around 40 years earlier.
However, the uptake of these more environmentally benign technologies
is still well below the level achieved in the sustainable development scenario, indicating that more vigorous policy support is required to realize
fully the capacity of fuel cells to transform the global transport system.
Importantly, this is not necessarily a goal in itself and the alternative scenarios described above help to illustrate that such a transformation is
required only when very stringent climate change mitigation and resource
management policies are pursued as part of a relatively rapid realization of
sustainable development.

If sustainable development is a long-term social goal, this analysis highlights the approximate level of policy intervention needed to promote such
development in the transport system specifically, and the energy system
more broadly. The analysis above has shown that additional technological
development of fuel cells and production technologies for alternative low-
or zero-emissions fuels is needed to improve the cost and performance of

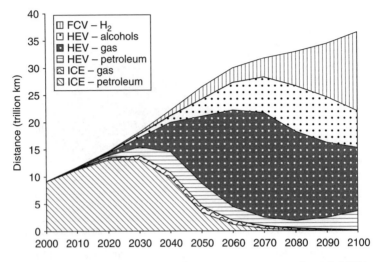

Figure 6.6   Technologies and fuels for passenger car travel, with $500/t C-e tax

these technologies and make them more commercially attractive. However, only a successful combination of research, development, and demonstration (RD&D) efforts, as well as commercial deployment would lead to the necessary technology improvements and cost reductions. Intensive R&D efforts are still required in a number of areas and policy support for the deployment of the renewable energy sources is essential (Barreto et al., 2003). Importantly, however, even with such technology–push support, additional intervention to ensure appropriate market signals (or demand–pull) may be needed to direct technology adoption in the transport sector. The next part of this book investigates and describes some of the important policy interventions that may play a role in promoting a sustainable transport system.

NOTES

1. There is a slight resurgence in the use of petroleum products at the conclusion of the 21st century because by this stage gas resources are almost exhausted.
2. This is because they represent performance under test conditions of a new vehicle, rather than actual in-use fuel consumption (which is reported in Table 6.1). Furthermore, in the scenario represented in Table 6.1 conventional ICE vehicles still account for a large proportion of the car market, and so the reported fuel consumption rates reflect the weighted average of hybrid and conventional vehicle efficiencies. Note, that the Ford Escape hybrid efficiencies were obtained from www.ford.com.

3. Note that this total is different from the equivalent estimate shown in Figure 5.7 owing to the much larger share of synthetic petroleum fuels in the sustainable development scenario, compared to the no-policy scenario illustrated in Figure 6.3. However, this larger share of synthetic petroleum comes about entirely owing to a decline in the use of conventional petroleum.

4. That is, around \$40 per tonne of CO_2-equivalent. This is comparable to the excess emission penalty of €40 per tonne of CO_2 equivalent levied under the European Union Emissions Trading Scheme (European Parliament, 2003, Article 16 (4)).

5. Equivalent to a tax of around \$135 per tonne of CO_2-equivalent.

PART III

Policy measures for sustainable transport

7. Policy instruments to reduce GHG from passenger road transport

Transport contributes greatly to global greenhouse gas emissions and is forecast to remain a significant source of concern in this regard in the future. Some of the possible implications, and ways to address these concerns, were presented in a number of scenarios in Chapters 5 and 6, modelled under various assumptions. For instance, the main scenario shown in Chapter 6 estimates potential energy and transport system development, and greenhouse gas emissions in the future, under the assumption that no policies to address sustainable development are pursued, and market forces alone determine energy and transport system characteristics. Other scenarios, such as that presented in Chapter 5, illustrate the potential impact that a more aggressive policy approach to greenhouse gas abatement and sustainable development can have on technological change, leading to efficiency improvements, adoption of new vehicle technologies and fuel switching. The divergence in future greenhouse gas emissions from transport between these scenarios is significant, and the analysis in the previous chapters tells us what kind of a reduction in greenhouse gas emissions can be anticipated if improvements in technology are achieved.

However, the scenarios themselves do not provide specific information on the best way to achieve the technological changes required for longer-term sustainability. The model tells us what kind of technological change is necessary to achieve greenhouse gas emissions mitigation from road transport at least total system cost, but not which policy instruments will achieve this goal most effectively, taking into account transaction costs, political feasibility and other institutional or social factors. A range of government initiatives, such as regulations, agreements and economic instruments, can all play an important role in correcting market failures to promote automobile technological development which is more compatible with sustainable development. To illustrate with a specific example, although the analysis in Chapters 5 and 6 identified targets for vehicle emissions performance, the results in these chapters do not themselves explain how best to involve governments and automobile manufacturers in achieving these targets, such as the current voluntary agreement between European governments and the European, Japanese and Korean automobile manufactures in their pursuit of a new-vehicle tank-to-wheels CO_2 emissions performance of 140 g/km in the EU.

Policy instruments are necessary to influence both the supply and demand for transport. Chapters 7 to 10 in Part III present a review of the range of policy instruments available to promote technology improvements and hence achieve reductions in greenhouse gas emissions from passenger cars. Where possible we provide recent examples of policies to mitigate CO_2 emissions from transport. In many cases we focus on policy implementation and experience in Europe because this region currently provides many of the best examples and evidence of the impact of prospective policies aimed at reducing greenhouse gas emissions from transport.

7.1 POLICY INSTRUMENTS APPLIED TO GREENHOUSE GAS MITIGATION

The word 'instrument' derives from the Latin 'instrumentum', meaning an apparatus or tool. We think of a musical instrument the playing of which produces music, or a medical surgeon's instruments, applied to remove an appendix or insert a heart valve. Thus described, the word creates an association in the mind with skill in application, with precision, with a direct and predictable relationship between cause and effect.

However, when we turn to the use of policy instruments to shape environmental behaviour, we find that technical engineering exactitude is not characteristic. Instead of precision, we talk of moving performance in a more environmentally positive direction, with considerable uncertainties as to the outcomes in this regard.

Typically, we recognize the following broad classes of policy instrument applied in the environmental field:

(1) *Command and control, or regulation,* whereby a standard of environmental performance is set and enforceable by law, and often administered using an integrated pollution control licensing scheme. Regulations mandating minimum average fuel efficiency, minimum insulation standards in new buildings, or requiring that combined heat and power be used in certain circumstances, are of this character.

(2) *Direct market-based instruments*, whereby a direct price signal is given to polluters that emissions impose a cost on society, and that they will pay a penalty per unit of emission every time they pollute. There are two types of direct market-based instruments: environmental taxes and charges, whereby a charge that in theory reflects the marginal

external cost being imposed at the optimum point is imposed; and emissions trading, whereby typically the total quantity of emissions per unit time is fixed and this 'envelope' allocated to emitters, and they then trade, with the proviso that, at the end of the trading period, emitters always hold sufficient permits to 'cover' their emissions.

(3) *Indirect market-based instruments*, including grants and tax and other subsidies, the removal of subsidies (environmentally perverse subsidies) and government regulations that encourage environmental degradation, and 'green purchasing' and procurement policies by governments and companies. Special capital write-off provisions relating to pollution abatement equipment (environment-enhancing subsidies) are also of this character.

(4) *Direct investment* that facilitates emission reduction: for example, investment in the electrical grid so that it can 'take' additional wind power, and investment in a gas pipeline interconnector that provides additional natural gas to substitute for more carbon-rich fuels, fall also into this category.

(5) *Information* that allows producers and consumers to know and understand the implications of the choices they face. Examples include energy audits and performance labelling that allow buyers of buildings, cars and appliances to know what are the energy performance characteristics of their prospective purchase.

(6) *Voluntary or negotiated agreements*, whereby a firm or group of firms in a sector commit themselves to meet a particular standard, for example carbon emissions per unit of output, typically within a defined period. Such agreements are often encouraged by tax and regulatory concessions.

(7) *Investment in research, development and demonstration (RD&D)*, which can produce new choices that did not exist before, which reduce the costs of meeting standards, or develop entirely new products and processes that change the nature of products and services.

7.1.1 Evaluation of Instruments

Each of these instruments has advantages and disadvantages and is suitable for different situations. An assessment is needed on an individual case basis so that policymakers can establish the benefits and costs of each instrument applied to a particular task. Economics evaluates the efficacy of instruments on the basis of several criteria:

a. *Static economic efficiency*: does the instrument achieve the environmental objective at minimum cost?

b. *Dynamic efficiency*: does the instrument create a continuing incentive for improvement over time and place?

c. *Distribution*: there are two aspects to this dimension, which do not necessarily work in the same direction. First, in its effects, is the application of the instrument 'fair' in the sense of protecting the well-being of those most vulnerable. Secondly, are the interests of those who most powerfully influence the shaping of policy (the 'stakeholders') sufficiently protected that they are willing to at least not block the use of the instrument?

d. *Administrative and political feasibility*: will key organizations and individuals in the relevant bureaucracies and political establishments back its implementation?

e. *Environmental effectiveness*: are environmental objectives met?

Table 7.1 summarizes the strengths and weaknesses of policy instruments based on the criteria above (Convery et al., 2003a). It is clear that no individual instrument will be the panacea to greenhouse gas reduction, but that rather different instruments will suit different technological, economic and cultural situations.

Although historically the most common instrument implemented in the area of environmental policy has been command and control policies, these have been found to be frequently inefficient. Standard regulation can be statically inefficient in that it may not achieve environmental objectives at minimum cost, and it may be dynamically inefficient, since there may be no incentive for polluters to continually improve. In recent years demand-side market-based instruments such as taxes, green subsidies and emissions trading have become more popular, as they provide an incentive to continually improve environmental performance. The revenue generated by market-based instruments can provide a double dividend if they are used to reduce other taxes which may be slowing economic growth[1] or creating inequity in society.

Supply-side policy instruments such as voluntary agreements and investment in research and development are relevant as they provide a push to bring new technology to the market. The voluntary agreement between passenger car manufacturers and the European Commission is the main instrument at EU level explicitly used to reduce CO_2 emissions from passenger cars (described in Chapter 9), whereas the Bush Administration has selected research and development (R&D) as the policy instrument of choice for addressing climate change.[2]

While information is a policy instrument in its own right, it is also fundamental to all other policy instruments. Without good information policymakers cannot understand the underlying environmental problem, their impacts or the cost of resolving them.

Table 7.1   Taxonomy of environmental policy instruments

Instrument	Main strength	Main weakness
Command and control (regulation)	Well established, familiar, few set-up costs to implement in developed countries	Potential for regulatory capture, high total costs of compliance
Direct market-based instruments		
Taxes and charges	Can reduce total costs of compliance and enhance economy-wide performance	Politically difficult to raise charges to 'optimal' level
Emission trading	Wide coverage, improved stakeholder acceptability, reduce total costs of compliance and (perhaps) enhance economy-wide performance	Free allocation of trading permits can reduce stakeholder acceptability, equity and potential effectiveness
Indirect market-based instruments		
'Green' grants and subsidies	Highly popular with beneficiaries	Difficult to avoid 'dead weight' losses and high costs relative to benefits at margin
Removal of environmentally perverse subsidies	Simultaneously reduces the burden on taxpayers and improves their environment	Very difficult to achieve because of beneficiary dependence, for example the coal industry
Direct investment	Very large and continuing impact with large investment	Issues in unfair competition and 'State aid' in EU context
Information	Can be very cost-effective, and empowering for consumers	Response limited if choices not market reality need to combine incentives
Voluntary agreements	High degree of acceptability with some stakeholders	Can have high transactions costs and low credibility with environmental NGOs and others
RD&D	Imposes no pain on emitters	Effectiveness doubtful in absence of strong complementary market signal

In an ideal world the optimal emissions abatement level can be estimated as the intersection of the marginal damage and marginal abatement cost curves. However there is generally great uncertainty with respect to the shape of these curves. Often the abatement costs are not known to the policymaker, owing to incomplete information on abatement technologies. In many cases also the technology has not been fully developed and therefore the future costs of abatement may not yet be known even to the manufacturer. The marginal cost of abatement curve may be neither smooth nor linear, since abatement technologies may be much more costly for increasing abatement levels. On the marginal damage cost curves, since greenhouse gas emissions represent, in terms of environmental economics, a Pareto-relevant externality,[3] the private damage costs usually do not equal the social damage costs. It may be very difficult to estimate the damage costs, both social and private, since the cost function in the real world is most likely non-linear and dependent on the number of 'victims', time, pollutant composition and perhaps location (Sterner, 2003). An important consideration in the estimation of greenhouse gas emissions costs is uncertainty regarding the future concentration of greenhouse gases in the atmosphere as a result of current emissions. The intertemporal dimension adds complexity to the issue since it is not certain what the impact of any given greenhouse gas concentration will be on future global and regional climates.

Figure 7.1 illustrates a situation where, for simplicity, the marginal damage costs are linear and decrease as the pollution or greenhouse

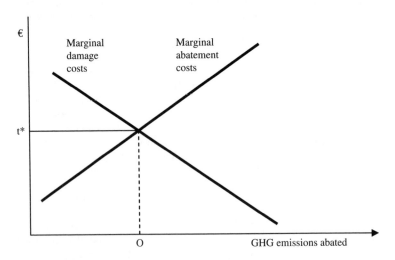

Figure 7.1   Schematic illustration of optimal abatement level

emissions are abated. Similarly the marginal abatement costs to reduce greenhouse gas emissions in this figure increase linearly as more abatement is carried out. In general, marginal abatement costs increase with increasing abatement level because it becomes more difficult to find lower cost methods to reduce greenhouse gas emissions as the amount of emissions to be abated decreases. Standard environmental economics tells us that the optimal level of greenhouse gas emissions abatement is at the point where the marginal abatement cost is equal to the marginal damage cost (point O in Figure 7.1).

In the case of optimal regulation, polluters would be required to abate to the level O. Similarly if a policy instrument of taxes or charges were preferred, the charge would be set at t^{*4} to produce an abatement level O or if a system of permits were implemented the quantity of permits issued would be equal to O. So, theoretically at least, under ideal conditions the optimal abatement level can be achieved with any policy instrument.

In the real world, conditions are rarely ideal and policymakers must settle for a second or even third best policy solution. This is because, even if it were possible to estimate the optimal abatement level, there are often political constraints related to the implementation of the first best policy selected using the criteria above. Particular conditions, for example the socioeconomic situation, information availability and structure, technology availability, environmental problem at hand and political system demand different policy instruments. Sterner (2003) has suggested that, really, a three-dimensional policy selection matrix is necessary for Table 7.1, which would include policy instruments, conditions and the evaluation criteria.

In the case of greenhouse gas emissions, there are several features that distinguish this environmental problem from others. Firstly, the pollutants act globally and therefore a successful abatement strategy requires a large majority of emitting countries to cooperate and abate, which complicates the political implementation of policy measures. Additionally, CO_2 emissions[5] are mainly a direct result of the combustion of fossil fuels and therefore are essentially a by-product of the industrial world. Abatement is different from that of other pollutants since end-of-pipe abatement of greenhouse gas emissions is not efficient and therefore modifications to the combustion process are usually necessary, such as improvement in efficiency or fuel switching. However, this kind of abatement can provide side benefits since, when the combustion becomes more efficient, it also saves the operator energy or fuel costs. A third feature of greenhouse gas emissions is that the consequences of abatement or lack of it will not be felt in the present but in the future.

7.2 POLICY CONTEXT FOR GREENHOUSE GAS EMISSIONS FROM TRANSPORT

The agreement of the Kyoto Protocol in 1997 and its subsequent ratification in 2004 has provided the policy backdrop to initiatives in Europe to reduce greenhouse gas emissions. Table 7.2 presents the emissions targets under the agreement (which entered into force on 16 February 2005). There are three flexible policy mechanisms called joint implementation (JI)[6], the clean development mechanism (CDM)[7] and emissions trading established in the Protocol. These are designed to help Annex I Parties[8] 'cut the cost of meeting their emissions targets by taking advantage of opportunities to reduce emissions, or increase greenhouse gas removals, that cost less in other countries than at home' (UNFCCC, 2005).

Although there are many instruments available to policymakers to tackle the reduction of greenhouse gas emissions from transport, it is still proving a difficult task to accomplish. Passenger road transport (that is, primarily cars) represents a non-point source of emissions with many independent users and a global pollutant. It is difficult to monitor and implement an abatement policy with so many small users, since measurement of individual vehicle emissions is near impossible on a wide scale. Passenger cars are

Table 7.2   Countries included in Annex B to the Kyoto Protocol and their emissions targets

Country	Target (2008–2012, relative to 1990**)
EU-15*, Bulgaria, Czech Republic, Estonia, Latvia, Liechtenstein, Lithuania, Monaco, Romania, Slovakia, Slovenia, Switzerland	−8%
US***	−7%
Canada, Hungary, Japan, Poland	−6%
Croatia	−5%
New Zealand, Russian Federation, Ukraine	0
Norway	+1%
Australia***	+8%
Iceland	+10%

*   The EU's 15 member states have redistributed their targets among themselves, taking advantage of a provision under Kyoto Protocol.
**   Some economies in transition (EITs) have a baseline other than 1990.
***   The US and Australia have indicated their intention not to ratify the Kyoto Protocol.

Source: UNFCCC (2005).

durable goods with a long product development and user life cycles. It is difficult to influence consumer behaviour over a long period and long-standing policies are required. Since passenger cars are mainly operated on fossil fuels, and CO_2 emissions are directly related to fuel consumption, one option would be to implement a user charge as a fuel tax. However, fuel taxes are subject to political feasibility and increases may be very unpopular. Another challenge is the lack of harmonization of initiatives between countries to reduce greenhouse gas emissions from passenger cars, which clouds the incentives for manufacturers to supply fuel-efficient vehicles to the market.

The OECD, under the guise of its Working Group on 'Analytical Methods of Road Transport Sector Strategies to Reduce Greenhouse Gas Emissions' (OECD, 2002a), has produced a catalogue of existing measures to reduce greenhouse gas emissions from road transport. It also created an evaluation framework with which to assess the impact of the reduction measures. It is in this context that governments have begun to design policies to reduce the emissions of greenhouse gases from transport. The OECD has identified the following three categories of existing measures to reduce greenhouse gas emissions from transport: (a) improvement of fuel efficiency, (b) alternative fuels and technologies, and (c) traffic demand management. The policy instruments associated with the first two categories tend to relate to supply-side management of transport, while the third category focuses on the management of consumer demand for transport.

The OECD Environmental Policy Committee's Task Force on Transport conducted the project 'Environmentally Sustainable Transport', which defined the concept of sustainable transport and germane criteria for evaluation. The Task Force estimates that, under their business-as-usual (or 'no new policy') scenario, greenhouse gas emissions will make the largest contribution, both absolutely and relatively, to the increases in external costs of transport in 2015 (OECD, 2002b).

The decoupling of economic growth from resource utilization has become a centrepiece of EU sustainability policy. The EU White Paper for transport[9] lists 60 measures to improve the quality and efficiency of transport in the EU. Highlighted is the need for transport to contribute to sustainable development and many of the measures identified affect greenhouse gas emissions directly.

Also in the EU, the TERM project has been developing indicators for assessing the effect of transport on the environment (EEA, 1998). One of these is ecoefficiency, described in Box 7.1. In the international community this concept is enshrined in the Agenda 21 update (UN, 1997), which notes the need to consider a tenfold improvement in resource productivity in industrialized countries.

BOX 7.1   ECO-EFFICIENCY (EEA, 1999)

The goal of eco-efficiency is to 'decouple resource use and pollutant release from economic activity'. This requires breaking the link between the use of nature, as measured by environmental indicators, and economic development as measured by output indicators such as GDP, or transport activity. Decoupling involves a reduction in the negative environmental effects per unit of economic output. This is achieved by either increased efficiency through technological change or a shift to a less environmentally damaging product.

While improvements in efficiency through technological change are crucial in reducing greenhouse gas emissions from transport, Part II showed that a complete transformation of the transport sector is necessary to achieve overall levels of abatement consistent with long-term sustainability. Without such a transition, there is a very large risk that more incremental technological developments and product shifts will be unable to reduce absolute energy use and greenhouse gas emissions because of demands for higher standards of living (EEA, 2002).

An example is passenger cars in Europe where the average amount of CO_2 emissions per km from new cars has decreased over the past decade thanks to technological advances, yet the absolute amount of CO_2 emissions of the passenger car fleet has still increased owing to the rise in the total number of cars in use.

Indicators of eco-efficiency are energy consumption and emissions as a function of GDP.

The following chapters describe how these policy instruments can be applied to transport in order to achieve the desired technological and behavioural change needed to reduce greenhouse gas emissions from passenger cars. Although, as shown in Part II, it may be possible to realize a sustainable transport system with the concerted effort to promote and deploy new technologies, changing travel demand behaviour is a complementary policy that may reduce the need for more expensive or radical technological change. Moreover, changing travel behaviour and consumer preferences may itself encourage the uptake of transport technologies more compatible with sustainable development.

The following sections examine each relevant policy instrument and ascertain their suitable application to the abatement of greenhouse gas emissions from passenger car transport. As we will see, what is perhaps most characteristic about the realities of policy intervention is, firstly, that a mix of policy instruments is increasingly used, which have either deliberate or coincidental interactions, and therefore analysis of such hybrid policies is essential; and, secondly, the design and micro implementation of the instrument(s) in question is as or more important than the choice of instrument itself.

We devote a chapter to demand-side market based instruments: taxes and charges, emissions trading and information. These are favoured by economists as a first best choice, as they address the public good feature of greenhouse gas emissions that is generally associated with environmental problems and provide consumers with the information needed to inform decisions. Another two chapters are dedicated to supply-side policy instruments: voluntary agreements and investment in research and development. The voluntary agreement between passenger car manufacturers and the European Commission has been the main instrument at EU level explicitly used to reduce CO_2 emissions from passenger cars. And, as already mentioned, since the Bush Administration has selected research and development (R&D) as the policy instrument of choice for addressing climate change, we also devote a chapter to this instrument. However, before moving on to these instruments, let us first examine the traditional method of environmental regulation in the context of passenger car transport, namely command and control.

7.3 COMMAND AND CONTROL AS A POLICY INSTRUMENT FOR PASSENGER CARS

Traditionally, command and control was the most frequently used policy instrument in environmental management. This stemmed partly from a desire to 'forbid' harmful activities and a belief that it was the only way for governments to get industry to achieve the desired reduction in pollution. The transport sector is no exception and the emission of pollutant gases from cars has been regulated in many OECD countries since the 1970s. The mechanism utilized is for manufacturers to certify that each new vehicle and model type they produce meets the specified emission limits for that year, based on a standardized laboratory driving test. The pollutants regulated are nitrogen oxides, (NO_x), carbon monoxide (CO), hydrocarbon (HC) and, for diesel, particulate matter (PM) emissions. However since greenhouse gases (carbon dioxide (CO_2), methane (CH_4)

and nitrous oxide (N_2O)) are not toxic as such and do not cause damage to health at a local level, they have generally not been regulated in many countries in the past. In the EU, vehicle airborne pollutant levels will continue to decrease, with new standards proposed that would reduce diesel car particulate emissions by 80 per cent and nitrogen oxides by 20 per cent, and NO_x emissions and hydrocarbons by 25 per cent from petrol cars in 2008 (CEC, 2005a).

It is only since the effect of greenhouse gases on the environment began to be understood that policymakers' interest has grown in regulating the emission of these gases. However, the emission of CO_2 from petrol and diesel cars is directly related to the amount of energy consumed. This explains in part why these emissions were not regulated with similar 'one size fits all' regulations as for other pollutants, since smaller cars have a CO_2 emissions advantage over larger more fuel-consuming cars and therefore arguably require a different design of regulation. While the emission of greenhouse gases from transport generally remains unregulated (directly), it is mainly through the regulation of other related characteristics such as fuel economy that their reduction is encouraged. Therefore command and control related to greenhouse gas emissions is implemented more often through the regulation of passenger car (fleet average) fuel economy, technology or fuel type. In contrast to regulated air quality pollutants from passenger cars, characteristics related to fuel economy are generally regulated as a fleet average or per segment class to allow manufacturers some flexibility in their sales of a range of vehicle sizes. The command and control instrument focuses on the supply side of reducing greenhouse gas emissions by requiring the production and sale of fuel-efficient vehicles. While this is important, it has the drawback that it will not guarantee a reduction in aggregate greenhouse gas emissions, since no signal is directed at driving behaviour. In fact purchasers of fuel-efficient vehicles may even drive more, which is termed the 'rebound effect' (see Box 7.2).

Efficiency gains, as a result of fuel economy regulations or other market-based incentives, reduce per-km vehicle operating costs, which encourages increased vehicle travel. This means that, if incentives cause motorists to choose vehicles that are 10 per cent more fuel efficient, this does not usually result in a full 10 per cent fuel saving (Greene and Schafer, 2003). It is estimated that there is a rebound effect of between 20 and 40 per cent (VTPI, 2006), so that a 10 per cent improvement in fuel efficiency leads to a 2 to 4 per cent increase in vehicle mileage, resulting in a net fuel saving of only 6 to 8 per cent. So, while there is still a net reduction in fuel consumption, the increased vehicle mileage may exacerbate other transportation problems, such as traffic congestion, road and parking facility costs, crashes, pollution and urban sprawl (VTPI, 2006).

BOX 7.2   REBOUND EFFECT

A *Rebound Effect* (also called a *Takeback Effect* or *Offsetting Behaviour*) refers to increased consumption that results from actions that increase efficiency and reduce consumer costs (Musters, 1995; Alexander, 1997; Herring, 1998, in VTPI TDM Encyclopaedia, 2006).

The rebound effect is an extension of the 'Law of Demand', a basic principle of economics, which states that, if prices (costs perceived by consumers) decline, consumption usually increases. A programme or technology that reduces consumers' costs tends to increase consumption. These effects are not limited to financial costs; they may involve reductions in time costs, risk or discomfort. For example, strategies that increase fuel efficiency or reduce traffic congestion, and therefore reduce the per-mile cost of driving, tend to increase total vehicle mileage. Similarly, strategies that make driving seem safer tend to encourage somewhat more 'intensive' driving (that is, faster, closer spacing between vehicles, more distractions) than what would occur if vehicle use appears riskier to drivers.

This is not to suggest that rebound effects *eliminate* the benefits of efficiency gains. There are usually net congestion reductions or energy savings after the rebound effect occurs. In addition, consumers benefit directly from increased vehicle travel or higher vehicle speeds. However, the rebound effect can significantly change the nature of the benefits that result from a particular policy or project.

There are three types of transport rebound effects defined in the literature:

Generated traffic: additional vehicle trips on a particular roadway or area that occur when roadway capacity is increased, or travel conditions are improved in other ways. (This may consist of shifts in travel time, route, mode, destination and frequency).

Induced travel: an increase in total vehicle mileage due to increased motor vehicle trip frequency, longer trip distances or shifts from other modes, but which excludes travel shifted from other times and routes.

Latent demand: additional trips that would be made if travel conditions improved (less congested, higher design speeds, lower vehicle costs or tolls).

7.3.1   Regulation of Passenger Car Fuel Economy

Vehicle fuel economy has been the target of regulation in several countries, and minimum standards established. Since fuel economy is directly linked to CO_2 and other greenhouse gas emissions, this measure reduces not only energy consumption, but also the emission of greenhouse gases. The next paragraphs will provide an overview of fuel economy standards implemented in different regions globally.

Japan
As a consequence of deteriorating energy efficiency and the signing of the Kyoto Protocol, Japan revised its Energy Conservation Law in April 1999 with the goal of strengthening the legal underpinnings of various energy conservation measures. The Ministry of Economics, Trade and Industry, with the Ministry of Land, Infrastructure, and Transport together have implemented the 'Top-Runner' Programme. The objective of the Top Runner Standard is to advance energy efficiency of machinery and equipment in the residential, commercial and the transportation sectors. Passenger cars are included as one part of this programme.

Fuel efficiency targets are set for 2005 for diesel passenger vehicles and by 2010 for petrol and LPG passenger vehicles, see Table 7.3. It is estimated that, if the targets are met according to schedule, there will be an improvement in vehicle efficiency of 23 per cent for petrol cars, 11.4 per cent

Table 7.3   Top Runner Programme targets

Category by vehicle weight	Standard fuel consumption efficiency (km/l)[a]		
	Petrol	Diesel	LPG
Less than 703 kg	21.2	18.9[b]	15.9
703–827 kg	18.8	18.9[b]	14.1
828–1015 kg	17.9	18.9[b]	13.5
1016–1265 kg	16.0	16.2	12.0
1266–1515 kg	13.0	13.2	9.8
1516–1765 kg	10.5	11.9	7.9
1766–2015 kg	8.9	10.8	6.7
2016–2265 kg	7.8	9.8	5.9
Greater than 2265 kg	6.4	8.7	4.8

[a]   Fuel efficiency measured over the Japanese regulation test driving cycle (10–15 mode).
[b]   One category for diesel vehicles weighing less than 1015 kg.

Source: Energy Conservation Centre Japan (2005).

for LPG cars and 14 per cent for diesel cars compared with 1995 levels (ECCJ, 2005). LPG vehicles are the latest to have been included in the Top Runner Programme. Compared to petrol-powered cars, CO_2 emissions from LPG vehicles are about 10 per cent lower. Most of the 230 000 taxis in Japan operate on LPG, which began replacing petrol from 1963 onwards. Since taxis travel about seven times further than private passenger cars, the new standards are expected to contribute significantly (reduced emissions of up to 500 kT CO_2 annually (Japan for Sustainability, 2004)) to global warming prevention.

The third amendment to the Energy Saving Law was enacted in Japan in 2005, with a special emphasis on the enhancement of energy-saving measures in the transport, housing and construction sectors. The amended law entered into force in April 2006. In the transport sector, large transportation companies using trucks, buses or aircraft, and shippers will be obliged to submit an annual strategic plan and report on their energy consumption. Manufacturers, for example, will be urged to work toward a modal shift to public transportation systems and to consolidate their ordering systems. Transportation companies and manufacturers are to make collaborative efforts to further reduce CO_2 emissions, and penalties will be applied to firms if their efforts are found to be insufficient.

BOX 7.3   COMPARISON OF METHODS TO REGULATE ENERGY EFFICIENCY

There are three main methods for setting standards for machinery and equipment energy efficiency. The first is a minimum standard value system, under which machinery and equipment covered by the system are required to exceed a certain level of performance. The second is an average standard value system, under which the average performance of machinery and equipment products are required to exceed standard values. The third is called a maximum standard value system (Top Runner Standard). Under this system, target performance levels are set, based on the value of the most energy-efficient products on the market at the time of the target-setting process.

The most popular minimum standard value system worldwide is the Minimum Energy Performance Standard (MEPS). Under MEPS, the target machinery and equipment products must exceed a minimum performance standard (or be subject to sanctions such as suspension of product shipments). At first glance, the system appears extremely simple. However, to establish MEPS values that all products must achieve or exceed, evaluation of the economic validity of the standard values is necessary. In the US, which employs the minimum standard value system, several alternative approaches to evaluating economic fairness, such as life cycle assessment, are applied to set performance standards. Long periods of time and substantial coordination with manufacturers are necessary to establish final standards.

The second system, the average standard value system, was introduced in Japan when the Energy Conservation Law was enacted in 1979 as an equipment energy consumption efficiency value system. Target values are determined after consideration of a number of factors, such as potential technical improvements and potential impact of categorical improvements that may contribute to overall improvements, based on information provided by manu-facturers (through hearings, supplemental materials and other methods). Under this system, designated machinery and equip-ment products are required to achieve a weighted average effi-ciency performance by a target fiscal year. The system provides flexibility to manufacturers, but on the other hand may have less impact on energy conservation than expected, since the estab-lishment of standard values is partly dependent on manufacturers' provision of good information.

The Top Runner System uses, as a base value, the performance of the most energy-efficient product on the market to set future standards, taking into account potential technological improve-ments. As a result, target standard values are extremely high com-pared to the other approaches described above. Manufacturers are required to achieve targets using weighted average values by shipment volume, similar to the average standard value system. The implication of using weighted average values is the same as the average standard value system; that is, the system is meant to give manufacturers flexibility to develop energy-efficient equip-ment. An advantage of the system is that negotiation of the targets can proceed smoothly in a shorter period. While this system gives manufacturers substantial technological and economic burdens, the industry can conduct substantial prior negotiations on possi-bility of achieving standard values and adopt sales promotion measures for more energy efficient products.

Source: The Energy Conservation Centre, Japan, 'Developing the World's Best Energy-Efficient Appliances (Japan's "Top Runner" Standard)', http://www.eccj.or.jp/top_runner/index_contents_e.html.

USA and Canada

In the USA, one of the repercussions of the oil crisis in the 1970s was the introduction of Corporate Average Fuel Economy (CAFE) legislation to reduce the fuel consumption of passenger cars. This legislation indirectly regulates CO_2 emissions from passenger cars since most cars in the United States are operated on fossil fuels. This is a flexible command-and-control instrument with intracompany trading and therefore has some common characteristics with economic instruments, since the fuel consumption limit is applied at automobile company fleet level to permit some flexibility between model types within a company. Each car manufacturer must meet the Corporate Average Fuel Economy (CAFE) standard, which currently stands at 27.5 miles per gallon (mpg) for passenger cars and 20.7 mpg for trucks (this latter standard increased to 22.2 mpg in 2007).

The National Academies' National Research Council (NRC) (2003) estimates that the CAFE standards have reduced petrol consumption by roughly 2.8 million barrels per day from where it would be in the absence of the CAFE standards. Without these energy savings, total US CO_2 emissions would be more than 14 per cent higher. However, the NRC's findings show that setting fuel economy standards may not be the most efficient way to reduce fuel consumption, and instead recommend the introduction of tradable fuel economy credits with a cap on the price. Like CAFE, such a system could provide incentives for manufacturers to improve fuel economy continually, but would afford additional flexibility to meet efficiency targets. As an instrument, tradable fuel economy credits could also provide better information to regulators about the costs of increasing fuel economy (National Research Council, 2003). We discuss such tradable systems in more detail in Chapter 8. Figure 7.2 illustrates the development of the CAFE standards and the average fleet fuel economy over the same period.

The National Highway Traffic Safety Administration (NHTSA) has stated recently that the CAFE standards are due for overhaul. Since 1995, US agencies have been restricted from spending funds to 'prepare, propose, or promulgate any regulations . . . prescribing corporate average fuel economy standards for automobiles'. This restriction was lifted in 2001 and since then the NHTSA has introduced light truck CAFE standards. The agency has issued notification of intention to reform the CAFE agreement.[10] Modifications are likely to include both tighter standards and changes to the system of regulation.

Canada introduced voluntary Motor Vehicle Fuel Consumption Standards for passenger cars in 1978. These standards replicate those of the CAFE programme in the USA; however the standards are not binding and

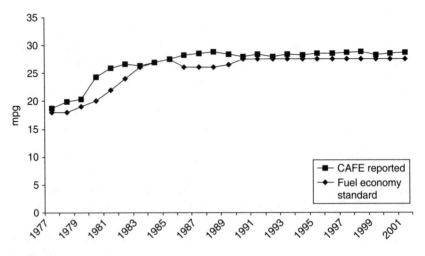

Source: NHTSA (2006).

Figure 7.2   Development of fuel economy standard and reported Corporate Average Fuel Economy (CAFE), 1977–2001

are described in more detail in Chapter 9 which discusses voluntary agreements. There has been compliance for 98 per cent of the passenger cars sold in Canada with these standards.

China
Fuel economy standards do not exist in the EU; however there are further examples in other regions such as China. Weight-based fuel economy standards have been introduced in China for passenger vehicles from 2005. Different standards are applied to automatic and manual transmission vehicles and prescribe fuel economy targets for each vehicle weight class (see Figure 7.3 for automatic transmission model standards). There are two phases for the implementation of these standards: the first phase began in 2005 and the more stringent second phase in 2008.

Although under the Chinese fuel economy standards the fuel consumption permitted for heavier vehicles is higher than for lighter vehicles, nonetheless the standards are designed to be relatively tighter for heavier vehicles than lighter vehicles, compared to performance in 2003. The objective is to improve the efficiency of SUVs and heavier vehicles sold in China, which are increasing at a high rate. There are 16 weight classes for passenger cars and light duty trucks, in contrast to the US CAFE system, which has just one standard for passenger cars and another for light trucks. Overall, it is estimated that Chinese fuel economy standards are more

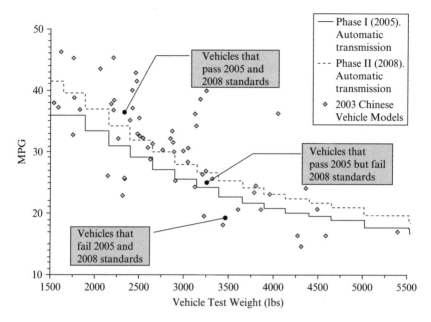

Source: reproduced from Sauer and Wellington (2004) with permission from the authors.

Figure 7.3   *New Chinese fuel economy standards and 2003 Chinese vehicle model performance*

stringent than the US CAFE system (Sauer and Wellington, 2004). An improvement in fuel efficiency of 5 per cent in 2005 and 10 per cent in 2008 would be required for the US new vehicle fleet to meet the new Chinese fuel economy standards. Analysis of the Chinese 2003 vehicle fleet demonstrates that 66 per cent of vehicles sold in 2003 met 2005 standards, while 35 per cent met the Phase II standards.

Sauer and Wellington (2004) examined the implications of the efficiency standards described above for automakers operating and manufacturing in China. They show that the impact of the regulations varies widely between the firms, since the relevant cost of compliance for each manufacturer varies according to the efficiency of the vehicles produced. The fuel economy improvements necessary for automobile manufacturers to meet Phase I standards range from 0 to 16 per cent, while for Phase II improvements of 0 to 24 per cent are required. Commentary on the new standards has differed, with some applauding the introduction of standards that might halt the increasing fuel consumption of cars in China, while others bemoan the lost opportunity to implement a more effective policy.[11]

7.3.2 Regulation of Technology

In California, legislators created the Zero Emission Vehicle (ZEV) Program in 1990 to mandate the introduction of low-emission vehicles to the market (CARB, 2003a). The ultimate objective of the programme was to reduce total emissions by requiring a percentage of vehicles to achieve zero emissions, and to drive technology development forward. The original target was for 10 per cent of vehicles produced for sale in California to be ZEVs by 2003.

The implementation of this technology regulation has not been straightforward, with the programme being adjusted or modified in 1996, 1998, 2001 and 2003 as a result of pressure from manufacturers, who were able to show that the technology was not mature enough for introduction to the market on the scale foreseen. The modifications in 2001 allowed auto manufacturers to meet their ZEV obligations by producing a mix of pure ZEVs, AT–PZEVs (vehicles earning advanced technology partial ZEV credits) and PZEVs (extremely clean conventional vehicles). The ZEV obligation is based on the number of passenger cars and small trucks a manufacturer sells in California.

The modification to the Rule in 2001 permitted manufacturers to meet some of their ZEV quota with 'partial' ZEVs. Vehicles are classified as partial or advanced technology ZEVs if they contained advanced technology, are low emitters, and have low fuel consumption. This last criterion caused a lawsuit to be filed against the Californian Air Resources Board (CARB) in 2002 and so the introduction of the rule was postponed until there was clarification. The lawsuit asserted that CARB could not include a provision requiring vehicles with low fuel consumption since this was pre-empted by the federal CAFE standards. This led to the modifications of 2003, where all references to fuel economy or efficiency (through an efficiency multiplier) have been removed from the definition of advanced technology partial ZEVs (CARB, 2003b). The problems faced by the ZEV programme illustrate the potential barriers associated with regulating fuel economy and CO_2 emissions from passenger cars.

The programme restarted in 2005 and manufacturers can earn and bank credits for vehicles produced prior to 2005. An additional alternative ZEV compliance strategy has been introduced to provide manufacturers with flexibility, which allows them to meet more of their ZEV requirement with AT–PZEVs if they have met the criterion of producing at least 250 fuel cell vehicles by 2008. The remainder of their ZEV requirements can be achieved by producing 4 per cent AT–PZEVs and 6 per cent PZEVs. There is an increase in the required number of fuel cell vehicles in the alternative ZEV compliance strategy to 2500 from 2009–11, to 25 000 from 2012–14 and to

50 000 from 2015 to 2017. Failure to comply with the requirements of the ZEV programme from 2005 will result in a fine based on the number of non-compliant vehicles. There have been many criticisms levelled at the ZEV programme, for example the rigidity with which advanced technology is specified and the high costs for manufacturers, particularly non-North American manufacturers. Moreover, there is no direct requirement to produce ZEV vehicles that incorporate reduced greenhouse gas emissions. However, the programme does encourage advanced technology vehicles that will have the side-effect of improved fuel economy (CARB, 2004).

There can be no doubt that the programme is currently one of the main driving forces worldwide for the development of non-fossil-fuelled vehicles. CARB states that over 4000 battery-operated vehicles were brought to the market in California between 1998 and 2003. It is rivalled only by the fiscal treatment of hybrid vehicles in Japan in terms of encouraging new technology to the market.

Other examples where vehicle technology has been regulated exist in Brazil and Tokyo, Japan. In both cases diesel vehicles were banned. The consequences of this and additional subsidies were that the bioethanol share of the transport fuels market in Brazil and the use of LPG vehicles as taxis in Tokyo increased significantly, as described in other parts of this chapter.

7.3.3 Regulation of Fuel

The implementation of legislation to mandate the substitution of fossil fuels with alternative low carbon fuels can assist in the reduction of CO_2 emissions from passenger cars. There are several regions where this kind of regulation has been introduced. In most cases, such as the European example, further instruments such as fiscal incentives are initiated in order to encourage suppliers and consumers to increase the production and consumption of the alternative fuel.

Under the European Directive on the promotion of the use of biofuels or other renewable fuels for transport,[12] member states are instructed to 'ensure that a minimum proportion of biofuels and other renewable fuels is placed on their markets' and reference values for national targets are given as 2 per cent, by 2005, and 5.75 per cent, by 2010. These targets are indicative rather than mandatory but failure to meet them requires member states to explain the discrepancy in their annual biofuels progress reports. The bases for this Directive were provided in the Communication from the Commission to the European Parliament, the Council and the Economic and Social Committee of the Regions on alternative fuels for road transportation and on a set of measures to promote the use of biofuels.[13]

A partner Directive exists to promote biofuels by allowing member states to reduce excise duty on them.[14]

The motivation is to reduce the EU's dependency on oil and to find ways to reduce greenhouse gas emissions in order to comply with commitments under the Kyoto Protocol to the United Nations Framework Convention on Climate Change (UNFCCC). One way to do this is to encourage the use of biofuels and other renewable fuels in road transport. The Commission has an objective to replace 20 per cent of the petroleum fuels used in the road transport sector with alternative fuels (biofuels, natural gas and hydrogen) by the year 2020. Importantly, the sustainable transport scenario in Part II also identified the potential for these fuels to achieve greenhouse gas and energy security goals. Since the filling station infrastructure is not yet widely available for natural gas as a transport fuel and vehicle technologies are not yet mature for hydrogen fuel, biofuels are seen as the first step that can be taken in this process. The Green Paper 'Towards a European Strategy for Energy Supply' supports this initiative and it is also appropriate in the context of the reforms of the Common Agricultural Policy that focus on supporting rural economies, while decoupling subsidies from food production.

There are multiple challenges facing alternative fuels before gaining market acceptance and penetration of the fossil fuel market, as noted in the sustainable transport scenario in Part II. The predominant use of petroleum fuels with internal combustion engines (ICE) in private transport is a result of the many advantages that these systems offer to customers. The public is accustomed to vehicles that are flexible and cheap. And, although petroleum fuels are highly flammable, fuel containment systems are sufficiently developed for vehicles to be safely parked anywhere. The driving range has also improved greatly with refuelling required for passenger cars on average only every 400–600 km, or even every 1000 km for diesel vehicles. The fuelling infrastructure for petroleum is standardized and extensive coverage is available.

Currently the alternative fuels that are viewed as capable of achieving performance similar to petroleum fuels are biofuels and natural gas. Nearly 2.5 million tonnes of biofuels were produced in the EU in 2004, reflecting a 26.6 per cent increase on the previous year. Figure 7.4 illustrates the growth in biofuels in EU15 between 1992 and 2004. Germany leads in the production of biodiesel while Spain is a major producer of bioethanol. In addition to biofuels, there is much discussion of the potential of hydrogen to be the transport fuel of the future. However, owing to infrastructural, cost and technical challenges remaining, it is likely to be a medium- to long-term rather than short-term solution even under optimistic assumptions. Because of the low cost of production in other regions, such as Brazil, compared

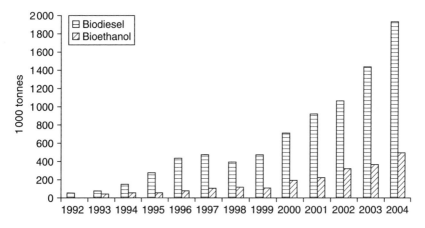

Source: EurObserver (2005).

Figure 7.4   Biofuels production in EU15

with the EU, there is a potential trade issue, as it is likely to be cheaper to import bioethanol from Brazil than to produce it domestically in Europe.[15]

Turning to other world regions, there appears to be very little utilization of biofuels in transport in Japan. In June 2004, the Ministry of Land, Infrastructure and Transport set up a project team to develop within two years an engine that can operate on diesel blended with biofuel. Several projects are going on with NEDO (New Agency and Industrial Technology Development Organisation) and the Ministry of Economy, Trade and Industry, as part of the Renewable Portfolio Standard regulation that was introduced in 2001 (Yagishita and Ueda, 2003). This regulation imposes a requirement on electric utilities to produce 7.3 GWh of energy in 2003 and 12.2 GWh in 2010 from New Energy (representing 1.35 per cent of total electricity production in 2010), although this provides only peripheral support to transport applications. There are also subsidies available for the installation of bioenergy conversion and utilization facilities. One of the 'Projects of Demonstration Test and Supporting New Energy Operators' involves the production of biodiesel. In Japan, there are 35 biodiesel production facilities using waste frying oil as feedstock. Figure 7.5 illustrates the distribution of the size of biodiesel plants in Japan and shows that the majority produce under 100 l per day. However, the total amount of waste frying oil in Japan is around 400 kl/year and hence biodiesel produced from this feedstock is unlikely to develop significantly. In comparison, biodiesel production from soybean oil is increasing.

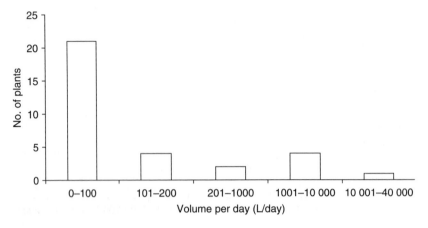

Source: Yagishita and Ueda (2003).

Figure 7.5   Distribution of size of biodiesel plants in Japan in 2003

Japan also plans to require fuel producers to blend all petrol with 10 per cent bioethanol by 2008 (Fulton et al., 2004). This would translate to sales of six billion litres of bioethanol per year. Before proceeding with this measure, the Japanese government is sponsoring a number of studies to test vehicle engine compatibility with bioethanol. The government also subsidizes bioethanol fuel blends at the petrol pumps in some regions. Since Japan does not have any surplus agricultural production, bioethanol will most likely be imported from Brazil and Thailand.

In the USA, there is a history of biofuel use as a result of legislation promoting ethanol production and use as a motor fuel in the 1970s. Large-scale production of biofuels consists mainly of bioethanol: 8151 million litres in 2002 (Fulton et al., 2004). One of the factors encouraging biofuel production and use in the USA in the 1990s was the oxygenated fuel programme, which has its root in the 1990 Clean Air Act and required that 'gasoline sold in carbon monoxide (CO) non-attainment areas must contain 2.7 per cent oxygen' (Fulton et al., 2004). Also the reformulated petrol programme obliges 2 per cent oxygen content in gasoline sold in the nine worst ozone non-attainment areas. As a result, average bioethanol consumption rose by approximately 2.5 per cent per annum in the 1990s. Recently the EPA has decided that MTBE (an oxygen fuel additive) must be phased out and thus bioethanol demand is increasing again in the US. Biodiesel has not been as common in the US, with 70 million litres produced in 2002, although production from soybean oil is increasing.

Brazil remains the biggest bioethanol producer and market in the world. In response to the oil shock of 1973, the Brazilian government instigated the Brazilian National Alcohol Programme in 1975. This encouraged the production and use of biofuels from sugarcane. It was extremely successful in terms of promoting biofuel production and market penetration was 92 per cent of transport fuels in 1988. In recent years, the incentives have not been so high and so the sales of petrol are growing again, although the Alcohol Programme has resulted in significant reductions in cost, as illustrated in Figure 4.3.

The policy measures that have been designed to promote the introduction of biofuels in Brazil, Europe and the US are varied. The main method by which the introduction of biofuels has been encouraged is through price incentives to compensate for the higher price of biofuels compared with petroleum fuels. In Europe, this has meant exempting biofuels from excise duty in many places (see section 8.2.4). Also, under the reform of the Common Agricultural Policy, subsidies for some grain and sugar crops will be significantly reduced, while energy crops will be subsidized at a rate of €45 per hectare. In the US, there is a tax credit of 14.3 cents per litre of bioethanol (Fulton et al., 2004).

7.3.4   Regulation of Greenhouse Gas Emissions from Passenger Cars

As mentioned above, the emission of CO, HC, NO_x and PM by passenger cars is regulated, with emissions standards in nearly all countries worldwide. Most regulation related to greenhouse gas emissions from passenger cars is indirect: that is, a greenhouse gas-emitting characteristic of the vehicle is regulated rather than the emissions themselves. There is, however, one case where policymakers have decided to impose CO_2 emissions standards for passenger cars. In California, a proposal has been made to regulate the emission of greenhouse gases from passenger cars in 2009.[16] The California Air Resources Board (CARB) has 'reviewed baseline vehicle attributes and their contribution to atmospheric climate change emissions, and evaluated technologies that have the potential to decrease these emissions' (CARB, 2004). Based on this assessment, CARB has chosen CO_2-equivalent emissions fleet standards, which should be phased in between 2009 and 2012. The result of these emissions standards will be a 22 per cent reduction in greenhouse gas emissions from the passenger car fleet compared with 2002 levels. The mid-term standards 2013–2016 will reduce CO_2 emissions by 30 per cent compared with the 2002 fleet. The emissions standards proposed are presented in Table 7.4. The standards require the measurement of CO_2, CH_4 and N_2O emissions[17] directly from the vehicle, the CO_2 emissions due to increased fuel consumption as a result of

Table 7.4 CO_2-equivalent emissions standards proposed for new passenger cars and trucks

Tier	Year	CO2-equivalent emissions standard (g/mile)	
		PC/LDT1 (passenger cars and small trucks/SUVs)	LDT2 (large trucks/SUVs)
Near-term	2009	323	439
	2010	301	420
	2011	267	390
	2012	233	361
Mid-term	2013	227	355
	2014	222	350
	2015	213	341
	2016	205	332

operation of the air conditioning system, and hydrofluorocarbon emissions from the air conditioning system due to leakage during recharge, or release from scrappage at the end of the life of a vehicle.

Full cycle well-to-wheel emissions are taken into account. CARB estimates that the simplest way to do this is to take as a baseline the upstream emissions for vehicles that use conventional fuels. This provides a reference against which the upstream emissions from alternative fuels can be compared and a conversion factor accounting for the difference estimated. Therefore, to measure the greenhouse gas emissions from an alternatively fuelled vehicle, the tank-to-wheel greenhouse gas emissions are measured and then the conversion factor is applied, to take into account the upstream emissions.

This new regulation is strongly opposed by automobile manufacturers. The automobile industry sued in state and federal courts, once California adopted the regulations in their final form in September 2004. At the time of writing, this process is still going on. The industry argues mainly that fuel economy regulations can only be set at federal level. However, Californian regulators counter that 'they have authority to take action on any emissions threatening public health' (Hakim, 2005). The consequences of the challenge are considerable, since ten other states have stated that they too will introduce the same regulation if California is successful. Whether the rule is implemented or not, it remains an example of one way in which greenhouse gas emissions from passenger cars could be regulated, if so desired. Some insights into the difficulty of introducing CO_2 emissions legislation may be gleaned for other policymakers from this process.

While stakeholder consultation on the proposed legislation took place, there does not appear to have been a serious attempt at negotiation with the industry on least-cost alternatives to reach the same target. Interaction between the regulator and industry at an early stage in the policy design process can bring industry on side and improve the likelihood of policy success (see, for example, the EU voluntary agreement described in Chapter 9). In the Californian case the type of regulation, namely command and control, had already been decided upon before industry was included in the discussion and may have hindered agreement between parties.

In 2007, the European Commission announced that the strategy to reduce CO_2 emissions from passenger cars, which until then had been based mainly on a voluntary agreement with car manufacturers, would be revised to include legislation to regulate CO_2 emissions from passenger cars. The Commission stated that it would propose legislation by mid 2008 that would require average CO_2 emissions from passenger cars in EU27 to reach a target of 120 g/km in 2012. Vehicle technology improvements should be responsible for the reaching 130 g/km, while 'complementary measures' should contribute a further emissions reduction of 10 g/km, leading to achievement of the target of 120 g/km overall. The Commission added that

> These complementary measures include efficiency improvements for car components with the highest impact on fuel consumption, such as tyres and air conditioning systems, and a gradual reduction in the carbon content of road fuels, notable through greater use of biofuels. Efficiency requirements will be introduced for these car components. (CEC, 2007)

Further elements of the revised strategy include fleet average CO_2 emissions targets for vans of 175 g/km by 2012 and 160 g/km by 2015; support for research which will lead to cars with an average of 95 g CO_2/km by 2020; improvement of the vehicle labelling sheme and encouragement of member states to base vehicle taxes on vehicle CO_2 emissions; and to draw up an EU code of good practice to promote more sustainable consumption patterns through marketing and advertising (CEC, 2007).

7.4 SUMMARY

- Policy measures are required to achieve a reduction in greenhouse gas emissions, such as the level estimated in the sustainable development scenario (Chapter 5).
- Historically command and control regulations have been the most popular instrument for environment management policy.

- There is little or no direct regulation of greenhouse gas emissions from passenger cars worldwide. More common is the regulation of fuel economy, vehicle technology and fuel choice, all of which are related to greenhouse gas emissions from vehicles.
- The Corporate Average Fuel Economy standards in the USA are probably the best-known example of fuel economy regulation.
- An assessment by the USA National Research Council has shown that, although regulation has reduced fuel consumption in the US, a more efficient method would be to introduce fuel economy credits trading. This would be less costly, and provide more flexibility to industry and better information on the cost of fuel economy improvements.
- With regard to vehicle technology regulation, California has introduced the Zero Emission Vehicle (ZEV) programme, which regulates the introduction of advanced technology. Although the main objective is to improve air quality, the technology will most likely show improvements in greenhouse gas emissions and fuel economy also.
- Another example of command and control policymaking for passenger cars is the instruction by the European Commission to member states in Europe to introduce a proportion of biofuels to the fuel market. Some biofuels show substantial reductions in greenhouse gas emissions over their life cycle.
- California has proposed to regulate the emission of greenhouse gas emissions from passenger cars; however, it remains uncertain whether the rule will be implemented.
- A legislative framework to regulate CO_2 emissions from passenger cars to an average of 120 g/km by 2012 has been announced by the European commission; the details are not yet available at time of writing (2007).

NOTES

1. An example is the eco tax in Germany where a tax was levied on transport fuels to reduce transport externalities and the revenue was used to reduce labour taxes.
2. The White House (2005), Statement from George W. Bush, *Climate Change Fact Sheet*; The White House website available at http://www.whitehouse.gov/news/releases/2005/05/20050518-4.html.
3. Baumol and Oates (Baumol and Oates, 1988) define a (Pareto-relevant) externality as present, firstly 'whenever some individual's utility or production relationships include real variables, whose values are chosen by others without particular attention to that individual's welfare' and secondly when 'the decision-maker, whose activity affects others' utility levels or production functions does not receive or pay in compensation for this activity an amount equal in value to the resulting benefits or costs to others'.

4. When the charge or tax is set at the intersection of the marginal abatement cost and marginal damage cost the tax is referred to as a Pigovian tax.
5. There are six greenhouse gases listed under the United Nations framework convention on climate change. Of these gases, CO_2 emissions are estimated to be responsible for over 60 per cent of the greenhouse effect (http://unfccc.int/essential_background/feeling_the_heat/items/2903.php).
6. 'Under JI, an Annex 1 Party may implement an emissions-reducing project or a project that enhances removals by sinks in the territory of another Annex 1 Party and count the resulting emissions reduction units (ERUs) towards meeting its own Kyoto target' (www.UNFCCC.org).
7. The clean development mechanism (CDM) allows Annex 1 Parties 'to implement projects that reduce emissions in non-Annex 1 Parties, or absorb carbon through afforestation or reforestation activities, in return for certified emission reductions (CERs) and assist the host parties in achieving sustainable development and contributing to the ultimate objective of the Convention' (www.UNFCCC.org).
8. Annex 1 Parties are those countries listed in Annex 1 to the framework convention on climate change. Almost all of these countries are required to undertake greenhouse gas emissions reductions under the Kyoto protocol.
9. European Commission (2001), White Paper, 'European transport policy for 2010 : time to decide'.
10. NHTSA (2005), 'Reforming the Automobile Fuel Economy Standards Program', *49 CFR Part 533* [Docket No. 2003-16128]. RIN 2127-AJ17.
11. *The New York Times*, 23 November 2003: 'Like the U.S., China Favours Fuel Standards, Not Taxes.'
12. Directive 2003/30/EC.
13. COM 2001, 547 final, Brussels, 7.11.2001.
14. Directive 2003/96/EC.
15. A regulation has been passed that requires member states in Europe to monitor sales and imports of bioethanol; if it is deemed 'necessary', tariffs may be raised in the future (Council Regulation No. 670/2003).
16. Chapter 200, Statutes of 2002 (AB 1493, Pavley) directs CARB to adopt regulations that achieve the maximum feasible and cost-effective reduction of greenhouse gas emissions.
17. Greenhouse gas emissions are converted to CO_2-equivalent using the IPCC global warming potentials, where CH_4 and N_2O are estimated to cause the equivalent of 21 and 310 times, respectively, the global warming of CO_2 emissions over a 100-year period (IPCC, 1996).

8. Demand side: market-based instruments

Market-based instruments have become popular in recent times among economists and subsequently policymakers because they address some of the failings of command-and-control policies such as static and dynamic inefficiency.

Two important demand-side measures include emissions trading, which can provide flexibility to reduce aggregate greenhouse emissions at lower cost, while taxes and charges, in addition to emissions trading, advance the polluter pays principle, requiring polluters either to pay for their emissions or to carry out abatement actions. Both instruments provide an incentive for firms to invest in innovation in order to abate at lower cost than the price of an emissions permit or the tax. When the costs of abatement are passed through to consumers, these instruments act as demand-side charges to consumers and encourage the demand for less polluting goods. From the demand side, transport has relatively low fuel price elasticities: -0.12–-0.31 (short run) and -0.5–-1.39 (long run) and so charges will likely need to be high to have an impact on the passenger car sector. Price sensitivity or elasticity tends to increase if alternative destinations and transport modes are available and of good quality. For example, the extent to which travel demand is reduced as a response to an increase in vehicle or fuel price will be influenced by the alternatives available (VTPI, 2006).

In theory, under perfect conditions,[1] as shown in Section 7.1, taxes and emissions permits should have the same effect. However, Weitzman (1974) pointed out in his seminal paper that there is rarely adequate information and therefore policymakers are likely to be unsure about the cost functions to determine the optimal abatement/price level (as seen in Figure 7.1). When the cost functions are not certain, it is likely that implementation of an emissions tax or permit system will not provide the optimal result and therefore a combination of policies is often employed; policymakers must design policy instruments suitable for their particular situation.

8.1   EMISSIONS TRADING

There is a large and growing literature examining emissions trading in the context of greenhouse gas emissions abatement (see Convery et al., 2003a; Redmond and Convery, 2005) and only the main points that are relevant to transport are discussed here. Dales (1968) proposed the idea of emissions trading, and showed theoretically that, when the rights to pollute are limited and freely tradable, polluters are encouraged to reduce emissions at least cost. Emissions trading is a 'flexible mechanism' permitted under the Kyoto Protocol.[2] The advantage of a transnational mechanism is that it allows greenhouse gas mitigation to be undertaken where the abatement cost is lowest. The two largest emissions trading schemes worldwide are in the EU and USA.

Much experience has been gained with emissions trading from the US acid rain programme, which was established by Title IV of the 1990 Clean Air Act (Montero et al., 2000). This was the first large-scale emissions trading programme worldwide. The focus was the reduction of sulphur dioxide (SO_2) emissions from electricity utilities through a credit banking and trading programme (see Box 8.1 for a description of different trading systems). The programme came into effect in 1995 with two phases: phase 1 (1995–1999) included the 263 dirtiest generating units and, in the second phase (2000–2009), nearly all fossil-fuelled electricity generators were included. The programme put an aggregate cap on SO_2 emissions and gave utilities 'with multiple fossil-fired generating units enormous and unprecedented flexibility in complying with emission limits even if they trade[d] no allowances at all with each other' (Montero et al., 2000). Further flexibility was afforded by provisions for banking of allowances from one period for use in a future period.

The acid rain programme is judged to have been a success, since there was 100 per cent compliance in phase one by all those included with lower than expected allowance prices. The programme demonstrates that emissions trading reduces compliance costs compared with a similar command and control style of regulation (Montero et al., 2000). When compliance costs vary between emitting units across a sector, then, in an efficient trading programme, there should be a divergence between the emissions allowances allocated and the emissions produced on a plant level, resulting in the equalization of marginal abatement costs.

The EU greenhouse gas emissions trading scheme was approved in 2003[3] and the first phase began in 2005 with a three-year pilot period 2005–2007 (Convery et al., 2003). All 27 EU member states are covered by the scheme and it is the first international trading system for CO_2 emissions. It is a cap and trade scheme, which covers some 12000 installations representing close

BOX 8.1   EMISSIONS TRADING SYSTEMS (ETS)

To date emissions trading programmes have used one of three systems: baseline and credit, cap and trade, or off-set schemes. The latter system cannot operate alone but must be linked to an absolute or relative constraint.

Cap and trade

This is the system used in the EU ETS. An aggregate emission target or cap is agreed upon by the regulator or government. The emissions under that cap are then allocated to individual installations. Since the amount allocated is finite this effectively limits the amount of emissions permitted under the scheme. The method of allocation of the allowances is hugely important in terms of the efficiency of the system and is a highly political process. This system provides certainty with regard to environmental effectiveness and less administrative and transaction costs compared with baseline and credit trading.

Baseline and credit

In this system, which was used in the acid rain programme, emission credits are awarded when an emitter reduces emissions below a defined baseline. When the baseline represents an absolute cap on emissions, this system is equivalent to the cap and trade system. However, credits may also be based on relative criteria (such as emissions per unit output). A weakness associated with baseline and credit trading is that it does not guarantee achievement of absolute reduction targets.

Project-based or off-set systems

Emitters can earn credits under a project-based system for projects that reduce emissions more than required by pre-existing regulation or other such benchmark. These can then be traded with other firms and may be used for compliance with a regulatory requirement. This system does not provide environmental certainty and suffers from high administrative costs due to extensive involvement of the regulatory authority.

Source: Redmond (mimeo, 15/09/2006).

to half of Europe's estimated emissions of CO_2 in 2010. Non-compliance penalties of €40 per tonne of CO_2 apply from 2005 and will rise to €100 per tonne in 2008. After the three-year pilot period, allowances will be allocated for the five-year period 2008–2012, which coincides with the first commitment period under the Kyoto Protocol.

The European Commission is considering including the aviation sector in the EU Emissions Trading Scheme (EU ETS) in 2008. This would be the first time a mode of transport was incorporated directly in an emissions trading scheme.[4] A number of economic instruments are already applied to various modes of transport, many of which are described in other chapters in this book. For example, fuel used in road transport is subject to duties, while rail transport is already indirectly included in the emissions trading scheme, through its electricity consumption. Aviation remains the only mode of transport without economic instruments related to greenhouse gas emissions applied to it, while it is probably the easiest to include in emissions trading thanks to the relatively small number of operators and centralized fuelling characteristics. Emissions trading would send a carbon price signal to the sector and provide an incentive to reduce CO_2 emissions. The EU Emissions Trading Directive anticipates a review of the trading scheme to consider 'how and whether [it] should be amended to include other relevant sectors, inter alia the chemicals, aluminium and transport sectors and emissions of other greenhouse gases'. A Working Group has been set up under the European Climate Change Programme to examine the options available to incorporate the aviation into the European emissions trading scheme (CEC, 2005b). Legislation is expected by the end of 2006 on the inclusion of aviation after 2008 in the second phase of the EU emissions trading scheme.

The International Civil Aviation Organisation (ICAO) has studied several market-based instrument options to reduce greenhouse gas emissions from aviation. The ICAO passed a resolution in October 2004 that allows for aviation to be included in greenhouse gas (GHG) emissions trading regimes (Karmali, 2005). This means that it is not necessary for the ICAO to approve the inclusion of aviation in any country or regional (such as the EU) emissions trading scheme. However, there remain several issues to be considered before the inclusion of aviation in emissions trading schemes is possible. CO_2 emissions constitute only one-third of greenhouse gas emissions from aviation,[5] with emissions of NO_x and the production of contrails and cirrus cloud formation representing the remainder of the climate change impact. If the full climate change impact of aviation is to be included in an emissions trading scheme, a conversion factor for the non-CO_2 radiative forcing emissions to CO_2-equivalent emissions is needed to enable aviation to trade on a genuine CO_2-equivalent basis. Consideration must also be given to the way to treat domestic and international aviation emissions. Only domestic aviation emissions are included in the Kyoto Protocol country targets, however the EU Commission has recommended that international aviation emissions be included in a post-2012 climate change regime.[6]

It is anticipated in emissions trading schemes that aircraft or airports could be treated as if they were 'installations'[7] and therefore flight operators or airport operators would be responsible for emissions from aviation. The international nature of the aviation sector means that there is concern that regional emissions trading schemes will cause the sector to face a significant loss in competitiveness vis-à-vis their international competitors. While operators apply pressure to limit the economic impact of such schemes, it is unsure whether this can be guaranteed while preserving environmental integrity. A study for the UK Department of the environment has shown that the inclusion of the aviation sector into the second phase of the EU emissions trading scheme would have a small impact on the price of EU allowances (ICF Consulting, 2006).

Japan undertook (in 2003) a greenhouse gas emissions trading simulation, in which 30 companies participated. The objectives were to design a regulatory structure that allows cost-effective emissions reductions and subsequently to make a proposal for a Japanese emissions trading scheme. The simulation showed that Japanese companies would not abate greenhouse gases by more than 5 per cent but would rather buy credits from abroad (Ogushi and Kure, 2003).

A review of the Japanese Climate Change Policy Programme by the Central Environmental Council in 2004 stated that emissions trading would be useful to help Japan achieve its Kyoto targets but that more experience for both industry and government was necessary before implementing a mandatory emissions trading scheme. In light of this, the Ministry of Environment began to prepare a large-scale voluntary emissions trading scheme (Japan's Voluntary Emissions Trading Scheme – J-VETS) in 2005. Under the scheme, participating companies declare greenhouse gas emissions reduction targets. As an inducement to the scheme, the government provides a subsidy of one-third of the investment in abatement technology, new more efficient facilities or in renewable energy promotion to help the companies meet their targets. Emissions trading began on 1 April 2006 and finishes on 31 March 2007. A further three months is then provided for firms that do not meet their targets at the end of the period to buy credits, either internally or abroad from CDM projects. If they still do not possess enough credits at the end of these three months they must repay the government subsidy (MRI, 2005).

The road transport sector is thus far not included in any of the greenhouse gas emissions trading schemes globally; industrial sectors are facing most of the emissions trading-related abatement challenge. Nonetheless, interest has grown in Europe to apply an emissions trading scheme to the transport sector and there is a small amount of literature on the subject of including road transport in emissions trading schemes.. The British Environment Minister has stated, 'There is no reason why the Emissions Trading Scheme should not be expanded to include surface transport emissions.'[8]

There are several mechanisms by which road transport could be included in an emissions trading scheme (Bergmann et al., 2001).

1   Downstream
    A CO_2 emissions trading system applied downstream is aimed at trans-port users. A total emissions cap is estimated for transport for the entire period (for example, 2008–2012) and using current data the regulator can allocate (for example by grandfathering) CO_2 emissions permits between different transport subsectors (for example freight and pas-senger transport). These allowances can be further divided down to per capita CO_2 emissions allowances for passenger transport or per firm allowances for freight transport.

    One way for these allowances to be used is to apply a carbon levy on transport fuels, which would be a reflection of the price of carbon in the emissions cap. Customers can then either use their emission allowances to avoid the levy or pay the levy. Users can at any time pur-chase additional allowances on the open market at the current price or undertake private trading with other individual users (Bergmann et al., 2001).

2   Midstream
    A midstream emissions trading system describes a scheme where the transport vehicle manufacturers or service providers are held responsi-ble for CO_2 emissions. This scheme encourages the reduction of trans-port CO_2 emissions by technological improvements. All transport vehicles are characterized in terms of their emissions performance and then emissions permits are allocated to vehicle producers according to the number and type of vehicles sold historically. At the end of the trading period, all new vehicle registrations are examined and com-pared with the emissions permits held by each producer (that is, high CO_2-emitting vehicles require more permits). If the producer is not covered by the allocation of permits received, he is obliged to purchase more on the emissions trading market, which may be cross-sectoral or limited to the transport sector. Costs of the trading scheme may be passed on to the vehicle purchasers and may thus influence the pur-chase of more fuel efficient vehicles.

3   Upstream
    The upstream approach focuses on reducing transport CO_2 emissions
    by requiring transport fuel suppliers (refineries, fuel trading companies
    or importers) to possess a specific amount of emissions allowances.
    Since there is a direct relationship between fossil fuel combustion in
    transport and CO_2 emissions, this method can capture all CO_2 emis-
    sions from the sector. Emissions allowances or permits can be allocated
    to all sellers in the fuels market and at the end of the trading period each
    compares the amount of fuel sold and its carbon content with the
    number of allowances held. Any deficiencies are made up on the emis-
    sions trading market. Additional costs can be passed through to con-
    sumers in fuel prices and should therefore influence the demand for fuel.

The German Federal Environment Agency commissioned a study
on the potential to develop emissions trading for the transport sector
(Ewringmann et al., 2005). The focus of the research was to examine the
three mechanisms and assess the feasibility of their practical implementation. The study finds that the upstream approach is the most 'cost efficient,
effective and manageable approach' and it is considered to be relatively easy
to implement. For the purposes of economic efficiency, the authors recommend that any emissions trading scheme for the transport sector be linked
to the existing multi-sectoral emissions trading scheme.

Ten Brink et al. (2005) carried out a study for the Commission on the
economic impacts of an emissions target of 120 g/km on average per car
using emissions trading. The emissions trading scheme is assumed to be a
downstream system with a starting point of 140 g/km in 2008. The study
estimates that the additional cost to manufacturers of achieving 120 g/km
would be €577/car on average and the net costs to society (excluding externalities) would be between €127 and €252/car.

Albrecht (2000, 2001) has proposed that emissions trading be used cross-
sectorally and take in emissions produced both from manufacture and
during the life of the product. In this manner, automobile manufacturers
would be responsible for both the CO_2 emissions emitted during the manufacture of the vehicle and those emitted during the operation of the vehicle.
It is possible that a future phase of the EU emissions trading scheme will
include the CO_2 emissions produced from automobile manufacturing
plants.[9]

Albrecht estimated that an average petrol car emits 25 times as many CO_2
emissions during its lifetime than are produced with the manufacture of the
car. If a manufacturer were held responsible for the operational emissions
as well as the production emissions, it would shift the abatement emphasis
to the product technology. A reduction of 5 per cent in CO_2 emissions from

Table 8.1   Example calculation comparing the impact of abatement from vehicle production with abatement from vehicle operation

	Emissions (tonnes CO_2)	Share of total emissions (%)
Vehicle production	1–2	2.7–5.3
Vehicle use (lifetime, 150 000 km)	37.5	94.7–97.3
Total	38.5–39.5	100
Impact of abatement		
• Five per cent abatement of emissions from production	0.05–0.1	0.13–0.25
• Five per cent abatement of emissions from operation	1.875	4.7–4.9

vehicle operation would reduce the life cycle emissions by nearly 5 per cent overall, whereas a reduction in production emissions of 5 per cent would only reduce the life cycle emissions by around 0.2 per cent, as shown in Table 8.1.

Therefore if policy instruments focus on the reduction of emissions from the use of transport products rather than the production of the product, the total abatement of transport emissions will increase. There are a few advantages to this mechanism. It can be argued that the know-how of the car manufacturer lies more in the development of vehicle technology that is fuel efficient than in improving manufacturing processes and therefore they should be encouraged to concentrate on that aspect of abatement. Albrecht states that it is also more likely to be cheaper to reduce CO_2 emissions in the use of each car rather than in its production, although anecdotal evidence suggests that this may not necessarily hold true. However, it depends on the units of calculation: if the costs are calculated over the life of a vehicle then perhaps indeed this may be the case. Unfortunately, customers generally do not calculate the price of the vehicle over its lifetime. The study shows that in any case emissions trading of vehicle life cycle CO_2 emissions could provide an interesting opportunity for vehicle manufacturers to capture returns from improvements in vehicle technology. Such returns will not be directly yielded, for example, by the main instrument used in the EU to reduce CO_2 emissions by 2008 (voluntary agreement described in Chapter 11), as there is no financial revenue earned directly from emissions reduction.

We can compare in principle the efficiency of a cross-sectoral emissions trading scheme that includes manufacturing as well as product life, with a combination of emissions trading for the manufacturing process and a voluntary agreement for the vehicle CO_2 emissions. To make a detailed comparison, knowledge of the marginal abatement costs of both production and vehicle technology advancement are needed.

In a cross-sectoral emissions trading scheme, the allocation of permits would clearly be difficult. The calculation to distribute the proportion of permits between the different stages of a product life could be exceedingly complicated, and even then it could only succeed if all sectors, at every stage, were part of the emissions trading scheme to avoid any gaps in the energy cycle. For example, a car manufacturer could save emissions permits by the employment of aluminium in the vehicle body, thus achieving better energy efficiency through lighter weight. However aluminium itself is very energy-intensive to produce and hence, if the responsible sector was not included in the emissions scheme, the car manufacturer could perversely benefit through the use of an energy-intensive material. However, if the aluminium sector were part of the scheme, the increased use of energy in the production of aluminium would cause the aluminium producer to use permits, whose cost would then be passed on to the car manufacturer and would be included in the car design and manufacturing decision. Therefore, cross-sectoral emissions trading can potentially only work if all sectors are included. There can remain a problem with energy-intensive imports and possible 'carbon leakage'. Carbon leakage occurs when imports coming into the system are not part of an emissions trading scheme and therefore the original producer has avoided the requirement to ensure their emissions are covered by sufficient permits. In this sense, carbon is considered to have 'leaked' from the region covered by the scheme to the region outside the scheme.

Another issue with regard to the allocation of emissions permits to vehicle models is the determination of baseline emissions. Without a credible estimate of baseline emissions, it is difficult to establish fair criteria for the allocation of credits for CO_2 emissions reductions (in a baseline and credit scheme). Apart from the difficulty of determining the 'no policy' level of emissions, another challenge arises in deciding the method of measurement. Should, there be one absolute baseline for all vehicle model types? Should, for example, a mini have the same baseline as a sports utility vehicle or a luxury saloon? There are several options for units including absolute and relative or attribute-based emissions. The question as to the most suitable type of CO_2 emissions from passenger cars to measure remains pertinent for all passenger car policy instruments related to CO_2 emissions, be it for taxes, command and control or voluntary agreements.

One way to include transport in emissions trading is to restrict the scheme to commercial fleets[10] and then to treat fleet operators as emissions sources. The greenhouse gas emissions allowances are based on the amount of fuel consumed by the fleet of vehicles. A disadvantage of this scheme is that this method would not be applicable to private drivers, as it would be too complex to require individuals to participate as the emissions credit holders, owing to the numbers involved, at least without the development of new systems. Since CO_2 emissions from private passenger cars have the highest growth within the transport sector, and commercial fleet operators are already extremely conscious of fuel consumption for cost reasons, this must be considered as a major downside to the scheme.

Emissions trading, as with other market instruments, transmits a price signal to polluting activities so that there is an incentive to invest in greenhouse gas-reducing technology. If this type of policy instrument is applied to passenger car fleets, there could be a price incentive for fleet operators or manufacturers to purchase or produce, respectively, low-emitting vehicles. It appears that the US acid rain programme accelerated innovation in the main abatement technology used for compliance (scrubbers) because there was a significant fall in scrubber costs from the early 1990s (Montero et al., 2000).

Some modelling work has been carried out to simulate the effect of emissions trading on technology diffusion in other sectors, which may be relevant to the discussion on the application of emissions trading to passenger cars. Barreto and Kypreos (2004b) showed, using MARKAL,[11] that carbon abatement activities for the electricity sector in general tend to stimulate technological change, and this can spill over to other regions. They also found that cheaper mitigation opportunities exploited under an emissions trading scheme can discourage the development of more advanced low-carbon technologies in regions that are buying permits. Simultaneously, however, trade could encourage their penetration into the selling regions. The learning potential and extent of spillover effects can have a strong influence on the diffusion of technology between firms, sectors and regions. Similarly research has simulated the effect of emissions trading on R&D investment and demonstrated that there could be a significant impact (Buchner et al., 2002).

8.1.1 Summary of the Main Points

- Emissions trading is a policy instrument that may enable CO_2 emissions abatement to be achieved at lower cost compared with command and control regulations, by equalizing the marginal cost of abatement across sectors.

- International emissions trading is a flexible mechanism permitted under the Kyoto Protocol.
- Transport CO_2 emissions are not included in any emissions trading schemes but this may change in the near future with a review by stakeholders in Europe on the potential to include aviation in the EU emissions trading scheme in 2008.
- Some studies show that emissions trading schemes, which include the CO_2 emissions during the life of operation of the vehicle, would be more efficient than schemes which only include the emissions from the manufacture of the vehicle.
- The allocation of permits to the transport sector in an emissions trading scheme could be very complex, and would need to account for the life cycle emissions.
- The effect of emissions trading in other sectors will most likely affect investment in R&D and technology development trends and will probably be relevant to the passenger car sector.

8.2   TAXES AND CHARGES (FISCAL MEASURES)

Taxes and charges have gained in popularity as measures to reduce greenhouse gas emissions from transport, since they can influence consumers' purchasing and travel behaviour. The terms 'taxes' and 'charges' are often used interchangeably in environmental economic literature. They are essentially the same instrument in the sense that they apply a fee to the use of an environmental service. The difference between them is that taxes are often decided as part of fiscal regime at a national level, whereas charges mainly refer to locally administrated fees. The destination of the revenue generated can also differentiate the terms, since taxes generally are sent to the national treasury, unless they have been earmarked for an environmental fund, whereas the revenue from local charges usually remains in local use.

8.2.1   Design of Passenger Car Taxes and Charges

Historically there are few examples of an optimal tax applied by governments to passenger car greenhouse gas emissions because of either political or information constraints. Generally, vehicle and fuel taxes have been designed with the objective of raising revenue rather than with any particular environmental target planned. Therefore there often remains scope for redesign of the taxes in order to promote vehicle purchase and operation with specific environmental targets taken into account. It should be noted that this does not always mean raising the current taxes but 'greening' them to prioritize certain goals to be achieved.

As stated in the previous chapter, the design of an instrument can often influence its effectiveness more than the choice of the instrument itself. In the case of taxes and charges, setting the level of tax is complex. It is often difficult to estimate the marginal abatement cost and the actual environmental damage cost, in order to pinpoint the optimal tax, as illustrated in Figure 7.1. Frequently environmental targets and the related environmental tax are set on the basis of engineering or technological estimates and what is politically feasible, without further economic assessment. This may be reasonable where there is an obvious emission threshold above which pollution is detrimental to human health; however greenhouse gas damage is a global problem and hence it is difficult to estimate the marginal damage costs leading to a local optimal emission level. In the real world adjustment of the tax based on trial and error is often necessary, which is generally undesirable since policy stability is a requirement for investment. However the difficulty associated with environmental target setting in taxes is a feature of many other policy instruments too. Another issue is the declining revenue nature of environmental taxes. If environmental taxes act as an efficient incentive to stop producing an environmentally harmful good, then the tax base is reduced and tax revenues fall. Sometimes this can also result in an increase in the implicit tax rate or require an increase in taxes on other goods and services to maintain the same total tax revenue (CEC, 2002b).

Taxes and charges applied to passenger car transport can be generally categorized as follows:

- taxes on acquisitions, mostly referred to as registration tax;
- periodic taxes in connection with ownership such as annual motor taxes, termed 'circulation tax' here;
- fuel taxes; and
- other, such as road user fees, congestion charges, parking and so on.

The European Commission established the Expert Group on Fiscal Framework Measures, who commissioned a study by the consultancy company COWI to assist the Commission in considering the potentials of fiscal measures in achieving a target of 120 g/km on average per vehicle. The study was completed in 2002[12] and modelled scenarios of different changes to the current vehicle tax systems in nine member states (COWI, 2002). The analysis results led to several conclusions that are relevant to a general discussion on taxes and charges related to the reduction of greenhouse gas emissions from passenger cars and are paraphrased here:

- It is essential to apply a tax scheme, which is directly or indirectly CO_2 related in order to provide for significant reductions in the average CO_2 emissions from new cars.
- Differentiation of the taxes is necessary in such a way that promotes energy-efficient cars over cars with poor energy efficiency.
- The largest reductions are estimated to be achieved when the existing vehicle taxes are replaced by purely and directly CO_2-related taxes that are sufficiently differentiated.
- The level of the potential CO_2 reductions does not depend on whether the tax is an annual circulation or registration tax, but rather on the CO_2 emissions and the level of tax differentiation.
- Simple increases in vehicle tax, if the parameters upon which the tax is based remain the same and are unlinked to vehicle CO_2 emissions, do not have much impact on vehicle CO_2 emissions per km.
- Fuel tax increases lead to very small reductions in average new vehicle CO_2 emissions, compared to vehicle taxes. They may however be effective at reducing the CO_2 emissions from the overall passenger car fleet.

The model used in the COWI analysis estimates the levels of differentiation required, given a budget constraint, to achieve a 1 per cent reduction in CO_2 emissions for both replacing the existing registration and circulation taxes with CO_2-dependent taxes, and adding a CO_2-dependent tax to the existing taxes. In both cases, the tax differentiation required to achieve a reduction of CO_2 emissions through circulation tax is significantly lower than when using registration taxes. This is perhaps not surprising, considering that a circulation tax is applied annually and a registration tax is only applied once at the time of purchase. Since the CO_2 emissions considered are measured per kilometre travelled, the study does not consider the impact on travel demand and hence absolute emissions.

In the EU, fiscal instruments represent the second pillar of the European Commission strategy to reduce CO_2 emissions from passenger cars. In consequence, the European Commission has made a proposal for a Directive on passenger car-related taxes,[13] to reform and harmonize registration and annual circulation taxes on passenger cars in EU member states. The proposal has two objectives: to 'remove tax obstacles and distortions to free movement of passenger cars within the internal market' and also to restructure 'existing vehicle taxes to put more emphasis on environmental objectives in line with Community policy and Kyoto Protocol'. The Communication recommends abolishing registration taxes across the EU and relating annual vehicle taxes directly to their CO_2 emissions. The main points of the proposed Directive are the following:

- The abolition of car registration taxes over a transitional period of five to ten years.
- A system whereby a member state would be required to refund a portion of registration tax, pending its abolition, where a passenger car that is registered in that member state is subsequently exported or permanently transferred to another member state.
- The introduction of a CO_2 emissions element into the tax base of both annual circulation taxes and registration taxes.

Other challenges associated with greenhouse gas taxes are common to most taxes. There can be equity issues associated with taxes, where for example a car tax may represent a greater share of poorer drivers' incomes and hence they are priced off the road. Distribution of the revenue can also provide a concern. When one sector is taxed, there can be pressure to use the revenues to the benefit of that sector. This leads to the subject of earmarking and the option to refund tax revenues to low polluters. A charge or tax that is partially refunded to polluters who reduce their emissions provides an incentive to abate and may lower resistance to the introduction of a charge. Although this measure is more generally applied to industrial sectors, it could be potentially feasible with motorists, for example where the revenue from fossil fuel taxes could be used to subsidize alternative fuels and related technologies. Care is needed in measures such as these to ensure that they remain general or performance-based, to avoid the technology development becoming locked in.

The following subsections describe how these instruments are currently applied to reduce greenhouse gas emissions from transport. Observed examples of their use in various parts of the world are provided, although the focus is on the EU (see Box 8.2). There is a wide literature on this subject and, for a more detailed discussion, the reader is referred to the referenced literature in each section.

8.2.2 Taxes on Vehicle Acquisition

Most countries worldwide apply taxes on vehicle sales such as Value Added Tax (VAT) or vehicle registration tax. Vehicle registration tax represents the tax payable once only upon purchase of a vehicle. These are primarily applied as revenue raisers, rather than with any particular environmental objective in mind. However, in recent years, there have been increasing examples where vehicle sales taxes have been used to encourage the purchase of more environmentally friendly vehicles. In the past governments have designed these taxes to promote a particular technology rather than focusing on the emissions or environmental problem directly. Many countries provide a tax reduction on advanced fuel vehicle technologies, such as hybrid, fuel cell and electric vehicles.

The drawback of registration and VAT on vehicles is that they do not influence travel behaviour. However, if they are CO_2-differentiated they can influence consumer purchasing behaviour and encourage the purchase of fuel-efficient vehicles. This sends the right price signal to consumers and supports the CO_2 vehicle labelling requirements in the EU (see Section 8.3).

There is VAT on new cars in all EU member states of between 15 per cent and 25 per cent. However, registration charges and taxes exist in 16 countries

---

BOX 8.2 CONTEXT FOR FISCAL MEASURES ON PASSENGER CAR TRANSPORT IN EUROPE

Already in 1992 the European Council proposed reducing CO_2 emissions from new passenger cars to a target of 120 grams per kilometre by 2005, or by 2010 at the latest. Fiscal measures were to be a part of this target. Owing to disagreement between the European Council, Parliament and Commission, in 1996 the Council agreed with the Community strategy to reduce CO_2 emissions from passenger cars and improve fuel economy by means of a 'three-pillar' strategy, which included:

– Voluntary commitment of the car industry to reduce average specific CO_2 emissions to 140 g/km by 2008/2009,

– Fuel-economy labelling,

– Fiscal measures.

The commitments with the car industry to lower CO_2 emissions to 140 g CO_2/km leaves a shortfall of 20g CO_2/km from the original target. Vehicle labelling and fiscal measures are intended to assist the reduction of the remaining amount. Therefore, the voluntary agreement target provides the baseline from which further CO_2 emissions reductions are expected to ensue, as a result of the other two measures specified in the pillar strategy.

Since unanimous agreement is required in the Council of Ministers to pass EU tax regulations, fiscal measures are generally implemented by individual member state governments rather than at EU level (Commission of the European Communities, 2000). EU labelling, on the other hand is promulgated EU-wide as a result of the EU Labelling Directive (Directive 199/94/EC).

in the EU25, and vary in their design. Some countries impose registration taxes based on the value of the car, and some on the engine size. In general, countries with a car manufacturing industry tend to impose low registration taxes, whereas countries importing passenger cars have higher registration taxes (CEC, 2002b). The proposal to gradually scrap registration taxes is motivated by the desire to remove obstacles to trade between member states rather than by any environmental goals. The reduction of registration taxes can be carried out in a revenue-neutral manner by adjusting the annual circulation taxes to compensate.

In the EU, registration taxes often influence the pre-tax prices of passenger cars. Car manufacturers set recommended pre-tax prices for each member state, taking into account the registration tax that will be applied in each member state. This leads to high variation in pre-tax prices, since pre-tax prices in member states applying low registration taxes are set higher than in member states with high registration taxes. It is estimated that the variation in registration taxes between member states explains approximately 20 per cent of the price differentials (CEC, 2002b).

In the Netherlands from 1 January 2002, fuel-efficient passenger cars have been awarded an energy bonus in the form of a reduction in registration tax (CEC, 2002b) and Denmark has introduced tax reductions in the registration tax for the most efficient new cars.[14]

The Portuguese state budget for 2001, introduced in 2000, provides for a 50 per cent reduction of the tax on the purchase of vehicles when they use exclusively liquefied petroleum gas (LPG) or natural gas. When they are powered by engines that use conventional fuels but can also use LPG, natural gas, electricity or solar energy, a 40 per cent reduction of that tax is provided (IEA, 2004b). These measures create an incentive for the market penetration of low-carbon fuels.

In April 2001, the Japanese government introduced a broad green taxation scheme, which reduces the automobile acquisition tax on low-polluting vehicles (methanol, hybrid, compressed natural gas and electric) and on certain fuel-efficient and low-emissions vehicles (IEA, 2004b). It also increases the tax on old polluting vehicles in order to promote the acquisition and social acceptance of environmentally sound new vehicles. These measures aim to curb global warming and control local air pollution. In the six months before the lower taxes for low-emission vehicles came into force, the rate of newly registered low-emission vehicles (defined as electric, methanol-fuelled, natural gas and hybrid vehicles) was 21.1 per cent small or medium cars, but after the tax was implemented this amount increased to 34.2 per cent within six months and reached 57.3 per cent in the first half of 2002. The green tax scheme became stricter in 2003, with higher standards for cars to qualify and a shorter period of tax breaks. As it stands, for cars qualifying as 'green' 300 000 yen (approx. US$2500) is deducted from the value of the car in calculating the acquisitions tax. The acquisitions tax for fuel cell-powered cars is cut by a further 2.7 per cent.

In the USA the purchase of new hybrid and electric vehicles was eligible for a tax reduction of up to $2000 until 2005. Hybrids purchased after this date are no longer eligible for these deductions but may be eligible for a federal income tax credit, depending on the vehicle's fuel economy, estimated fuel savings and other factors (US DoE, 2005).

8.2.3   Taxes on Vehicle Ownership

A periodic tax, such as an annual circulation tax (ACT), is applied in many countries to passenger cars. As with registration taxes, the objective factors employed as the basis of the tax vary widely, that is, cm^3, kW emissions. Similar to registration taxes, since the level of ACT is independent of the distance travelled during the period for which it is paid, there is little scope to influence travel behaviour through ACT differentiation. Instead, through the greening of ACT, passenger car customers are encouraged to buy vehicles with low greenhouse gas emissions with lower ACT payments. There is more scope than with registration taxes to do this, since an ACT is paid on all vehicles every year, whereas in many countries the customer only pays the registration tax once, at the time of purchase of the vehicle. Ryan et al. (2006) find in their examination of vehicle and fuel taxes between 1995 and 2004 in EU15 that the registration and fuel taxes have an effect on whether customers purchase a vehicle and its fuel type, whereas circulation taxes may have a stronger influence on the CO_2 emissions of the vehicle purchased.

In the EU, all member states (apart from the Czech Republic, Estonia, France, Lithuania, Poland, Slovenia and Slovakia) impose some sort of periodic circulation tax on passenger vehicles. Although low-emitting vehicles qualify for reductions in some countries, these reductions are based on emissions relevant to local air quality rather than greenhouse gas emissions. The UK is the only member state that applies a CO_2-based annual circulation tax: a passenger car emitting less than 150 g CO_2/km is charged €159, while more polluting cars are charged by an amount increasing incrementally to €246 (cars emitting more than 185 g CO_2/km) (CEC, 2002b). Annual circulation taxes in the EU varied from an average of €30 per car in Italy to an average of €463 per car in Denmark in 1999 (CEC, 2002b). Insurance is another significant annual outlay for passenger-car drivers. Germany allows an exemption in the annual tax for cars that meet very advanced emissions standards or have very low fuel consumption.

As part of the Green tax system in Japan, in addition to the lower acquisition tax discussed above, low-emission vehicles are also subject to lower circulation tax rates for the first two years after purchase, although this was reduced to only the first year in 2003. Under the modifications to the tax in 2003, the annual tax for three-star (highly efficient) LPG and fuel cell-powered vehicles was reduced by 50 per cent for one year. As a result of this scheme and other green tax measures, Japan's Ministry of Land, Infrastructure and Transport reported that the number of registered low-emission vehicles (LEVs) had reached 5.75 million by the end of September 2003, accounting for about 11.4 per cent of all vehicle ownership.

The COWI report described above estimates the extent to which vehicle taxes could be adjusted in order to reduce vehicle CO_2 emissions towards the Community target of an average 120 g CO_2/km by 2008. They assume vehicle CO_2 emissions have already decreased to 140 g/km on average in 2008, thanks to technological improvements by then, and model the use of circulation and registration taxes to reduce average emissions by a further 10 per cent split equally between the two taxes. The study finds that the largest CO_2 reductions could be achieved when the existing vehicle tax systems were replaced by CO_2-dependent registration and circulation taxes. Table 8.2 and Table 8.3 show the results of this study for the modification of circulation taxes on petrol and diesel vehicles. They illustrate the taxes that would have to be applied on new diesel and petrol cars, taking the current and future circulation tax systems in each country into consideration in order to achieve a CO_2 emissions reduction of approximately 5 per cent overall. The vehicle taxes can be restructured either by enhancing the existing taxes by adding a CO_2 element or by replacing the existing taxes with another completely CO_2-dependent tax. Both concepts are compared with the reference scenario in 2008 of continuation of the current system of circulation taxes.

The results show the estimated effect of replacing current circulation tax systems with CO_2-dependent circulation taxes on the level of tax levied per year. Across the nine countries studied, changing the taxes in order to achieve on average 4.4 per cent CO_2 emissions reduction would require average circulation taxes to increase by between 26 and 169 per cent for petrol cars and between 0 and 50 per cent for diesel cars. The UK values are deemed unreliable, since the UK already applies CO_2-differentiated vehicle taxes, and therefore are not included in these ranges. The base scenario represents average circulation taxes in existence in 1999 and their projected values in 2008.

The COWI results show that either registration or circulation taxes can be used to reduce CO_2 emissions from transport, although the respective taxes increase by a significant amount. The additional costs to consumers are lower for circulation taxes than registration taxes for the countries modelled in the COWI study. The European directive on vehicle taxes proposes to

Table 8.2 *Estimated CO$_2$-differentiated circulation tax on diesel vehicles compared with reference circulation taxes for 2008*

Country	Base scenario values Average circulation taxes		Scenario calculations 2008					
			Adding CO$_2$ element to existing taxes			Replacing existing taxes with CO$_2$ taxes		
	Average circulation tax €1999	Average circulation tax €2008	€/g CO$_2$ per 1% emissions reductions	Average circulation tax	% CO$_2$ emissions reduction	€/g CO$_2$ per 1% emissions reductions	Average circulation tax	% CO$_2$ emissions reduction
Belgium	384	395	2.6	480	2.0	8.8	483	3.4
Germany	282	321	1.1	366	2.4	2.0	369	3.4
Denmark	574	403	5.9	513	1.9	17.3	525	1.8
Italy	190	193	1.5	266	2.7	2.0	269	3.7
Netherlands	986	1005	3.6	979	1.9	10.3	997	4.3
Portugal	31	32	0.5	46	2.7	1.2	48	3.2
Sweden	659	678	1.1	746	4.3	2.2	753	4.4
Finland	572	579	1.4	573	2.5	2.8	578	4.3
UK	236	182	0.9	414	–	1.2	415	4.4

Source: COWI (2002).

Table 8.3   Estimated CO_2-differentiated circulation tax on petrol vehicles compared with reference circulation taxes for 2008

Country	Base scenario values		Scenario calculations 2008					
	Average circulation taxes		Adding CO_2 element to existing taxes			Replacing existing taxes with CO_2 taxes		
	Average circulation tax €1999	Average circulation tax €2008	€/g CO_2 per 1% emissions reductions	Average circulation tax	% CO_2 emissions reduction	€/g CO_2 per 1% emissions reductions	Average circulation tax	% CO_2 emissions reduction
Belgium	177	200	1.0	310	4.0	4.1	307	5.2
Germany	88	97	0.7	230	5.0	1.4	232	5.5
Denmark	404	227	2.6	411	5.4	4.9	440	5.9
Italy	151	163	1.1	239	3.6	3.9	241	4.3
Netherlands	433	471	1.3	581	4.7	4.1	606	6.5
Portugal	35	37	1.8	89	1.9	6.5	91	2.1
Sweden	150	155	1.5	297	3.2	2.1	300	3.9
Finland	118	118	1.3	292	3.2	1.8	295	3.4
UK	231	167	1.2	449	–	1.6	450	4.7

Source: COWI (2002).

harmonize vehicle taxation in the EU and transfer revenues from registration to circulation taxes. This would involve phasing out registration taxes and restructuring circulation taxes to allow tax differentiation in favour of low CO_2-emitting cars. If vehicle tax revenue were to be kept constant, they estimate that this would raise annual circulation taxes, for example in Ireland, by 100 per cent by 2015, since the registration taxes in Ireland are high. The Commission recommends that strict budget neutrality be observed and that the overall tax burden on passenger cars should not increase.

The implications for a reform of registration and circulation taxes in Europe to CO_2 differentiated taxes on the development of passenger cars globally could be considerable. The car industry is a global sector and the development of low CO_2-emitting vehicles for sale in the EU could have spillover effects elsewhere.

8.2.4   Taxes on Fuel

Fossil fuel consumption is directly related to the production of greenhouse gas emissions. All countries apply transport fuel taxes as revenue raisers. Recently, as part of the drive to reduce greenhouse gas emissions, countries have begun to introduce carbon taxes across a wide range of sectors. Fuel taxes are included in governments' plans to reduce their carbon dioxide emissions and internalize the externalities of personal car usage. In the transport sector this translates to a levy on fuels based on their carbon content. Carbon taxes are generally small relative to other fuel taxes, although the relative size of the carbon tax varies according to the type of fuel (US EPA, 2004).

The rationale behind differentiating fuel taxes according to carbon content is that, by increasing fuel taxes, consumers embark on strategies that will allow them to consume less fuel, such as buying a more fuel-efficient vehicle, driving less or switching to an alternative mode of transport. Carbon taxes have been adopted in several European nations, including Belgium, Denmark, Finland, France, Italy, Luxembourg, the Netherlands, Norway and Sweden. A fuel tax escalator was adopted in the UK to raise revenue and constrain transport demand (described in Box 8.3). Poland has a small tax on CO_2 emissions. ECMT (2003a) provides a review of these and other energy taxes in OECD countries. Fuel taxes vary considerably between countries and can cause distortions in the market where citizens from one country drive across the border to buy transport fuel and benefit from cheaper prices. Fuel taxes in the US are the lowest of developed countries and are not CO_2-differentiated.

A differential between types of fuel taxes has shown itself to be a very successful way to change consumption patterns from one type of fuel to another, for example in promoting the switch from leaded to unleaded petrol in the USA and the EU (see Hammar et al., 2004). It is more difficult to apply this to the carbon content of fuels with the limited choices available in conventional fossil fuels. An additional problem with the application of fuel taxes is their acceptability: while increases in fuel taxation do have a part to play in attributing to motorists the 'correct' costs of their decisions, they are unlikely to achieve all the desired reductions on their own at politically acceptable levels of taxation (see the example in Box 8.3). Raising fuel taxes can lead to an increase in inflation and hence governments are often reluctant to consider this option. There are also equity issues associated with all transport taxes, as mentioned at the beginning of this section.

An advantage of a fuel tax over vehicle acquisition and registration taxes and VAT from an environmental perspective is that it acts as a user charge per kilometre. Fuel prices are the most obvious charge a driver faces in the operation of his vehicle. In this manner a fuel tax can influence passenger car travel demand as well as vehicle purchasing behaviour. An increase in fuel taxes can encourage vehicle manufacturers to develop more fuel-efficient vehicles.

BOX 8.3   THE RISE AND FALL OF THE FUEL ESCALATOR IN THE UK

In Britain the fundamental stumbling block to environmental taxation has been more the attitude of the public than of business and this is exemplified in the story of the road fuel duty escalator (Dresner et al., 2006).

In the March 1993 budget, it was announced that road fuel duties would increase by 3% in real terms each year as a means of reducing emissions from transport. This was reaffirmed by the new government in 1997 in the White Paper: 'Increasing fuel duty has proved an effective way of directly influencing CO_2 emissions from road transport as part of our strategy for tackling climate change . . .' (paragraphs 4.118–4.121). At the end of 1993, the rate was raised to 5 per cent and from June 1997 further increased to 6 per cent per annum. For the first few years the tax was remarkably successful at raising revenue. It had a low profile, since until 1999 oil prices were falling and therefore offset the increase in fuel tax. According to Glaister (2001) the fuel tax did manage to keep traffic constant between 1998 and 2000 (when economic growth would have predicted a rise of 7 per cent and so from a policy perspective it was successful. In 1999, however, the impact of the escalator began to be noticed by motorists and road haulage companies; the Conservative Party (who had introduced the escalator but were now in opposition) and some newspapers started to campaign vociferously against the escalator. Petrol that had been cheap by European standards was the most expensive in Europe and a tax that hardly anyone had been aware of for six years started to become a political issue. Lorry drivers embarked on a campaign of civil unrest, claiming that the high diesel prices due to the escalator were making them uncompetitive with competitors in other European countries, and appeared to attract a large amount of public sympathy despite the disruption they caused. While the government pointed out that overall taxes on haulage companies were actually higher in other European countries, nobody appeared to believe them.

Finally, in November 1999, Gordon Brown announced that the escalator would be abolished and announced a freeze in fuel duty. He did not rule out future increases in fuel duty, but pledged that it would not be automatic and that future increases would be hypothecated for expenditure on public transport and road-building. However, at the beginning of 2000, responsibility for transport was transferred to the Department of Environment, Transport and the Regions (since 2002 Department for Transport). Although increased investment in public transport is now promised, the commitment to reduce car use has been diminished and road building has again increased as a measure to reduce congestion (Dresner et al., 2006).

There can be two distinct effects from changing to a policy of differentiated fuel taxes proportional to carbon content in order to reduce consumption and reduce greenhouse gas emissions. The first is that more fuel-efficient cars could be purchased. In the immediate future perhaps this would most likely mean a higher share of diesel and other fuels such as LPG or biofuels, or increasingly hybrid passenger cars (observed to be an important development towards longer-term sustainability in Chapters 5 and 6).

In terms of impact on CO_2 emissions factors as a result of vehicle purchasing behaviour, which are measured per vehicle per kilometre, the COWI study (COWI, 2002) has found that an increase in fuel tax by as much as 25 per cent has very little effect on CO_2 emissions factors (g/km) if other vehicle taxes are not CO_2-differentiated in tandem. The study estimates that a 25 per cent increase in fuel price would only decrease CO_2 emissions per kilometre by 0.2–2 per cent across the nine countries modelled by 2008. It postulates that fuel taxes are ineffective in terms of emissions factors, as they apply equally to both fuel-efficient and fuel-inefficient vehicles in terms of costs per litre. They do not have the scope to increase the price differentiation between low and high fuel efficiency vehicles, therefore providing less incentive for consumers to switch to more advanced technologies. There is evidence in other fuel elasticity literature, however, that higher fuel prices lead to fuel-switching and the purchase of more fuel-efficient vehicles in the longer term (VTPI, 2006).

The COWI report estimates the effect of increasing diesel share on CO_2 emissions in EU countries. It is estimated that, in the nine countries studied, the effect of doubling the diesel passenger vehicle share would reduce CO_2 emissions by 5 to 9.4 per cent. Increasing the diesel share to 50 per cent of the total passenger vehicle stock would reduce CO_2 emissions by between 6 and 11.8 per cent. The total cost to society of increasing the diesel share of the passenger car fleet is not clear, since, although conventional diesel technologies generate lower CO_2 emissions than petrol cars, they produce relatively higher NO_x and particulate emissions (Mayeres and Proost, 2001). However, the new vehicle emissions standard in EU for 2008 (EURO 5) will most likely be so stringent that most new diesel vehicles will need to be equipped with particulate traps and NO_x storage devices in order to meet the emissions limits. This should eliminate the problem of diesel pollutant emissions. The rising demand for diesel fuel is predicted to have adverse impacts on the security of energy supply, the well-to-wheel energy efficiency per kilometre, and the cost of diesel fuel (Kavalov and Peteves, 2004). This is due to the rise in world diesel consumption, which will necessitate the expansion of oil refinery diesel fractions. Refinery output fractions are technologically determined to achieve minimum energy losses and greenhouse gas emissions. Increased diesel production, at the expense of the petrol fraction, will result in higher energy use, greenhouse gas emissions and costs.

Apart from the incentive to purchase more fuel-efficient vehicles, the second effect of differentiating fuel taxes on the basis of emissions is the impact on travel demand. It is sometimes observed that fuel taxes have little or no effect on fuel consumption demand (that is, there is a low fuel price elasticity of demand), since people may be unable to change their consumption pattern. Although this may be true in the very short run, there is evidence that people change their consumption of fuel in the long run (Sterner, 2003). This can occur because they buy a less fuel-consuming car, or they change the mode of transport to work, or they move job or house and so reduce the distance travelled, or change their driving behaviour.

Table 8.4   Elasticity estimates in OECD countries (1963–1985)

Calculation method	Price elasticity		Income elasticity	
	Short run (1 year)	Long run	Short run (1 year)	Long run
Pooled OLS[a]	−0.12	−1.39	0.05	0.58
Pooled (fixed effects 'within')	−0.22	−1.27	0.13	0.75
Cross-section ('between')		−1.19		1.09
Mean group estimates	−0.25	−0.85	0.37	1.15
Aggregate time-series	−0.31	−1.28	0.29	1.19

[a]   Ordinary least squares.

Source: Sterner (2003).

There is a large literature on estimated price elasticities of transport fuel demand, which comprise the change due to both consumers switching to more fuel efficient vehicles and the reduction in travel demand. These values give an indication of the percentage change in demand for fuel, given an increase in fuel price by 1 per cent. Sterner (2003) has summarized the results from some studies in OECD countries to estimate the elasticities of fuel demand with price and income and these are presented in Table 8.4. The models used to measure fuel price and income elasticity of demand affect the values estimated. In this table it is shown that the elasticity in the short run is in fact quite low for both price and income effect by most methods of estimation. The long-run elasticity values are much larger, indicating that a change in price does affect the demand for fuel. Another large review found the short-run price elasticity of fuel demand to be −0.25 and the long-run value to be −0.6 (Goodwin et al., 2004).

Fuel taxes increase the cost of car transport relative to other modes. The elasticities from most of the literature in Table 8.4 suggest that an increase in the price of fuel of 10 per cent would lead to a reduction in fuel consumption from passenger cars of approximately 1.2–3.1 per cent in the short run (within a year) or 8.5–13.9 per cent in the long run as a result of the two effects described above.

Some economists favour an increase in fuel tax, which is revenue-neutral and funds a reduction in economically harmful taxes such as income or labour. An example of this kind of fuel tax is the 'eco' tax in Germany. Between 1999 and 2003, taxes on petrol, diesel, electricity, heating oil and natural gas were increased in five stages and the revenue was mainly used

Table 8.5   Change in number of passengers using public transport in Germany

1999	2000	2001	2002	2003
0.4%	0.8%	0.8%	0.5%	1.5%

Source: GBG (2004).

Table 8.6   Change in road transport fuel consumption compared to previous year in Germany

2000	2001	2002	2003
−2.8%	−1.0%	−2.3%	−2.9%

Source: GBG (2004).

to reduce pension contributions. This tax appears to have significantly reduced fuel consumption (see Table 8.6) and hence transport CO_2 emissions in Germany. For the first time since 1949, fuel consumption, and hence CO_2 emissions in the transport sector as well, fell for four years in a row (2000–2003), whereas prior to this they had increased almost every year without exception. As a result, CO_2 emissions were cut by around 6 to 7 per cent compared with the high of 1999. Although fuel tourism and a worsening economic situation confounded the situation, it is expected that the adoption of more fuel-efficient driving practices, a reduction of the mileage driven and the availability of vehicles with reduced specific consumption on the market were a partial result of the ecotax. The number of passengers using public transport had been falling until 1998, but began to increase in 1999 (see Table 8.5). Other effects were the increase in sales of fuel-efficient and alternatively fuelled cars.

Of course, all of the price increases cannot be attributed to the ecotax alone; other factors contributed to increased fuel prices over the period from 2000 to 2003 and hence the reduced road transport fuel consumption reported in Table 8.6 and therefore CO_2 emissions also. It is estimated that the ecotax contributed to only 25 per cent of the rise in fuel prices in Germany and that the remainder was due to high world market prices for crude oil and the strong dollar exchange rate (GBG, 2004).

Fuel taxes in many countries are earmarked to fund road transport projects, in particular roads and other infrastructure. Wachs (2003) has estimated that fuel taxes are insufficient in the US to cover road costs, especially if the external costs of transport are taken into consideration.

Because they influence consumer preferences, environmental taxes may encourage vehicle manufacturers and fuel producers to develop innovative products, thereby supporting the deployment and diffusion of new technologies. This is seen in Chapter 6, where it is shown how taxes on greenhouse gas emissions may accelerate the adoption of low- and zero-emission vehicle technologies, supporting a transition towards a more sustainable transport system. The technological change due to environmental taxes in one region of the world may become pervasive, as the technologies developed will spill over to other regions of the world. In any case, all of the car manufacturers operating in the EU sell vehicles globally and therefore R&D in vehicle environmental performance tends to have an impact on vehicles sold worldwide.

Alternative fuels tax policies
Many countries have reduced fuel taxes on alternative fuels. Alternative fuels represent a way to achieve several goals simultaneously. They can provide an opportunity to reduce greenhouse gases and other pollutant emissions, create new employment prospects (in particular in rural areas), improve security of energy supply and even support a rural economy. Worldwide, biofuels are growing in popularity. However, there are multiple challenges facing alternative fuels before gaining market acceptance and penetrating significantly the transport fuel market, as stated in section 7.3.3.

One of the main barriers to biofuels, as well as other alternative fuels, is the higher cost compared with fossil fuels, although, as seen in Figure 4.3, biofuels are competitive in Brazil. Biofuel production costs are higher than fossil fuel costs, however they are varied and are very dependent on market prices of crude oil, seed prices and the extent of refining undertaken. Biofuels are therefore generally not competitive with conventional fossil fuels in Europe, Japan and the USA unless an excise duty rebate is given.

In the EU, member states are permitted to reduce or abolish taxes on alternative fuels as a result of the Energy Taxation Directive.[15] These tax concessions are considered as state aid, and may not over-compensate the biofuel producers. Since the costs of biofuel production vary considerably, particularly for bioethanol, the Commission is investigating the optimal way to do this. The Commission also recommends that a 'framework of incentives be established to encourage and promote the use of market-driven and demand-side measures for biofuels' (CEC, 2006a). One study, which estimates the cost of exempting biofuels from excise duty as a greenhouse gas mitigation strategy, has calculated that the cost of revenue forgone, due to an excise duty exemption of European biofuels per tonne of CO_2 emissions saved, ranges between €202 and €1289 (Ryan et al., 2005). This is significantly higher than the simple average market price of CO_2 allowances in 2006 of approximately €17 per tonne. However, it is expected that the cost of biofuel production will reduce with time (Fulton et al., 2004).

There are many instances of excise duty exemption as a means to providing an incentive to alternative fuel sales. The main fuels for which tax exemptions are currently provided are biofuels, CNG and LPG. The UK government, for example, has supported the use of LPG as an alternative fuel since 1996. In 1999, the duty was reduced by 29 per cent and in 2001 by 40 per cent. This cost the government £50 million in lost revenue in 2002. Conversion of petrol engines for use with LPG has been funded through the PowerShift programme (£8 million spent) and it is estimated that there are now nearly 100 000 vehicles using LPG.

In the US, the federal excise tax on 10 per cent bioethanol fuel blends is 13.2 cents instead of the standard 18.4 cents per gallon of petrol. This equates to a tax credit of 52 cents per full gallon of denatured ethanol, which is expected to remain in force at least until 2010. Furthermore, E85 blends (85 per cent bioethanol and 15 per cent petrol) are also eligible for an additional tax incentive, up to 52 cents per gallon 'Income Tax Credit for Alcohol Used as Fuel'.[16] The credit only applies to the alcohol portion of E85, and the credits are reduced by what the taxpayer has already received via the federal excise tax reduction above. This tax credit is taxable as income at both the state and the federal levels.[17] Further tax credits are available on biofuels in most US states.

In the EU, many countries provide an excise duty exemption in order to encourage the market demand of biofuels.

Australia provides an excise duty exemption to domestically produced biofuels. There has been some opposition to the promotion of biofuels, mainly from oil companies and car manufacturers, and therefore the substitution of biofuels is restricted to a 10 per cent blend.

Impact of policy measures on EU passenger car sales and CO_2 emissions

In the EU, the Directorate General Environment commissioned an analysis in 2004 to examine to what extent the CO_2-specific vehicle CO_2 emission reductions achieved between 1995 and 2003 were attributable to technological improvements caused by the manufacturers (under the voluntary agreement described in subsection 9.2.3), or by market changes and policies and hence non-attributable to manufacturers.

The main policy measures affecting fleet emissions in the EU are a voluntary agreement by manufacturers to supply efficient vehicles and member state fiscal measures on vehicle purchase (registration tax), ownership (circulation tax) and operational costs (for example fuel taxes);

informational measures introduced by the labelling directive; scrapping incentives; and other EU related regulations connected with issues such as safety and other pollutant emissions. Safety and, to a lesser extent, emissions regulations tend to cause vehicle weight to increase substantially, thus affecting vehicle CO_2 emissions.

It is estimated that safety requirements due to EU regulations have caused an increase of 15 to 20 kg average vehicle weight over the period (Mehlin et al., 2004b).

Currently the EU emissions trading scheme does not include the transport sector. However, after the first phase, there exists the possibility of this sector's inclusion, and the resulting effect on travel costs could be similar to that of a rise in fuel taxes. The relative impact on prices would vary across member states in accordance with variations in fuel prices, which are illustrated in Figure 8.1 for real petrol prices over the period from 1995 to 2003. These differences are largely a reflection of the corresponding differentials in excise duties that apply across member states.

Further non-technical factors exist, such as socio-economic trends and consumer preferences (over which manufactures also have a strong influence) that can influence the new car fleet emissions. The level of income per capita, demographic structural changes and social trends all play an important role in determining the structure of the passenger car market, and hence the average fleet CO_2 emissions.

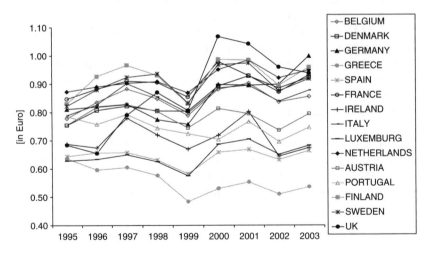

Source: Mehlin et al. (2004b).

*Figure 8.1   Real petrol prices for EU member states in €/litre indexed
                to 1995*

The large database collected for the EU by the market research company Polk on vehicle registrations, and their associated CO_2 emissions, is the basis for an econometric regression analysis carried out by Mehlin et al. (2004b) to examine the impact of technical and non-technical factors on fleet CO_2 emissions.

Mehlin et al., (2004b) developed a model to estimate the impact on CO_2 emissions of a range of vehicle technical characteristics (such as vehicle length, width, height and weight, type of transmission, engine capacity and power, and the number of cylinders), and non-technical factors, such as car price, price index of alternative cars, size of car, foreign car indicator, population density, percentage of population aged between 50 and 64 years, percentage urban population, per capita GDP, per capita GDP squared, fuel price (€/100km), fuel price squared, circulation tax and circulation tax squared.

The results for technical factors indicate that emissions have increased less than expected considering concurrent increases in vehicle weight, height and engine power, suggesting that manufacturers have been successful in improving some aspects of CO_2 emissions performance. Mehlin's results for non-technical factors are of more interest here, since these factors include many potentially important policy variables. Three of these are per capita incomes, fuel prices and circulation taxes. As expected, the factor with by far the greatest influence on the number of vehicle registrations is found to be per capita GDP. This is important, since it means that an expanding EU economy will cause higher numbers of vehicles sales and provide greater challenges to reduce CO_2 emissions from passenger cars.

Another study by Ryan et al. (2006) has examined the effect of socioeconomic, technical factors and vehicle and fuel taxes on new vehicle sales and average CO_2 emissions in the EU15. They also conducted an econometric regression analysis and found, in agreement with Mehlin et al., that GDP per capita and fuel prices have a strong influence on vehicle registrations. They also found that, while registration tax has an impact on vehicle registrations, that is, whether consumers purchase a vehicle, circulation tax has a stronger impact on fleet average CO_2 emissions.

Broadly the main results indicate that (i) different taxes (fuel taxes, vehicle registration and circulation taxes) affect individuals' purchasing behaviour differently; (ii) fiscal instruments affect total vehicle sales, vehicle petrol-to-diesel sales ratios, and CO_2 emissions intensity differently; and (iii) new fleet average CO_2 emissions intensity has fallen over the period 1995–2004 independently of the member state fiscal measures analysed by Ryan et al. (2006).

8.2.5   Congestion Charging[18]

For over 30 years, economists have endorsed congestion tolls based on the costs that an additional car imposes on all other drivers during periods of congestion, to help better align the private travel costs faced by individual drivers with the overall economic costs to society. Road charges and tolls are widely documented in the literature as effective instruments in transport demand management (TDM). Although most TDM schemes focus on congestion as the externality to be controlled, they may also serve the dual purpose of reducing greenhouse gas emissions from transport. Some researchers (Button and Verhoef, 1998) show that, while road prices can be a method of restricting total vehicle numbers and also that transaction and administration costs are low, fixed taxes such as vehicle registration tax or annual road tax are a very poor form of transport demand management. As with any fixed cost that does not vary with usage, in both cases, once paid, the incentive remains to use the car as often as possible to 'recoup' the investment made (Kelly, 2003).

Road pricing is often cited in academic TDM literature as a first-best approach to transport demand management. The European Conference of Ministers of Transport examined pricing reforms for transport and stated:

> The key to achieving the potential benefits of pricing reforms is to charge closer to the point at which the decision to travel is taken. This would enable rational decisions by individuals and firms, informed by price signals of the full costs of their travel demands, to determine traffic levels and trends in transport demand. (ECMT, 2003b)

Successful implementations include Singapore, Scandinavian cities such as Trondheim, Oslo and Bergen, and London, two of which are described in Box 8.4. There may be more road pricing schemes implemented in the UK in the future as the current transport act in the UK enables local authorities to introduce road use charging and workplace parking levies independently of the central government (Bonsall, 2000). Systems for tolling heavy duty vehicles (HDVs) have been introduced in several countries, particularly in environmentally fragile areas such as the Alps in Europe.

A modelling study undertaken in Europe on optimal charges for transport for five countries makes the following recommendations (ECMT, 2003a):

- For road transport, significantly higher charges in urban areas and some inter-urban routes for cars and HDVs should be implemented, mainly in order to charge for congestion. This would achieve large reductions in the number of passenger cars in urban areas, while total

---

BOX 8.4 ROAD PRICING IN SINGAPORE AND LONDON

Perhaps the most successful of the early implementations of road pricing occurred in 1998 with the ERP (Electronic Road Pricing) system in Singapore. Under the ERP system vehicles are required to be fitted with an in-car transponder that communicates with overhead gantries along the travel route, with road charges deducted automatically via a smart card debiting system. The advantage of this system is that journeys do not need to be interrupted. In addition the tolls are both time and congestion-sensitive, thus the charge can reflect more accurately the marginal cost of additional demand and thereby influence demand levels in the direction the policy desires. The road price charges in the ERP are calibrated to keep traffic flow at optimum levels. Since the system was introduced, there have been significant reductions in the number of vehicles entering the Restricted Zone (the central business district) during the morning peak hours and for the whole day. The daily reduction after the first year of operation was 15 per cent, with most of the reduced volumes resulting from a reduction in the number of multiple trips. The success of electronic road pricing in this case is demonstrated by the fact that optimal speeds were achieved along the major roads (Menon, 2000). However, there has been no shift from private vehicles to public transport, but this is probably because this system replaced another road pricing system. There is some extra congestion on the roads surrounding the restricted zone. Non-payment is tracked by examining the photographs of vehicles that passed through without a valid card or transponder. Goh (2002) highlights the success of the Singapore ERP scheme as being dependent on the provision of sufficient alternatives and also the education and involvement of those affected, with the former being an essential means of redressing the equity imbalance for road users/commuters that such a policy can generate. Indeed it is no coincidence that the success of the scheme elsewhere, notably London, is in an area where, prior to the scheme, 85 per cent of the populace used public transport anyway.

As regards the specific set-up of the charge in London, it applies only to an eight square mile area of central London (but may be expanded). The charge was set initially at £5 per day between 7 am and 6:30 pm Monday to Friday and has been raised to £8 since, and takes no account of journey distance, although hybrid, electric and alternative fuel vehicles are exempt. It was introduced in tandem with other key proposals for a properly integrated transport system for London and so far has shown a 40 per cent reduction in congestion during charging hours (TfL, 2006).

There have been other examples, such as the toll road scheme in Trondheim, Norway and the GPS charging system in Switzerland which offers great potential for more accurate and structured charging that takes account of distance travelled and prior routing. Indeed the technological developments such as GPS tracking should allow future developments of road pricing to become even more sophisticated and capable of adjusting the charge on a more individual and accurate level. This could, for example, enable a charging system to account for the emissions level of a particular vehicle based on the distance travelled, creating a system more closely resembling a Pigovian tax, levied at the source of the cost and at the value of the damage.

HDV volumes would not change significantly, although a small transfer from peak to off-peak travel would take place.

- The charges for public transport in some cities should be reduced relative to the costs of using cars and should be accompanied by improved service quality in public transport, which would encourage modal shift.
- Charges for transport in rural areas could be reduced, with little change in traffic volumes.
- Rail freight prices should be reduced, depending on the amount that the current level of charges lies above the marginal social cost. This should increase rail and decrease road freight volumes.

Common problems relating to road pricing lie in the implementation and public acceptability for such a programme. Road users tend to prefer other methods of TDM employed, such as public transport improvements (Kelly, 2003). Congestion charges and road user pricing represent additional taxes on passenger car travel, but in practice may result rather in diversion of traffic around the zone and postponement of non-essential journeys than in much reduction in total mileage and associated CO_2 emissions. However, congestion charges have been observed to result in some modal shift towards public transport for those who could otherwise not avoid the congestion charge. In the Los Angeles area, a joint study by the Environmental

Defense Fund and the Regional Institute of Southern California found that congestion tolls would decrease carbon monoxide emissions by 12 per cent, carbon dioxide by 9 per cent and NO_x by 8 per cent, while significantly reducing traffic congestion (Cameron, 1991). This study showed the importance of reducing the number of trips as well as the total number of miles (due to increased emissions when a car is first started).

Another type of road charging in TDM is the use of parking pricing to reduce the use of passenger cars. A study carried out by the UK Dept of Transport in 2002,[19] which questioned users as to the factor most likely to change their behaviour away from private car to using a bus service, found that, although frequency, availability and speed of the public transport mode were significant, the largest contributing factors to change were if 'parking were difficult to find' and if 'parking was more expensive' (UK Dept of Transport, 2002). Overall, 56 per cent of car users said they would use the bus more if parking places were more expensive, and 64 per cent said that they would also use the bus more if parking were difficult to find.

There has been much academic work examining the price level and structural possibilities of parking pricing policies. Indeed, appropriate pricing of parking is crucial to its effectiveness as a policy tool. Cheap parking has been shown in research to be a significant influencing factor with regard to trip generation decisions and modal shift (Higgins, 1992; UK Dept of Transport, 2002). An important influence on performance in this regard is the effectiveness of enforcement. As Cullinane (1993) highlighted, the policy must include a deterrent to non-compliance. If there is no enforcement of a given parking policy, there is no policy. However, given enforcement and appropriately structured pricing, Button and Verhoef (1998) note the justification for parking policy as follows: (a) on-street parking affects road capacity; (b) the cost of parking (for those who pay themselves) is a large and often the largest monetary component of a car trip; (c) parking pricing is an important part of urban policy and crucial where congestion pricing is not enforced; and (d) cruising for parking (search time) is a major contributor to city traffic congestion.

Some have considered the potential of parking policy if used in tandem with other policy tools. Specifically, Calthrop et al. (2000) show that the second-best means of pricing urban travel is that of pricing parking spaces, and that parking pricing measures, if combined with road pricing, can yield greater welfare gains than road pricing alone.

However, parking pricing policy is not without limitations. As a means of affecting traffic within a city, it is clear that parking pricing policy will have no effect whatsoever on 'through traffic' (vehicles which pass through a city but are not looking to park) and may in fact encourage this type of traffic if the pricing policy itself reduces overall congestion levels. There are also a number of equity concerns, in that it will bear more heavily upon those travelling short distances since, for these individuals, the parking cost will form a greater proportion of their total trip cost. Another aspect is that, if a parking policy cannot encompass all private vehicle use, then the incidence of the charging will fall upon those who are unable to avoid the charge.

As a further limitation to the scope of parking policy, it is noted that generally a city can have a significant amount of private non-residential (PNR) parking facilities over which policymakers have no direct control (Higgins, 1992). The potential for a parking policy to affect congestion or road use externalities is directly proportional to the percentage of the city's parking spaces affected by the policy.

However the equity concern can be addressed somewhat by seeking either to spread the influence of the pricing mechanism to include PNR parking, and/or by ring fencing revenue into improvements in modal alternatives and the traffic network, to make alternatives better for those who cannot afford to pay and travel better for those who do have to pay.

As with many TDM pricing policies, there are also acceptance and implementation measures to be considered. In this regard, while parking pricing is generally considered more easily implemented than road pricing, thanks to the fact it is a recognized and established system of charging in many facilities and countries across the world (Arnott and Rowse, 1999), people unsurprisingly would rather see improvements in public transport as a means of effecting modal choice than a new charging system (Verhoef, 1996). But this apart, people have come to accept parking charges as a reasonable request of payment for a scarce commodity, whereas, with respect to road pricing, individuals may consider they have already paid for roads with road taxes and so further costs on road usage are less acceptable, despite road space also being a scarce commodity in congested areas.

With any pricing measure the degree of price sensitivity of the consumers is paramount to understanding how they will react to the given price level. Kelly and Clinch (2003) examined the sensitivity of parking behaviour and modal choice to the price of on-street parking in the city of Dublin, Ireland. They utilized contingent valuation[20] data sets from two large-scale surveys of on-street parkers' reactions to parking price increases in a prime area for parking in the centre of the city. The results of their analysis revealed that business users are more responsive at lower price increases, and non-business travellers are significantly more responsive at high prices.

It is clear from the study carried out for Dublin that parking pricing had an effect on the behaviour of drivers. Road and parking pricing have the advantage that they influence the use of road transport. Thus, if road pricing could be linked to other measures such as taxes and improvements in public transport, then the total kilometres driven as well as the greenhouse gas emissions produced per kilometre would be reduced, leading to an absolute reduction in greenhouse gas emissions from road transport. It is difficult to quantify the amount of greenhouse gas emissions that could be saved as a result of pricing measures. Parking pricing is really only relevant in urban areas, whereas road pricing could influence driving behaviour over longer routes. The effectiveness of road and parking pricing is strongly linked to other measures such as public transport and fuel taxes. Separate estimates for the quantity of greenhouse gas emissions that could be saved as a result of pricing measures are not calculated but assumed here to be included as part of the range of estimates given for savings through public transport and taxes (see Sections 8.2.3, 8.2.4 and 8.2.6). As a regional TDM strategy, a parking policy needs to be implemented throughout a region in order to avoid simply shifting drivers from one area to another.

8.2.6 Other Mechanisms

Car sharing

Mobility Car Sharing Switzerland offers participants the shared use of 1750 vehicles at 1000 locations in 400 towns. Specific energy reduction goals include total savings of 3200 TJ pa, and motor fuel savings of 2 per cent (Mobility CarSharing, 2006).

Another example is a car-sharing system developed for the residents of a large-scale new suburb in the northern part of Osaka Prefecture. The development is located in the richly forested hills of Ibaraki and Minoh cities in Osaka Prefecture. The objective of the development is to realize the concept of harmonious coexistence between nature and human beings. This project includes research institutes and public facilities on its site of about 740 hectares, and is expected to serve a residential population of 50 000. Until public transportation facilities are completed, cars will be the major means of transportation. The introduction of a car-sharing system was chosen with the aim of reducing carbon dioxide emissions through decreasing dependence on automobiles and minimizing parking lots in order to keep more areas green.

Users apply to the control centre through the Internet or by telephone. User identification, payments and door locking/unlocking are performed through registered user integrated circuit (IC) cards.[21] The cars are managed by a remote control system that transmits information about the engine, oil levels, and so on, to the system's control centre. This attempt (in Kansai) is among the first car-sharing projects in Japan.

Although a vehicle-sharing scheme does not reduce specific vehicle fuel consumption, it reduces the number of vehicles owned and driven, which leads to a reduction in fuel consumption.

Company cars

Company cars are defined as cars which are made available to a director or an employee because of their employment, and are available for private use, or to a member of their family or household.[22] They comprise between 35 per cent and 45 per cent of new cars sold in the EU15 markets (except Ireland and Italy, which are much lower) (CEC, 2002b). Corporate tax treatment appears to be supporting the trend towards bigger cars because it provides tax benefits to the acquisition and operation of company cars. However, the use of a company car is generally seen as 'benefit-in-kind' and thus taxable income in many countries. Company car fleets are replaced frequently and the vehicles sold on the second-hand market. Thus, in countries where there is a large share of company passenger cars, the specific vehicle models chosen as company cars have a large influence on total passenger car emissions.

In the UK, from April 2002, the income tax charge and the National Insurance Contributions charge on a company car have been based on a percentage of a car's list price graduated according to the level of the car's carbon dioxide emissions. In the 2006/7 financial year the charge builds up from 15 per cent of the car's price, for cars emitting 140 g CO_2/km, in 1 per cent steps for every additional 5 g CO_2/km over this level. The maximum charge is 35 per cent of the car's price. The reformed company car tax scheme offers significant financial incentives for company car drivers to choose low-carbon vehicles. This has already had a big impact on purchasers' decisions, and has generated a shift towards diesel vehicles, which offer carbon benefits over their petrol equivalents (UK HM Revenue and Customs, 2007). As the company car share of the new car market is so significant, this should not be neglected in the portfolio of policy instruments.

Pay-as-you-drive vehicle insurance and other distance-based fees

Distance-based fees such as pay-as-you-drive (PAYD) vehicle insurance and other fees are variable fees, based on the mileage driven. This encourages drivers to drive less. There are a number of benefits:

- Increased equity (fees more accurately reflect the costs imposed by each vehicle).
- Increased affordability (motorists can minimize their insurance and registration fees by minimizing their mileage, which is not currently possible).
- Reduced uninsured driving (increased affordability can help lower-income and low-annual mileage motorists afford insurance coverage).

- Reduced crash risk (reduced mileage reduces crashes, and PAYD insurance gives higher-risk motorists the greatest incentive to reduce their mileage).
- Reduced traffic congestion.
- Road and parking costs savings (VTPI, 2006).

There are examples of PAYD schemes in Israel, USA (Texas, Philadelphia, Oregon), the Netherlands, South Africa and the UK.[23]

8.2.7 Summary of the Main Points

- Historically, the main taxes and charges applied to passenger cars are acquisition (registration and VAT), circulation (or motor) and fuel taxes.
- The original objective of most of the existing transport-related taxes and charges was to raise revenue, rather than to operationalize the 'polluter pays' principle (internalizing environmental and social costs such as infrastructure, accidents and CO_2 and other emissions) or encourage people to drive less or to stimulate innovation in the motor industry.
- An added problem with this revenue aspect is that, if taxes are effective and induce change in CO_2 emissions or km driven, the revenue will go down unless tax rates keep rising. Thus tax systems need to be constantly re-designed and modified.
- Vehicle taxes have the potential to improve the overall fuel efficiency of new cars. Current vehicle taxes should be reformed so that they are fully based on CO_2 emissions or some CO_2 aspect built into existing registration or annual taxes (CEC, 2002b). Thus registration taxes and annual vehicle taxes should be reformed into CO_2 taxes as much as possible if they are to provide incentives for the purchase of low CO_2 emissions vehicles.
- Fuel taxes have varied rates of success. On the one hand, they can influence drivers to switch fuels and technologies. On the other hand, they have been less successful in reducing fleet-average greenhouse gas emissions per km from cars and can bring about distribution problems. However they can influence driving behaviour and thus reduce total CO_2 emissions.
- Charges, such as road tolls and parking pricing, that have been specifically designed to diminish the negative external effects of road transport such as congestion and greenhouse gas emissions, can be implemented.

8.3   INFORMATION MEASURES

Good information permits customers to take greenhouse gas emissions and fuel consumption into consideration in making purchase choices. Without knowledge of the CO_2 emissions characteristics of a vehicle, it is more difficult for purchasers to evaluate any fiscal incentives that may be available for low CO_2-emitting vehicles, or to exercise their desire to purchase a less environmentally damaging vehicle. For this reason, it is important that complete and transparent information be provided on the features of vehicles during and before the purchase. CO_2 emissions and fuel consumption labelling enables purchasers to compare vehicles on the basis of these characteristics. This tool complements other demand measures such as fiscal incentives. Labelling can also encourage vehicle manufacturers to improve the CO_2 performance or other characteristics of their vehicles (Menanteau, 2003).

Worldwide, labelling has been used to rank domestic energy-using products such as refrigerators, washing machines, cookers, dishwashers and so on in terms of energy efficiency. There is a substantial literature on the influence of energy labelling on consumers' purchasing decisions, the conclusions from which may be relevant to CO_2 emissions and fuel economy labelling of passenger cars. For example in Japan, the New Energy and Industrial Technology Development Organization (NEDO) has created the 'CEV Eco Delivery Label', which is to be attached to goods and packages that have been delivered using clean energy vehicles (CEV). The label is certified in each case by NEDO and the delivery companies can be required to report on how the labels are being used. The label can be put on goods delivered, for example, by shipping or delivery companies, which deliver to local government offices or companies using trucks fuelled by compressed natural gas (CNG). The Tokyo metropolitan government and six prefectures and cities, including Kyoto and Osaka prefectures and Kobe City, have requested that only 'green delivery' – using eco-friendly vehicles – be used for goods that they purchase. NEDO is hoping that the new label will raise citizen awareness about low-emission vehicles.

In Europe, the Parliament and Council initiated the second pillar of the European strategy to reduce greenhouse gas emissions from passenger cars, when it adopted the European Directive on labelling in 1999.[24] This Directive promulgates consumer information to be made available in the form of fuel economy and CO_2 emissions labels, guides and posters in car dealer showrooms from 18 January 2001. The amended Directive on labelling requires dealers to provide information on fuel economy and CO_2 emissions to consumers via television, radio and the Internet, as well as electronic storage devices such as videotapes, DVDs and CD-ROMs.[25]

Car dealers are required to ensure that a label on fuel economy and CO_2 emissions is attached on or displayed near each new passenger vehicle on sale. The car showroom should contain a poster listing and ranking all the vehicles sold at that outlet according to fuel consumption and CO_2 emissions. Additionally, a complete guide to the fuel consumption and CO_2 emissions from all passenger vehicles offered on sale in that member state must be available in the form of a portable booklet free of charge to customers.

The Commission has issued general guidelines on the design of the CO_2 labels, requiring the presentation of values of the fuel economy, CO_2 emissions and the model and fuel type of the passenger car. Some Member States have created labels that provide a more vivid portrayal of the fuel economy of the vehicle, awarding a grade to the vehicle model based on its fuel economy and CO_2 emissions. Figure 8.2 provides an example of this with the Netherlands design (CEC, 2004a).

Energie	Personenauto
Fabrikant	**Merk X**
Model	Model Y
	3-drs hatchback
	handschakeling
Brandstof	Benzine
Brandstofverbruik	**7,2** liter/100 km
germeton volgens de test van de typegoecicuring	= 1 liter op 13,9 km
Zuinig A B C D E F G **Onzuinig**	B
CO_2-uitstoot CO₂ is het broeikasgas dat bij de wereldwijde klimaatverandering de belangrijkste rol speelt.	**173** gram/km
Jaar van toepassing	2001
Een gids betreffende het brandstofverbruik en de CO₂-uitstoot met gegevens voor alle nieuwe modellen personenauto's is gratis verkrijgbaar in elk verkooppunt. Naast de brandstofefficiëntie van een auto zijn ook het rijgedrag en andere, niet-technische factoren bepalend voor het brandstofverbruik en de CO₂-uitstoot van een auto. Richtlijn 1999/94/EG. Etikettering personenauto's	

Figure 8.2   Netherlands 'washing machine'-style vehicle label

There are merits to different types of label. The information disclosure type of label (where the CO_2 emissions and fuel consumption are disclosed but not illustrated on the label) such as the UK design is neutral and simply provides the consumer with the information needed to make an informed purchase. The 'grading' or seal of approval style of labels such as the Dutch design in Figure 8.2 are simpler to understand but not necessarily impartial. The label here provides information on the model, the version and fuel type of the vehicle in the upper part of the label. The label shows that the vehicle consumes 7.2L of petrol per 100 km driven, which classifies the vehicle as grade B.[26] There is a growing literature on the subject of green- and eco-labelling that suggests that clearer seal-of-approval labels are usually better understood by consumers than information-disclosure labels, although seal-of-approval labels are over-simplified and judgemental. 'Experience has shown that the proportion of consumers who are willing and able to use technical information effectively is low' (Banerjee and Solomon, 2003). Therefore several Member States have favoured the seal-of-approval labels in CO_2 emissions labelling. The car industry prefers direct disclosure labels that are neutral and do not rate or differentiate products.

In addition, the European labelling directive requires that member states produce a guide incorporating the values of all vehicle models' fuel consumption. The guide provides an opportunity for customers to compare CO_2 emissions and fuel consumption of vehicles across all makes and size classes and theoretically encourages a shift to more fuel-efficient vehicles.

It is difficult to estimate the effectiveness of fuel consumption labelling (Vine et al., 2001). The literature suggests that labelling is most effective when there is government involvement to win consumers' confidence (Banerjee and Solomon, 2003). Publicity is also important to gain consumer awareness and to impress upon manufacturers the significance of the programme. Good label clarity helps consumers make the right choices, and incentives to do so, such as tax relief, are an added bonus.

EU member states are required to report on the effectiveness of the labelling Directive following specific guidelines on the reporting format.[27] The German automobile association ADAC collated the preliminary results (ADAC e.V., 2004), which include information on the status of implementation of the Directive in the member states, any fiscal measures that affect car purchase decisions, as well as the effectiveness of the initiative, as judged by the individual member states. In general, in most member states it is the responsibility of the car manufacturers to supply the label and poster, whereas the guide tends to be produced by national Ministries or an independent authorized institution.

The results of surveys carried out on the effectiveness of the Directive show that the main factors influencing car purchase decisions in the EU are car reliability, safety, comfort and cost/price ratio. The fuel economy is only relevant in so far as it affects the cost of running the vehicle. Many countries say that customer awareness of the label, poster and guide is low and that the foremost sources of information are dealerships, sales brochures, car magazines and recommendations by family and friends. Customers prefer a label which compares the fuel efficiency between different cars in the same market segment and rates the vehicle using a simple energy rating system (A to G, for example).

Only the Netherlands has attempted to quantify the impact of the labelling Directive on CO_2 emissions from the vehicle fleet. It is estimated that, after the implementation of the labelling Directive in 2001, the market share of vehicle classes B and C (6.5 per cent and 41.4 per cent in 2000) increased slightly to 9.5 per cent and 45.7 per cent in 2001; the share of vehicles in classes D, E and F decreased, and classes A and G were unchanged. In 2002, a refund of the vehicle acquisition tax existed for vehicles in class A. It was observed that the increase in share in classes A and B vehicles went disproportionately from 0.3 per cent to 3.2 per cent and from 9.5 per cent to 16.1 per cent. The tax refund was abolished in 2003 and the share of vehicles sold in classes A and B decreased. The evidence from this member state demonstrates the effectiveness of fiscal measures over consumer information in influencing vehicle-purchasing behaviour.

Member states made proposals to improve the effectiveness of the labelling Directive. The main proposals are the following:

- Consumers need to be made further aware of fuel economy, CO_2 emissions and the information tools available to them through this Directive.
- Dealers need to be informed about the requirements and rationale of the Directive's provisions. Often the poster is ineffective since its production and updating requires too much effort and is not in line with the dealers' ideas for their showroom.
- Harmonization of the content and design of information tools would simplify the issue for manufacturers and reduce costs since the labels could be attached at the vehicle production stage.
- Harmonization of an energy-rating system for all vehicle labels would make vehicle labels more transparent for consumers. This is also corroborated in a previous study (Boardman et al., 2000).
- Since cost is a high priority for consumers when purchasing a vehicle, the fuel consumption and CO_2 emissions should be converted to vehicle running costs on the label.

From these first reports on the effectiveness of the labelling Directive, it appears that in the EU most policymakers regard this instrument as underperforming and not achieving the reduction potential desired. It is difficult to judge the effectiveness of any instrument in isolation from the other factors that are in place concurrently. It seems imperative that the information on technological advancements in passenger cars, achieved as a result of the Voluntary Agreement or other initiatives, reach consumers.

In the US, the Department of Energy and the Environmental Protection Agency (EPA) are responsible for managing the 'fueleconomy.gov' website which has a guide listing the fuel economy of all vehicles sold in the US. Customers can compare the fuel economy according to vehicle model and model year. The vehicles are also graded according to the fuel economy, informing consumers of the 'best' vehicle in its class. Other information on energy-efficient vehicles is available from the American Council for an Energy-Efficient Economy, who publish a list of the most environmentally friendly vehicles[28] on sale, and the Californian Air Resources Board (CARB) lists all low and zero emissions vehicles for sale in California on their website.[29]

In Japan, three Japanese ministries, the Ministry of the Environment, the Ministry of Economy, Trade and Industry, and the Ministry of Land, Infrastructure and Transport, jointly publish the 'Low-Emission Vehicle Guidebook' annually, as part of the government's low-emission vehicle (LEV) promotion policy, which is one of the main countermeasures against global warming and air pollution in urban areas.

The guidebook covers a total of 157 LEV models now available in Japan: electric vehicles (24 models), fuel cell vehicles (9), compressed natural gas (CNG) vehicles (63), hybrid vehicles (13) and others (48). It covers a wide range of data to aid purchasing decisions and maintenance for each of the 157 models, such as emissions performance, vehicle prices and maintenance services. It also provides a summary of the government's LEV-related programmes and subsidy systems. Starting with the fiscal 2004 edition, the guide also provides information on subsidy systems in municipalities and various sectors' activities to promote LEVs. The guidebook is distributed to governmental agencies and local authorities, and provided to the public through the Environmental Information Center. It is also open to the public by Internet as the 'Low-Emission Vehicle Pavilion 2004'.

Another climate change initiative in Japan is organized by the Japanese Automobile Federation (JAF), which encourages drivers to make declarations of environmentally responsible driving. Environmentally responsible driving is defined as fuel-efficient to reduce the emission of CO_2. Drivers who have made this declaration are issued with stickers and encouraged to affix them to their cars in order to increase awareness of the issue. The JAF website shows the number of people in real time who have made the declaration; the number is expected to reach 500 000 soon (Japan for sustainability website, 2004).

8.3.1 Summary of Main Points

- Information is used as a measure to reduce greenhouse gas emissions from transport by increasing customer awareness of fuel efficiency in passenger cars. Good information on the CO_2 and greenhouse gas-emitting properties of vehicles is necessary for consumers to differentiate between passenger cars and adjust their purchasing behaviour accordingly.
- Vehicle labelling is an information tool that should be implemented with fiscal incentives to encourage vehicle purchasers to choose vehicles producing low CO_2 emissions. The EU has passed a Labelling Directive requiring all new passenger cars sold in the EU to attach a label presenting the fuel consumption and CO_2 emissions values of the car.
- The design of vehicle labels can be influential in persuading customers to take CO_2 emissions into consideration in their vehicle purchasing choices. There is evidence to suggest that, although entailing several disadvantages such as lack of transparency and impartiality, the seal of approval style of label appears to be simpler for consumers to understand and hence more effective. Government backing is helpful to provide credibility for a labelling programme.
- First reports from member states on the effectiveness of the EU vehicle-labelling scheme demonstrate that CO_2 emissions and fuel economy labelling are most effective when accompanied by a fiscal incentive scheme, which encourages consumers to act upon the information and purchase more efficient passenger cars.
- Eco-labelling is in effect in Japan, however it is not applied to passenger cars as a measure to reduce greenhouse gas emissions. Fuel economy guides are also published in the US, EU and other countries.

8.4 SUMMARY

- Market-based instruments such as emissions trading and taxes and charges can provide an efficient way to reduce greenhouse gas emissions from transport by encouraging drivers to purchase fuel-efficient vehicles and to drive less.

- There are emissions trading schemes for greenhouse gas and other pollutant emissions in the EU, US and, on a trial basis, in Japan; however transport is not included in any of these, although this may change in the future.
- Taxes and charges applied to transport are well established in practice and well-studied in the literature. They have historically been used to raise revenue rather than to reduce CO_2 emissions, or address other environmental externalities.
- Increasingly CO_2-differentiated vehicle and fuel taxes are applied as part of a greenhouse gas abatement strategy in many countries.
- Fuel taxes and vehicle taxes affect passenger car CO_2 emissions differently, since fuel taxes affect drivers' travel behaviour and reduce mileage, whereas vehicle taxes tend to influence vehicle-purchasing decisions only.
- Distance-based and parking charges are effective, as they have an impact on vehicle mileage and hence reduce congestion, accidents, noise and emissions.
- Information is an important complement to fiscal measures to enable drivers to make informed decisions.

NOTES

1. Namely fully informed, honest, welfare-maximizing regulators and proper application of property rights (Sterner, 2003).
2. Two other project-based instruments, the Clean Development Mechanism (CDM) and Joint Implementation (JI), are the other flexible mechanisms permitted under the Kyoto Protocol.
3. Directive 2003/87/EC entered into force on 25 October 2003.
4. The USA SO_2 program includes indirectly emissions from electricity used to power some train and subway travel.
5. Communication from the Commission to the Council, the European Parliament, the European Economic and Social Committee, and the Committee of the Regions, *Reducing the Climate Change Impact of Aviation*, COM (2005) 459 final [online]. Brussels, 27.9.2005. Available at http://eur-lex.europa.eu/LexUriServ/site/en/com/2005/com2005_0459en01.pdf.
6. COM(2005) 35, 9.2.2005.
7. Similar to the definition used in EU ETS Directive 2003/87/EC.
8. At 'Carbon Market Insights 2006' conference. 28 February–2 March 2006, Copenhagen. Available at http://www.planetark.com/dailynewsstory.cfm/newsid/35367/story.htm.
9. Currently only CO_2 emissions produced from the electricity used in automobile manufacturing plants are included in the EU emissions trading scheme.
10. Fleets of vehicles operated by commercial firms.
11. MARKAL (acronym for MARKet ALlocation) is a widely applied bottom-up, dynamic, originally and mostly a linear programming model developed by the Energy Technology Systems Analysis Programme (ETSAP) of the International Energy Agency.
12. Available at http://europa.eu.int/comm/taxation_customs/taxation/car_taxes/co2_cars_study_25-02-2002.pdf.

13. Proposal for a Council Directive on passenger car-related taxes (presented by the Commission) SEC(2005) 809.

14. Danish Ministry of Taxation website: http://www.skm.dk/foreign/english/taxinden mark2007/5344/#104.

15. Directive 2003/96/EC of 27 October 2003 restructuring the Community framework for the taxation of energy products and electricity (OJ L 283, 31.10.2003).

16. IRS Publication 6478.

17. More information available at http://www.e85fuel.com/forsuppliers/docs/e85_primer_rack_to_retail.doc.

18. Acknowledgement is due to Andrew Kelly, School of Geography, Planning and Environmental Policy, UCD, for this section. Much of the material was sourced from his PhD thesis (2003).

19. July 2002 Omnibus survey samples 1850 adults representative of the British adult population.

20. The contingent valuation method involves directly asking people (for example in a survey) how much they would be willing to pay for specific environmental goods (Hanly et al., 2001).

21. Integrated circuit (IC) cards are embedded with a memory chip which can store large quantities of information. They have the advantage of allowing one card to be used to access multiple services.

22. UK HM Revenue and Customs (2006). Available at http://www.hmrc.gov.uk/cars/.

23. Described at http://www.vtpi.org/tdm/tdm79.htm.

24. Directive 1999/94/EC of the European Parliament and of the Council of 13 December 1999 relating to the availability of consumer information on fuel economy and CO_2 emissions in respect of the marketing of new passenger cars.

25. Commission Directive 2003/73/EC of 24 July 2003 amending Annex III to Directive 1999/94/EC of the European Parliament and of the Council.

26. There are seven energy efficiency classes rated A-G, showing the relative energy efficiency (from the CO_2 emissions perspective) of a car in comparison to the average energy efficiency of cars with the same size. Petrol and diesel are calculated separately.

27. Commission Decision 2001/677/EC of 10 August 2001 on a reporting format for completion by member states in accordance with Article 9 of Directive 1999/94/EC.

28. Available at http://www.greenercars.com/.

29. Available at http://www.driveclean.ca.gov/en/gv/home/index.asp.

9. Voluntary or negotiated agreements

In recent years there has been a trend towards voluntary approaches (VAs) in environmental policymaking in the EU and other OECD countries, particularly Japan, instead of the previously favoured command and control regulations. Voluntary approaches are defined as 'commitments from polluting firms or sectors to improve their environmental performance' (Higley et al., 2001) beyond regulatory requirements. They have become important in most regions as an alternative instrument in environmental policy and have been used to mitigate greenhouse gas emissions in many sectors. This chapter will begin generally, describing the types of agreements and the theory of their design. Box 9.1 describes the theoretical context of voluntary agreements in environmental policy. The chapter proceeds with specific examples of this instrument applied to greenhouse gas reduction in transport, where possible, and also to other environmental questions.

The policy and economic literature divides VAs into three categories: unilateral commitments made by polluting firms, public voluntary schemes and negotiated environmental agreements between a sector and public authorities (Higley et al., 2001). *Unilateral commitments* consist of environmental actions undertaken by firms and communicated to their stakeholders (employees, shareholders, clients and so on). There is no government intervention; the firms themselves determine the definition of environmental targets and the conditions of compliance (OECD, 2003). Firms can involve a third party (such as the International Standards Organisation, ISO) to certify the environmental effects of the commitment. *Public voluntary schemes* invite firms to meet specified standards established by public authorities such as environmental agencies. These standards can be related to environmental performance, technology adoption or management. Participation usually requires signing non-binding letters of agreement. Public voluntary schemes often provide participants with support in the form of information, public recognition, technical assistance and information subsidies to participants (Khanna, 2001). A *negotiated environmental agreement* is defined as a commitment to meet one or more environmental targets through bargaining between a firm, sector or group of sectors and a public

---

BOX 9.1 THEORETICAL CONTEXT OF VOLUNTARY AGREEMENTS

Voluntary agreements (VAs) find their theoretical framework and intellectual underpinning in the theory of collective action and public goods. Environmental quality is what economists call a public good – in being provided to one, it is provided to all. This creates other implications for the use of VAs in environmental policy. In his definitive work on public goods, Samuelson (1954) makes the point that, in regard to collective action regarding public goods, 'it is in the selfish interest of each person to give false signals, to pretend to have less interest in a given collective consumption or activity than he really has'. This non-revelation of prices is a crucial characteristic inhibiting economically efficient outcomes. It makes strategic behaviour (the 'free rider' problem) whereby each potential beneficiary of collective action seeks to secure the benefits, but avoid the costs: central policy challenge.

Olson (1965) supports the view that voluntary or spontaneous mechanisms will not provide the economically optimum quantity of public goods such as environmental protection. But he on the other hand makes the point that such strategic inhibitions can be overcome where a group can gain substantial benefit from collective action. In such cases, he notes that 'large groups that have been organized for collective action for any period of time are regularly found to have worked out special devices, or selective incentives, that are functionally equivalent to taxes, that enable governments to provide public goods'. A subsidiary literature focused on 'club goods' has emerged, identifying the incentive structures and performance characteristics when collective action is at issue, but where exclusion is possible, for example in the case of access to a highway (Sandler, 1997).

---

authority. This kind of agreement generally contains a pollution abatement target and a time schedule to achieve it. It is to the last category that voluntary agreements to reduce greenhouse gas emissions from passenger cars generally belong, and it is this literature that is mainly reviewed here.

9.1   VA DESIGN ISSUES IN ENVIRONMENTAL POLICY

VAs are perceived to hold several advantages for both firms and public authorities over other regulatory instruments. The increased flexibility in abatement opportunities over an equivalent command-and-control measure is a prominent reason for this.

Similar to other economic instruments applied in environmental management, such as emissions trading schemes, a potential strength of a VA is that the burden of meeting the environmental target can be borne mainly by those firms who do so at least cost, thereby minimizing the total costs to the sector as a whole. Firms or plants with lower marginal abatement costs can reduce more than those with higher marginal abatement costs and thus total abatement costs are minimized (OECD, 2003). However, achieving this objective requires that this least-cost behaviour actually happens; therefore an issue is how to induce (and perhaps compensate) those firms that can achieve better than average CO_2 emissions reductions to do so. Economists point out that there can be an incentive for all parties to the agreement to wait around for the others to do it: the 'free rider' problem (Millock and Salanié, 2000). VAs differ from other economic instruments, since by their nature the abatement commitment may be non-binding.

For public authorities the motivation to create a VA is to reduce transaction and administrative costs due to a shorter negotiation process and fewer enforcement procedures (Manzini and Mariotti, 2003). Superior VAs are defined by their economic efficiency, environmental effectiveness, low transaction costs and transparency.

Environmental groups have called the above advantages into question, asserting that VAs weaken environmental targets and often result in nothing more than the endorsement of an industry's 'business as usual' environmental strategy (WWF, 2000). The shortened negotiation time often means that there is not sufficient time to carry out a public consultation process, which results in a lack of transparency. Sometimes regulatory capture also results, whereby a public authority yields to industry pressure and either does not pass legislation or else implements an environmental agreement with zero costs to the firm (OECD, 2003).

The OECD has assessed VAs (OECD, 1999, 2003) and issued the following recommendations on the good design of VAs:

• Characterize a business-as-usual scenario before setting the targets to establish the baseline scenario in the absence of the agreement.

- Clearly define the targets; the targets should be quantitative, transparent and clearly defined. Interim objectives permit identification of any challenges in advance of the ultimate target.
- Provide credible regulatory threats in the negotiation stage and during the commitment period so that there is an incentive for firms to go beyond the business-as-usual scenario and achieve the targets.
- Perform credible and reliable monitoring in order to keep track of performance improvements. This is the key to ensuring that firms stay on target. Companies, public authorities and/or independent parties can carry out monitoring.
- Include third-party participation in the negotiation of environmental objectives and performance monitoring to increase the credibility of the VA.
- Set penalties for non-compliance, which make the VA a binding commitment, perhaps with links to regulatory consequences in cases of non-compliance.
- Provide information-related measures to maximize the potential of the VA to achieve the targets.
- Include provisions to avoid competition distortions, such as cartel behaviour as a result of collective VAs.

There has been some economic research into the merit of voluntary agreements in environmental policy compared with other regulatory or market-based methods. A review of the literature on VAs has been carried out by several authors (Brau and Carraro, 2004; Krarup, 2001; Khanna, 2001; Alberini and Segerson, 2002). Generally, the literature on VAs tends to focus on three issues: comparing the efficiency of VAs in terms of costs and benefits with other environmental policy instruments, mainly command and control and environmental taxes; target setting and whether VAs permit achievement of the optimal environmental target; and finally, an analysis of implementation issues of VAs.

The OECD has examined VAs in terms of these three criteria. The economic efficiency of a VA hinges upon whether there is static efficiency; that is, minimum total costs, and dynamic efficiency, which signals continual improvement so that the costs of abatement decrease over time. While the increased flexibility can provide an opportunity to equalize marginal abatement costs between firms in the agreement compared with a command and control instrument, the OECD concludes that additional mechanisms are necessary in the agreement to ensure marginal abatement cost equalization. VAs on their own are not enough to ensure static efficiency. In many agreements, the participating firms decide the abatement burden and this depends on the relative negotiating power of each firm. With regard to dynamic efficiency, the incentive to innovate in order continually to reduce pollution is weaker in VAs than with other economic instruments such as emissions permits or taxes. This is because there is little reward to abate beyond what a VA requires, compared with the fiscal incentive available in a tax or emissions trading regime. However Maxwell et al. (2000) point out that firms can use a voluntary abatement activity to provoke regulatory authorities to introduce stricter environmental regulations on other companies. Finally, VAs can affect efficiency through reduced competition, arising from increased cooperation between firms.

The main discussion related to target-setting centres on whether environmental targets under VAs tend to be set too low from an environmental effectiveness perspective, as a result of 'regulatory capture'. The environmental targets can be judged to have been set too low if the marginal social benefits of additional abatement are significantly higher than the marginal social abatement costs to achieve the targets. Another aspect is whether the environmental targets set are actually met in the VA. There are hundreds of VAs in existence and the evidence from the cases studied in the literature demonstrates that the targets set in most VAs have actually been met (Khanna and Damon, 1999; US EPA, 2004).

Another question is whether any abatement achieved actually occurred as a result of the VA or other factors. If the abatement takes place very shortly after the signing of an agreement, it is not credible to suggest that the abatement would not have taken place in any case. Asymmetric information is a feature of VAs, as with all environmental regulation, where firms tend to have far superior knowledge of their abatement costs than the regulator. The consequence of this is that public authorities may have very little insight into either the true costs of abatement or the investment plans in a particular abatement technology, which may have occurred anyhow. The solution to this lies in the establishment of a sound counterfactual – what is likely to happen over the commitment period in the absence of any regulation or VA. Millock (2000) postulates that the potential to gain information on firms' abatement opportunities is a significant incentive for public authorities to enter into an environmental VA with industry. Better information allows regulators to improve environmental target setting. The OECD (2003) provides several examples of VAs, which are deemed to have been environmentally effective. However they conclude that factors other than the VAs have caused the majority of abatement in these examples.

As stated previously, the design of a policy instrument is often more important than the choice of instrument itself. The universal issues which arise from environmental policy implementation – free-riding (Dawson and Segerson, 2003; Segerson and Dawson, 2003; Millock and Salanié, 2000), strategic behaviour, high transactions costs (OECD, 2003; Manzini and

Mariotti, 2003), incentives to foster collective action (Brau and Carraro, 1999), and so on – all find practical expression in the field of voluntary agreements and care must be taken to account for these in the instrument design.

In summary, the following potential weaknesses are associated with VAs (OECD, 1999, 2003):

- Regulatory capture: the public authority yields to industry demands and grants lower environmental targets than required.
- Lack of transparency: to save time, the negotiation process may not include a third party, which may result in lower environmental targets and less credibility for the agreement.
- The abatement costs are not always lower than regulations: the environmental targets must be set and designed so as to achieve equal marginal abatement costs for all sources of pollution.
- Transaction costs may not be lower if there is a lengthy negotiation process and high monitoring costs when the VA is in operation.
- The threat of free-riding exists if an agreement is made with a sector.
- Without a legally binding default mechanism, it is unlikely that targets will be achieved.

9.2 EMPIRICAL EXAMPLES

VAs have been used to address a broad spectrum of environmental issues. They are increasingly applied to reduce the impact of industry on climate change and the literature provides many examples of voluntary agreements between industry and public authorities worldwide. However, the closed-door nature of many of these agreements means that data is not always readily available. The literature has identified a need to collect ex-post empirical data on voluntary agreements in order to carry out theoretical and empirical analyses of the instrument (Krarup, 2001).

However, since there are few examples of VAs that have been in place for a long time with the achievement of the environmental targets, few empirical data are available for analysis. Empirical literature on VAs has mainly covered national programmes such as the German chemical industry VA (Heins and Luettge, 2002), the Netherlands negotiated environmental agreements (Immerzeel-Brand, 2002) or the Pollution Control Agreements in Yokohama City and Kitakyushu City (OECD, 2002b). The UK Climate Change Levy provides a practical example of a subsidy associated with a voluntary agreement and is described by De Muizon and Glachant (2004).

The next sections provide examples of the three types of voluntary agreements applied in environmental policy. VAs have been used as a substitute for traditional regulation or market-based instruments across a wide range of environmental themes; however the reduction of greenhouse gases from transport has mainly utilized the third category of VAs, negotiated environmental agreement (NEAs). For example, in Europe a NEA was signed between the European automobile manufacturers and the European Commission to reduce CO_2 emissions from passenger cars.[1]

9.2.1   Unilateral Agreements

Unilateral agreements are environmental improvement programmes initiated by either an individual or group of firms without government intervention. The goals of the action are communicated to stakeholders such as employees, customers, regulators and shareholders, and so on. Often the main objective of a unilateral voluntary agreement is to improve a firm's public image in the area of the environment and can be used as part of a public relations strategy communicated to policymakers and customers.

Individual firm unilateral actions are commonly commitments to produce products according to international guidelines or codes of conduct. There are several internationally recognized standards, such as ISO 14000 and the European Eco-Management and Auditing Scheme, which are employed for this purpose.

Another term given to unilateral agreements is 'self-regulation', where a firm appears to undertake abatement actions in the absence of government regulations. These kinds of abatement activities are often 'no regret' actions, which means they are pollution abatement activities that are profitable to firms. However, there are some examples where firms have an incentive to abate beyond the business-as-usual strategy. This can be motivated by a desire to improve a firm or sector's reputation or the threat of stricter regulation. An example is the Responsible Care Programme (see Box 9.2), which has been set up in over 30 countries globally and encourages the chemicals industry to abate beyond the level demanded by regulation. The scheme was initiated as a result of the environmental disasters in chemical plants in Italy, India and Canada. An analysis of the US Responsible Care programme concludes as follows:

> Responsible Care's greatest private benefits to date are in the form of improved public outreach in communities where member company plants operate. Responsible Care's persistent shortcoming is the voluntary initiative's lack of credibility among some U.S. environmental groups. Environmental group critics charge that the initiative lacks transparency. Indeed, few quantitative data exist with which to link changes in the environment to Responsible Care. The lack of

quantitative data has caused some to conclude that the initiative is unsuccessful. However, Responsible Care's focus on management practices, rather than quantitative environmental targets, makes performance measurement difficult. It is likely that no additional amount of performance data will be sufficient to silence some of Responsible Care's most strident critics. (Mazurek, 1998)

Further examples of collective unilateral agreements are found in Japan. A case study of the Keidanren Voluntary Action Plan (Imura, 1999) describes the features of this unilateral voluntary action by Japanese industry to reduce the greenhouse gas emissions from Japanese industry. Keidanren (Japan Federation of Economic Organizations) is the most powerful and influential business association in Japan. It represents the interests and opinions of Japanese business society, its member corporations and trade associations. The Keidanren Voluntary Action Plan on the Environment incorporates the unilateral commitments of its member associations.

BOX 9.2   COMPARISON OF THE FRENCH AND
         THE CANADIAN CHEMICAL INDUSTRIES'
         RESPONSIBLE CARE PROGRAMMES

The Responsible Care programme was created in Canada in 1984 and since then has spread to over 30 countries worldwide. The programme aims to accelerate environmental improvements in the chemical industry. The context of its creation was marked by a series of major accidents: Seveso in Italy, Bhopal in India, Love Canal in Canada. The Responsible Care Program is an international initiative promoting the adoption of rules for sound environmental management practice concerning the limitation of nuisances and the communication with local communities. The implementation of these general principles in a detailed action programme is undertaken by national professional associations. The contents and the implementation of the Responsible Care Programme therefore vary between countries.

In Canada, the Responsible Care Programme is characterized by relatively ambitious targets and strict control procedures. This is the result of the pressure the industry was confronted with in the beginning of the 80s: the threat of new legislation, consumer boycotts of certain products, and local pressure on the operations. In 1986, the programme was improved by the definition of six codes of practice, recommended by a group of independent consultants to the branch association. Whereas initially monitoring relied exclusively on self-reporting, this has been performed by third parties since 1993. Each plant is assessed by a group of four persons, two of which are members of the industry (but independent from the plant) and two who are from outside the industry (one from the local community). The assessment is then based on interviews with employees, suppliers, clients and residents. Companies that are not complying with the codes can be excluded from the branch association, although this sanction has never been applied. Additional legal sanctions are possible in court. Although the commitments have no legal value, they may have a negative impact on the verdict in a court case motivated by an environmental nuisance (Webb, 1999).

In France the Responsible Care Programme is implemented under the name of 'Engagement de progrès'. It has currently 360 signatory companies, accounting for 90 per cent of the industry's turnover. The French charter was adopted in 1990 in a context very different to the Canadian case. No major accidents had occurred in the recent past and no threat of new legislation existed at the time. The contents and the implementation of the French charter are therefore very different from those of its Canadian counterpart. It is less ambitious as to the targets (the codes of practice are not mandatory, but only recommended for implementation), monitoring is based on self-reporting and the only sanction is exclusion from the branch association (codes of conduct have no influence on French court decisions). These elements suggest that the French 'Engagement de progrès' will probably not have much impact on firms' environmental performance, which seems to be confirmed by recent monitoring data.

Source: OECD (1999).

As industry's representative, Keidanren negotiates with national and local governments regarding policies that affect them, such as energy, regional development and pollution control measures. In 1991, Keidanren published its Global Environment Charter, which stated, 'Grappling with environmental problems is essential to corporate existence and activities.' The Charter committed Keidanren to seek positive and voluntary methods for promoting environmental conservation. In addition, Keidanren issued a call to the Japanese business community to organize the Keidanren Voluntary Action Plan on the Environment. In response to this call, a number of industries and industrial associations drafted their voluntary action plans and, in December 1996, Keidanren presented the Industry-wise Voluntary Action Plans for 29 industries (represented by 131 organizations) from manufacturing, energy, distribution, transportation, finance, construction and foreign trade. The main areas included in the voluntary action plans[2] are (a) measures to combat global warming, (b) waste disposal measures, (c) environmental management systems (for example, good practices based on the purport of ISO 14000 series), (d) environmental conservation in overseas business activities.

Among these objectives, measures to combat global warming are given the highest priority, since Japanese industries are committed to achieve greenhouse gas emission reductions. Similar to the Responsible Care programme, the main motives for the implementation of the voluntary agreement were to avoid public criticism and to avoid regulation.

Although the unilateral actions were intended to avoid possible government regulation, this has not been completely successful. The unilateral commitment approach suffers from a perceived lack of transparency and a credible system of verification. Therefore, government utilizes the plans as a supplementary mechanism to guide traditional policymaking. The government takes into account voluntary action plans in its long-term plans for energy supply and demand and so, in this respect, administrative guidance by government and voluntary action plans of industries play complementary roles.

Overall, by adopting a voluntary approach, Japanese industry has generally avoided new government regulation but has not completely succeeded in avoiding administrative guidance. Communication with NGOs and the public can help to make the process more transparent and limit the perceived need for government intervention. However, while many trade organizations and corporations produce environmental reports to publicize their environmental activities, there are very few cases of public reviews by NGOs and citizens (Imura, 1999).

The regional examples of unilateral agreements presented above are aimed at environmental problems other than those related to transport; no equivalent examples could be found dealing with the reduction of greenhouse gas emissions from transport. Nonetheless most large auto manufacturers unilaterally produce annual environmental reports, which set out the improvements made and whether certain international environmental standards have been reached. To this end it can be construed that all large firms in the developed world environmentally self-regulate to some extent.

9.2.2 Public Agreements

This kind of voluntary agreement generally requires firms to commit themselves to targets related to environmental performance, technology or management, which have been set by public authorities. Public agreements have been popular with industry, since participation incentives have included R&D subsidies, technical assistance and positive reputation effects (OECD, 1999). The conditions of the agreement generally specify the environmental standards and the monitoring procedures, as well as the criteria for success. Public agreements have been used to deal with a wide range of environmental issues and have become particularly common as an instrument to reduce greenhouse gas emissions from industrial sectors. There are few examples of this kind of VA used to reduce greenhouse gas emissions from transport and examples from other sectors are provided as examples here. The public agreements in existence for transport management generally are at a local level between local authorities and transport firms and deal with closed fleet emissions. Owing to the prevalence of public voluntary agreements as an environmental management tool, there has been some empirical and theoretical research examining the principles of this instrument. Lyon and Maxwell (2003) have reached the following conclusions regarding public voluntary agreements.

- Public voluntary programmes are often proposed in the absence of strong legislative threats and in fact regulatory authorities often use public agreements because they lack the authority to implement legislation.
- Companies join public voluntary agreements in order to benefit from the incentives offered by government and therefore the benefits should be viewed as subsidies from government to firms.
- Public voluntary agreements are generally weak tools that are used when the political will to take stronger action is lacking.

The Climate Change Action Plan (CCAP) in the US is a form of public voluntary agreement to reduce greenhouse gas emissions. The Clinton Administration introduced the CCAP in 1993, when it became clear that a prior proposal for energy taxes could not be implemented because of political constraints. The CCAP embraces many public voluntary programmes such as Green Lights, Climate Wise, Motor Challenge and Energy Star Buildings, among others. Most of these programmes have encouraged investment in energy efficiency improvements, an initiative supported by the US government since the 1970s. Lyon and Maxwell (2003) in their review of these agreements found that there did not appear to be a significant regulatory threat driving the public voluntary agreements in the CCAP. Howarth et al. (2004) find that public voluntary programmes such as the Green Lights and Energy Star Products programmes have facilitated the introduction of cost-effective energy efficient technologies that achieved a low rate of market adoption before the programmes began. They estimate that the benefits have outweighed the costs to government.

The second Bush Administration has pledged to reduce the ratio of GHG emissions to total economic output by 18 per cent between 2002 and 2012. Industry has been asked to make voluntary commitments to meet this goal, with credits (early reduction credits (ERCs)) awarded to firms against future regulatory requirements. Negotiating the voluntary commitments under the ERC programme may result in high transaction costs due to the necessity of estimating an emissions baseline for producers and consumers. Accordingly, it is expected that measurement and data collection requirements will influence the development of any subsequent mandatory climate change programme. The award of ERCs is similar to grandfathering in emissions trading regimes, whereas allocation would be more efficient if credits were auctioned. However, this kind of award system not only reduces political opposition to climate change regulations but also creates industry support for the introduction of mandatory climate change standards. Lyon and Maxwell find that ERCs are similar to other public voluntary agreements in that they are weak subsidy-based programmes, implemented when more effective mandatory programmes are politically infeasible. Rent-seeking behaviour is encouraged if firms expect a voluntary programme with subsidies in the wake of failed regulatory proposals. The Bush Administration has also introduced other programmes designed to provide incentives for energy-efficient technologies, and these are discussed later on.

Baranzini et al. (2004) have examined the public voluntary agreements in place to reduce greenhouse gas emissions in Switzerland. These agreements follow from energy efficiency agreements that were established prior to the emergence of concerns about climate change. The Energy Law in 1998 provided for public voluntary agreements to reduce energy consumption. A two-stage approach to energy reduction is applied in the Energy Law: voluntary agreements are first encouraged, and then, if they are insufficient, a market-based instrument such as a CO_2 emissions tax is implemented. The local and federal governments promote voluntary agreements under the Energy Law by providing technical assistance and contributing to information dissemination. Under the umbrella of public voluntary agreements facilitated by the Energy Law, a declaration of self-regulation was issued by the Association of Car Importers in Switzerland in order to pre-empt a CO_2 emissions tax. The Association has committed itself to reducing the average fuel consumption of new cars from 8.4 l/100km in 2000 to 6.4 l/km in 2008, which represents an efficiency improvement of 24 per cent over the period.

Matsuno (2001) has performed a review of Japanese Pollution Control Agreements (PCAs). PCAs have been in use since the 1960s in Japan and there were more than thirty thousand in operation in 2001. However, PCAs have not been used to reduce greenhouse gas emissions from passenger cars in Japan. Matsuno carried out a survey in 1999 of all Japanese local governments on their use of PCAs as part of their environmental policy. The results from the survey showed that PCAs were seen by local governments to have advantages over other instruments thanks to the 'individual' nature of the agreements concluded with firms. They therefore provided flexibility to firms, albeit inviting some inequity between regulated firms. Matsuno questions the voluntary nature of these agreements, as it appears that the firms are often forced by regulation or fear of more stringent measures to reach agreement with authorities. The far-reaching power of local administrative authorities and the desire of Japanese firms to avoid conflict with government are cited as reasons for entering into many of the PCAs. As mentioned, there appear to be none in effect to manage greenhouse gas emissions from passenger cars in Japan.

9.2.3   Negotiated Environmental Agreements (NEAs)

In contrast to the two other types of voluntary agreements discussed above, negotiated agreements are not determined unilaterally by either firms or public authorities but are negotiated cooperatively by both. NEAs have become a popular instrument in environmental policy management and particularly in transport policy. In several regions NEAs constitute the main supply-side policy measure in place to manage the reduction of greenhouse gas emissions from passenger cars.

NEA contracts may be legally binding or not and studies show that more NEAs are non-binding than binding (Öeko-Institut, 1998). In Europe, for example, the German government is not permitted legally to enter into formal NEAs, therefore environmental targets are negotiated and the results announced informally through the press. In the Netherlands, on the other hand, NEAs are binding and have become the key environmental instrument preferred by stakeholders. Environmental targets can be set either for individual firms or for collectives such as an entire sector or a representative trade association. There are hundreds of NEAs worldwide and, since several pertain to the automobile industry, it is these that are focussed on here. Several NEAs have been implemented to reduce CO_2 emissions from the passenger car sector. In the EU, a NEA has been in operation since 1999 and, more recently, Australia and Canada have introduced similar schemes. These NEAs, since they relate directly to the reduction of greenhouse gas emissions from passenger cars, will be described in more detail here, with a focus on the experiences gained in the European programme.

In April 2003, the Australian government released details on an agreement reached with the automotive industry on a voluntary target of 6.8 l/100km (approximately 167 g/km, assuming 2.5 kg CO_2 emitted per litre petrol) for petrol passenger cars by 2010. This represents an 18 per cent improvement in the fuel efficiency of new vehicles between 2002 and 2010. The Australian Greenhouse Office commissioned two studies[3] to establish business-as-usual fuel consumption trends in 2010 on which to base reduction targets. The two studies included extensive consultations with the Federal Chamber of Automotive Industries, the Australian motor vehicle manufacturers, importers and other interested parties. The studies applied models accounting for the commitments made by all auto manufacturers operating in Europe to reduce CO_2 emissions by 2008/9.

Further negotiations are going on to develop National Average CO_2 Emissions (NACE) targets for cars, vans, four-wheel drives and light commercial vehicles up to 3.5 tonnes. The NACE target for passenger cars implements the strategy outlined by the Australian Prime Minister in 1997 for an improvement in average fuel consumption for new passenger vehicles by 2010.

As part of the Climate Change Plan for Canada, the Canadian government reached a Memorandum of Understanding with the Canadian motor industry in 2005. The NEA is designed to reduce the emissions of greenhouse gases produced by light duty motor vehicles operating in Canada. It sets out commitments by the auto sector to achieve emissions reductions through the deployment of more fuel-efficient and less greenhouse gas-intensive technologies and vehicles. Examples include advanced emission and diesel technologies, and alternative fuel and hybrid vehicles. The target is to improve vehicle fuel efficiency and associated greenhouse gas emissions intensity by 25 per cent between 2002 and 2010. This target had been publicly discussed since 2000, but was only agreed with industry in 2005. Rigorous monitoring and reporting requirements will be put in place to ensure targets are reached. The Climate Change Plan states that the Government 'remains ready with legislative and regulatory action as needed'. There is a history in Canada of using voluntary programmes to achieve fuel efficiency targets and some background is provided in Box 9.3. The Canadian budget in 2005 noted the need to study the potential of incentives promoting the purchase of fuel-efficient vehicles (Government of Canada, 2005).

A further NEA in the transport sector has been agreed in Canada to reduce greenhouse gas emissions from aviation. As domestic aviation accounts for approximately 4 per cent of Canada's transportation greenhouse gas emissions, the government agency Transport Canada and the Air Transport Association of Canada reached a voluntary agreement in November 2004 to reduce emissions from aviation. This agreement was

---

BOX 9.3   CANADIAN VOLUNTARY AGREEMENTS TO IMPROVE VEHICLE FUEL EFFICIENCY

The Canadian Motor Vehicle Fuel Efficiency Initiative is based on the earlier Motor Vehicle Fuel Consumption Program initiated in the late 1970s which encourages motor vehicle manufacturers to meet voluntary annual company average fuel consumption (CAFC) targets for new automobiles sold in Canada. The Motor Vehicle Fuel Consumption Standards Act was passed by Parliament in 1981, but the Act was not proclaimed as the Canadian vehicle manufacturers offered to meet the requirements on a voluntary basis. The manufacturers have made good on their offer and have met the programme objectives at a significantly reduced cost to both government and industry compared to a mandatory approach.

CAFC calculates a sales-weighted average fuel consumption for all new model year vehicles that are sold by each company. In 2001, the target goal for passenger cars was 8.6 l/100 km and 11.4 l/100 km for light trucks.

In late 1995 and early 1996, Natural Resources Canada (NRCan) signed a Memorandum of Understanding (MOU) with domestic and international vehicle manufacturers that renewed and expanded the Motor Vehicle Fuel Consumption Program. The MOUs embrace a more comprehensive, balanced approach to motor vehicle fuel efficiency aimed at vehicle owners and operators, as well as vehicle technology.

The elements of the MOUs are implemented through the Government Industry Motor Vehicle Energy Committee (GIMVEC) and its sub-committees. GIMVEC, initially created in the early 1980s, was revived in 1996 following the signing of the MOU on Motor Vehicle Fuel Efficiency between NRCan and the domestic and import vehicle manufacturers. GIMVEC is a forum at which energy-related motor vehicle issues are discussed. The committee includes representatives of the Canadian Vehicle Manufacturers' Association (CVMA), the Association of International Automobile Manufacturers of Canada (AIAMC), NRCan, Environment Canada, Transport Canada and Industry Canada. The committee has three co-chairs, one each from the CVMA, the AIAMC and NRCan, and it works in three areas: communicating and promoting vehicle efficiency, vehicle energy data and reporting and future vehicle technology. GIMVEC functions on a consensus basis and relies on funding and in-kind services from members in order to carry out its mandate. In addition, other stakeholders may be invited to sit on the main committee or sub-committees.

Progress has been achieved in Canada in increasing the level of consumer awareness, in particular as it pertains to the purchase of new vehicles. The EnerGuide label for Vehicles has been appearing on all new vehicles since January 1999. Improvements to the *Fuel Consumption Guide* and the submission of annual industry vehicle data were also made through this process. Guide available at http://www.tc.gc.ca/programs/environment/fuelpgm/guidsub.htm.

Source: Natural Resources Canada website.

---

formally signed on 29 June 2005 and it includes a greenhouse gas reduction target, an action plan to help organizations meet that target and an annual progress reporting mechanism.

Through this voluntary agreement, the Air Transport Association of Canada will encourage its members to improve their energy efficiency by an average of 1.1 per cent a year. This is expected to result in a collective greenhouse gas emissions reduction of 24 per cent by 2012, when compared to 1990 levels.

The terms of the agreement state that the agency Transport Canada will provide support to the commitment with technical assistance in estimating baseline emissions and identifying reduction potentials; assist in information-sharing activities between participating firms; address any barriers that exist to impede improvements in fuel efficiency; and publicize the emission reductions achieved. In return the Air Transport Association of Canada will monitor the progress of the emissions reduction goal and will

- share information with its members about operational opportunities and technologies;
- adopt and implement an action plan for reducing greenhouse gas emissions, which sets out technically feasible, cost-effective and commercially viable techniques and strategies to attain the emissions reduction goal;
- recognize and promote among its members the need to achieve reductions when considering future purchases of aircraft; and
- achieve appropriate emissions reductions in other industry sectors through emissions trading and other such mechanisms, if and when such opportunities become available.[4]

As part of the agreement, operational improvements, technology or equipment upgrades and other methods of improvement were discussed to be promoted to members of the association.

Negotiated agreement between the automobile industry and the European Commission to reduce CO$_2$ emissions from passenger cars

In 1999, the European Automobile Manufacturers Association (ACEA) reached a negotiated agreement with the European Commission to reduce CO$_2$ emissions from passenger cars.[5] An equivalent agreement was adopted by the Korean and Japanese Automobile Manufacturers Associations (KAMA and JAMA, respectively) with the Commission in 2000. This voluntary agreement represents the main mechanism in place in Europe to reduce greenhouse gases from the passenger road transport sector. It is the first of three pillars implementing the Community's strategy to reduce CO$_2$ emissions from passenger cars. The other two consist of fuel economy labelling and fiscal measures (described in Chapter 8). The automobile industry has committed itself to reducing the average CO$_2$ emissions intensity of passenger cars sold in the EU by approximately 25 per cent compared to 1995 emissions by 2008.[6]

The Agreement specified several goals to be met as indicative to meeting the final target of 140 g/km in 2008/2009:

a. achieve an intermediate target range of 165–70 gCO$_2$ per km by 2003/2004;
b. bring to the market by 2000 some individual car models with CO$_2$ emissions of less than 120 g/km;
c. review in 2003 the potential for additional improvements with a view to moving the new car fleet average further towards 120 gCO$_2$ per km by 2012;
d. undertake annual joint ACEA/Commission monitoring of all the relevant factors related to the commitments (ACEA, 2007).

The most recent year for which monitoring data are available is 2004. Average new car fleet CO$_2$ emissions in the EU were 163 g/km in 2004, equivalent to a 12.4 per cent reduction from 1995 levels. Figure 9.1 presents the progress made to 2004 by the three (European (ACEA), Japanese (JAMA) and Korean (KAMA)) car manufacturing associations in achieving the CO$_2$ emissions target. The European car manufacturers (ACEA) estimate that this has led to a reduction of approximately 35 million tonnes in CO$_2$ emissions compared to the case if CO$_2$ emissions had continued to grow on the trajectory of 1995. The further reductions needed to reach the target of 140 g/km may be more difficult and costly to achieve. On average,

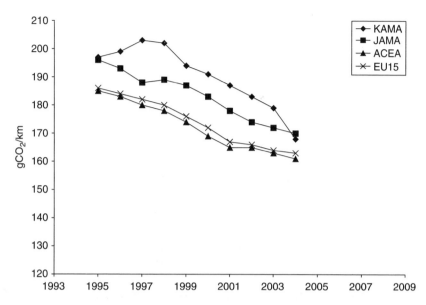

Source: Commission of the European Communities (2000, 2001, 2002a, 2004b, 2005c, 2006b).

Figure 9.1   Progress in CO_2 emissions from passenger cars from JAMA, KAMA, ACEA, and EU15 overall

an annual reduction of approximately 1.2 per cent has been achieved over the period 1995–2004; however it is estimated that, for the period remaining up to 2008, reductions in emissions must accelerate to a rate of 3.5 per cent per year to meet the 140 g/km target (CEC, 2006b).

As part of the conditions of the Voluntary Agreement, the automobile manufacturers and the Commission produce a joint monitoring report annually. These monitoring reports show that the intermediate CO_2 emissions target was met by ACEA in 2000 and that the upper end of the range was met by JAMA in 2002. KAMA still lags somewhat behind. Since 1995, the fuel efficiency of diesel passenger cars has improved more than the efficiency of petrol cars. ACEA and JAMA continue to make good progress, although the rate of reduction has slowed. KAMA remains behind, although it has been catching up in recent years.[7]

The proportion of fuel-efficient new vehicles sold in the EU in 2003 was higher than ever before, with the share of sales of vehicles generating less than 140 g/km reaching 23 per cent, up by 970 per cent from 1995. Sales of ultra-low CO_2 emitting vehicles (120 g/km) in Europe were 306 514 units in 2001 (approximately 2 per cent of vehicles sold). Future developments in passenger cars will involve more alternative fuels and technologies, in addition to advanced conventional technologies (described in Box 9.4). An EU study notes that total CO_2 emissions from the new passenger car fleet average are expected to stabilize as a result of the car industry's commitment to 140 g CO_2/km in 2008 (COWI, 2002). The aggregate emissions from passenger cars will decrease by only a few percentage points with the Community target being implemented (30 Mt CO_2 reduction in the car industry commitment alone).

BOX 9.4   ADVANCED CONVENTIONAL TECHNOLOGIES REQUIRED TO MEET THE 140 G/KM CO_2 EMISSIONS TARGET

Vehicle load reduction   Reduction of vehicle mass is important and generally achieved through increasing use of lightweight materials such as plastics, aluminium and high-strength steel. Average vehicle mass in Europe has remained stable even as the number of vehicle electronic devices and safety measures continue to mount. The Vehicle End-of-Life–Directive that was introduced in 2002 requires 85 per cent of vehicles to be re-used and recycled by 2006. This will mean that the use of some light-weight materials will be restricted, as last owners of vehicles are responsible for the disposal costs until 2007, but after that vehicle manufacturers will be required to meet all or a significant part of the costs of providing free take back if the car has no value.

Improved aerodynamics   Improving the vehicle shape to reduce aerodynamic drag can significantly reduce fuel consumption. Aerodynamic drag is measured by frontal area and coefficient of drag (C_D). The C_D of today's cars is 0.3–0.35, while that of light trucks is 0.4–0.45 (DeCicco et al., 2001). Ongoing work to reduce the drag coefficient could lead to a reduction (in C_D) by 10–25 per cent in the future (DeCicco and Ross, 1993).

Rolling resistance   Tyres are another area where fuel efficiency can be gained by changing the characteristics of the tyres, such as improved rubber, increased inflation pressures, and changes in tread design. These improvements can lower the rolling resistance of the vehicle.

Engine combustion   Direct injection diesel engines have been introduced since 1998 and paved the way for the widespread market acceptance of diesel passenger cars as a high-performance alternative to petrol cars. These technically advanced diesel engines include highly efficient unit injector and common rail technology. Gasoline direct injection technology is becoming available on the market with lean burn combustion that can result in fuel consumption savings of approximately 15 per cent. Challenges still exist in management of NO_x and particulate emissions.

Other developments have included the development of two-step variable valve lift, fully variable valve lift, a fully variable intake manifold, second generation common rail injection (high pressure) systems, application of advanced diesel technology to small cars, six-speed automatic gearboxes, integrated starter–generators and others.

Improved transmissions Continuous variable transmission (CVT) allows for an infinite number of variations in gear between minimum and maximum levels so that engine speed and torque can be chosen to maximize the engine efficiency over the whole engine map of operation. Past problems with CVT, which restricted use to small cars, have now been overcome and CVT is offered by many manufacturers in larger cars, although the torque limitations may restrict its use in light trucks. CVT offers a substantial improvement in efficiency over automatic transmissions, which generally have an efficiency of only 80 per cent. It is estimated that 20 per cent improvement in fuel economy can be achieved over conventional automatic transmissions.

Another option becoming more popular is the automation of manual transmissions. Manual transmissions have efficiencies in the mid-90 per cent range and automated manual transmissions combine the convenience of the automatic transmission with the efficiency of the manual transmission. Automated transmissions also allow manufacturers to preprogramme the transmission to select the most fuel-economic points of operation on the engine map. Nearly all of the new generation of 120 g/km cars are fitted with this technology.

The text of the Agreement in 1998 specified that the CO_2 target of 140 g/km be achieved through technological improvements and market changes linked to these advances. The European Commission's Directorate General for the Environment, which is responsible for the management and monitoring of the Voluntary Agreement with the automobile manufacturers, commissioned a study in 2004 to identify the reasons for the CO_2 emissions reduction achieved between 1995 and 2003 and assess their contribution to the total reductions achieved.[8] This study supported a broader review of the Agreement which concluded that the reduction in CO_2 emissions per vehicle has been 'overwhelmingly achieved by technological developments' (CEC, 2005c), and that all obligations specified in the Agreement were met. However, the review and the reports made by ACEA and JAMA to the Commission draw attention to the fact that measures under the other two pillars of the Commission's strategy have had low impact on the reduction of CO_2 emissions from passenger cars (ACEA, 2004; JAMA, 2004). Both associations in subsequent submissions state that the longer-term target of 120 g/km will be impossible to reach unless transport demand measures to influence consumer vehicle purchasing behaviour are introduced in support of the Agreement. In 2007 the Commission announced that 'the strategy has brought only limited progress towards achieving the target of 120g CO_2/km by 2012' and that 'the review of the strategy has concluded that the voluntary commitments have not succeeded and that the 120g target will not be met on time without further measures' (CEC, 2007). Therefore legislative measures would be proposed by mid 2008 to reduce CO_2 emissions from passenger cars (described further in Chapter 7). Box 9.4 provides an overview from the literature of the expected improvements to conventional vehicle technology that may be necessary to meet the CO_2 emissions target of 140 g/km.

As discussed above, the OECD has provided guidelines on the good design of voluntary agreements. Since the EU NEA has been in operation for several years longer than the equivalent NEAs in Canada and Australia, it is possible to assess it qualitatively, based on the guidelines.

Table 9.1 lists the OECD guidelines and assesses the EU NEA against that list. Not all information is available for the agreement, highlighting the lack of transparency of the negotiating process (Sauer and Wellington, 2004). In particular it appears that there was no baseline projection published for the counterfactual before the commitment (Jensen, 2003). Without the baseline projection, it is impossible to estimate the marginal CO_2 emissions abatement cost and therefore the optimal target at which total abatement costs are minimized. This suggests that this voluntary agreement may not be economically efficient. It is likely that the costs were not estimated publicly since this issue is very competitive between automobile companies. Companies would most likely prefer an instrument to operate inefficiently rather than reveal technological information to their competitors and the European Commission. The negotiation of this agreement did not take place with third-party involvement and it is therefore possible that regulatory capture did take place.

Table 9.1   OECD guidelines on NEA design compared with the automobile industry NEA

OECD recommendations	ACEA CO_2 agreement
Clearly defined targets	Short-term: yes; 140 g/km by 2008 Long-term: uncertain; perhaps 120 g/km by 2012. Methodology used is unclear
Characterization of a business-as-usual scenario	No
Credible regulatory threats	Moderate, threat of carbon tax or fuel economy standards but likely that Commission would fail to find agreement across EU
Credible and reliable monitoring	Yes, annually by industry and the Commission
Third-party participation	Unsure
Penalties for non-compliance	Introduction of legislation if the targets are not met
Information-oriented provisions	Indirectly, through the labelling directive (see section 8.3)
Provisions reducing the risk for competition distortions	No

9.3 SUMMARY

- Japan was an early leader in the use of voluntary approaches (VAs) in environmental policy but their use has become widespread across OECD countries.
- Among the types of VAs used in environmental policy, Negotiated Environmental Agreements (NEAs) have primarily been applied to greenhouse gas reduction in transport. There are NEAs to reduce greenhouse gas emissions from passenger cars in the EU, Canada and Australia.
- The main strategy to reduce greenhouse gas emissions from passenger cars in the EU has been managed by a Negotiated Environmental Agreement between the European Commission and the European, Japanese and Korean automobile manufacturers to reduce average CO_2 emissions of vehicles sold in Europe to 140 g/km by 2008. This represents a decrease of 25 per cent compared with 1990 levels.
- The literature on voluntary agreements has highlighted both merits and disadvantages to the implementation of this instrument. The

main merits appear to be flexibility for manufacturers and achieving least-cost abatement at lower transaction and administrative costs for public authorities. The pitfalls can be inefficiency through 'free-riding', lack of transparency, ineffective targets as a result of regulatory capture and unenforceability of the targets.

- The OECD has issued guidelines on good practice for voluntary approaches in environmental policy. The NEA between the automobile manufacturers and the European Commission fulfils some, but not all, of these recommendations: for example, the counterfactual emissions under a 'no policy' option were not estimated. The economic efficiency of the agreement has not yet been determined.

NOTES

1. Published in the Recommendation of the European Commission (1999/125/EC).
2. These voluntary action plans take the form of unilateral voluntary agreements.
3. Available at http://www.greenhouse.gov.au/transport/env_strategy.html#nace.
4. Media release June 29 2005: *Agreement to Reduce Greenhouse Gas Emissions in Aviation Signed*; http://www.tc.gc.ca/mediaroom/releases/nat/2005/05-h150e.htm#bg1.
5. Published in the Recommendation of the European Commission (1999/125/EC).
6. Published in European Commission Recommendation 1999/125/EC.
7. It should be recalled that the Council invited the Commission 'to present immediately proposals, including legislative proposals, for consideration, should it become clear, on the basis of the monitoring and after consultation with the associations, that one or more of the associations would not honour its commitments made' (Council conclusions, 1999).
8. DLR (German Aerospace Centre) was commissioned to perform this review (Mehlin et al., 2004a, 2004b).

10. Supply-side policy measures: R&D

Productivity-enhancing innovation is the lifeblood of modern economies. Without it, stagnation in growth and living standards is inevitable. What is true of economies is true also of sectors and companies. Those that lag in terms of innovation will lag also in terms of growth and market share; ultimately, their survival depends on their success or otherwise in embracing innovation. For firms in the automobile sector, new product development is the very essence of their craft; their survival depends on having a pipeline of new potentially successful products and services. For this reason, automobile industry analysts examine carefully what products are in the pipeline, and how much and to what effect expenditure is devoted to R&D.

As the number of vehicle manufacturers globally has shrunk through takeovers and mergers, there has been sluggish growth in major car markets and a rapid expansion of production capacities in emerging markets, leading to stronger competition in the traditional segments of the car market, and process innovation to keep production costs low (CEC, 2004c). This trend can have both a positive or negative effect for the development of environmental technology: either these technologies become increasingly important as a means by which companies can retain an edge over competitors, or margins become so narrow that companies are unable to afford to invest in technology research. Furthermore, large firms may be able to pursue more risky technologies, whereas small companies may lack the necessary capital or management resources. At the same time, consumer preferences can play an important role in determining whether car manufacturers attempt to minimize production costs or vehicle operating costs.

There is evidence to suggest that technological development may be the most important factor influencing climate change, since historically technological change has been responsible for up to half of total economic growth (Nakićenović and Swart, 2000), and this has generally resulted in increased greenhouse gas emissions.

Achieving multiple objectives of sustainable development in the future will require simultaneously reductions in greenhouse gas emissions and maintainance of economic growth. One method of reducing future greenhouse gases will be to improve energy supply and end-use efficiency by technological innovation and change. This will also lead to lower carbon intensity as a result of increasing availability and substitutability of fossil energy alternatives – also an effect of technological change. Some ways in which technological change can achieve multiple objectives, including satisfying growing energy and transport demands, while reducing greenhouse gas emissions, are explored in Chapters 5 and 6.

In this chapter, we focus on the use of research and development as an explicit policy instrument for 'accelerating' innovation leading to greenhouse gas abatement in transport. We outline the economic rationale for government support for R&D in general, how innovation and R&D are handled in the modelling of policy options, and the results from empirical research on the effectiveness of transport or energy-related R&D support as a significant driver of abatement. Finally we examine the main R&D policy proposals for passenger cars in the car-producing regions of the world.

10.1   CHARACTERISTICS OF TECHNOLOGICAL CHANGE

Technological improvement, especially in the area of energy efficiency, remains a goal for all sectors and transport is no different in this regard. The economics literature describes the process of technological change as a three-step development (Schumpeter, 1942). The first step is invention, the second is innovation and the third is known as diffusion or adoption. The first two steps are often combined under the term 'innovation'; in this step concepts are taken from initial idea to demonstration product. The final step, diffusion, is market-driven and represents the adoption or deployment of the commercial product. Research and development (R&D) contributes to the innovation process, while diffusion depends on market characteristics, technology clusters and the impact of learning-by-doing with new technologies.[1] Both steps play a major part in the process of technological change. Sagar and van der Zwaan (2005) and Turton (2005) demonstrate that R&D investment and deployment programmes together are often necessary in order to translate the gains from R&D to new technologies in the energy sector.

Technological change is achieved not just by corporate innovations (R&D) alone however; economic, social and cultural trends play an important role in many ways. It is highly situation-specific and often results from immediate local requirements. Technological change may be supply or demand-driven. Providing incentives for R&D encourages supply-driven technological change. This is pertinent since, until the external costs of climate change are included in the pricing of fossil fuels, there is unlikely to be much demand-driven R&D. This is unfortunate since historically many technologies were developed as a result of an immediate demand and it is therefore no surprise that many inventions were first deployed during wartime.

Market forces can also have a marked effect on demand-driven R&D; however these forces must remain in force throughout the product development cycle, that is, high fuel prices providing an incentive to improve fuel efficiency or develop alternatively-fuelled technology are only relevant if they remain over a sufficiently long period of time. This is important since there is almost always a time lag between R&D and the availability of a technology for deployment.

Another important aspect to technological change is the social acceptance of the innovation and the diffusion of the technology, in addition to its compatibility with existing physical and social infrastructure and systems. These factors can be as or more important than the performance of the technology in determining success, and whether the full benefits of that technology be realized. The length of time required for the diffusion of a new technology often depends partly on the definition of a technology, since technologies, once developed, continue to improve and be optimized over time. The diffusion of a technology has been described in the literature as a function of firm size, R&D expenditure, market share, market structure, input prices, the relative capital cost and price of the technology, epidemic and endogenous learning effects and stock[2] and order[3] effects in game-theoretic models (Karshenas and Stoneman, 1995).

Figure 10.1 illustrates a generic diffusion curve. Empirical observation in the literature has demonstrated that diffusion curves often have a sigmoid shape. The rate of diffusion of the use of a particular technology can vary widely, however, between industries, technologies and locations.

Often a new product must fulfil numerous needs in order for it to find market acceptance, other than the specific need for which it was developed. This can lead to 'lock-in' of the incumbent technologies that already provide for many of these needs and hence represents an important barrier to entry for new technologies. Table 10.1 lists a sample of technologies from the literature and the length of time taken from first commercialization for 50 per cent market penetration.

In Part II one possible future trajectory of technological innovation and deployment was presented that highlighted the role these processes may play in realizing a more sustainable global energy system. Indeed some groups contend that technological improvements can provide the main method by which climate change will be mitigated in the future. However technological innovation and change is a highly uncertain process and there is no guarantee that the necessary breakthroughs will occur, or that a purely technologically-driven solution will be low-cost or efficient. Accordingly, it is more prudent to assume that technology alone will not mitigate climate

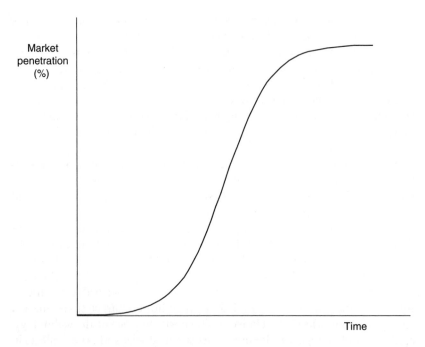

Source: Karshenas and Stoneman (1995).

Figure 10.1   A technology diffusion curve

change, but rather a combination of behavioural and technological change will be necessary to reduce greenhouse gas emission to a more sustainable level.

10.2   ECONOMIC RATIONALE FOR PUBLIC R&D

Economic theory tells us that private firms are unable to appropriate all the benefits of new technologies and there are large spillovers benefiting other firms and society as a whole. That is, the benefits of R&D are largely public, accruing across society and to future generations, and only a small fraction of the full benefits can be converted to returns on investment for firms (Chupka, 1997). Therefore in the absence of public policy there will be less investment in R&D than needed for optimal economic growth and efficient environmental policy. This is one reason why public, as well as private, funding of R&D is crucial. Government leadership is required to set policy and R&D direction, while industry/government partnerships in R&D are useful in order to incorporate market relevance into policymaking and to

Table 10.1   Diffusion indicators in the United States

Innovation	No. of years taken for half of potential adopters to acquire
Industrial robots	12
Diesel locomotives	9
Centralized traffic control	14
Continuous annealing	13
Tin container	1
High-speed bottle filler	6
Pallet loading machine	5

Source: Mansfield (1968).

tap specialist expertise. However, governments must not lose sight of their special role in advancing the achievement of long-term objectives, as distinct from the objectives of private firms.

Government often supports high-risk, precompetitive research in R&D collaborations. In the same way that government environmental policy must send the appropriate signals to R&D investment, so should government pave the way with R&D leadership, co-ordination and direction to create efficient economic, energy and environmental policy.

Investment in R&D, therefore, in part drives environmental technological change. Jaffe et al. (2005) point out two market failures, which cause a double underinvestment in technology to reduce pollution. Firstly, a negative externality is associated with pollution, which causes firms to pollute more than the social optimum. Environmental policy is necessary to correct this market failure and firms are required or encouraged to reduce pollution to the socially optimum level. Economic instruments have been shown to provide more dynamic incentives than command and control measures for lower cost abatement through technological change (Requate, 2005).

Secondly, several unpriced positive externalities are created through investment in technology, which leads to firms investing too little in R&D. The first derives from the 'public good' nature of R&D, whereby the benefits of innovation are often available to all of society and only a fraction is appropriated by those who undertake the research. As Goulder (2002) puts it: 'because not all the knowledge can be appropriated by the private firm (due to spillover effects to other firms and free riders), the private return tends to fall short of the social return. The firms therefore tend to engage in less R&D than the amount that would maximize net social benefits' (Goulder, 2002). The more 'basic' and fundamental the research (further away from the market place) the more likely is this to be the case.

The second externality reflects the uncertainty associated with high-risk investments such as investment in innovation. The asymmetry in information between the developer of the technology and the investor makes it difficult for a firm to raise capital for an untried technology and investors can demand a premium for the investment. This effect exacerbates the spillover effect and discourages firms from investing in R&D at the socially optimum level.

A third market failure is highly relevant to greenhouse gas emissions and closely related to the first described above, in that it derives from the fact that the prices of many commodities do not adequately reflect the external costs they impose. In addition to causing firms to pollute more than is socially optimal, this situation means that developers of innovations that reduce externalities (e.g., through efficiency) cannot appropriate the benefits of avoided external costs again leading to underinvestment in R&D.

Finally, Parry (2003) describes a negative externality that encourages overinvestment in R&D. It occurs when a firm does not take into consideration the impact its investment in R&D and the resulting patents have in reducing the probability that other firms will obtain patents. This is the old problem of overexploitation of a common good. However, the literature seems to indicate that the other externalities (particularly the 'spillover' externality) dominate, leading to 'social rates of return that are substantially higher than the private rates of return' (Parry, 2003).

The problem can be expressed using parameters as follows:

X = proposed R&D investment,
A = value of energy consumption reduced,
B = value of positive spillover effects to others that the investor in R&D cannot capture,
C = value of external costs that are reduced as a result of the proposed R&D investment.

The incentive problem is that the investors in R&D can only capture return A, and will only invest if they expect A to exceed X. If the spillover benefits (B) and reduction in external costs (C) could be captured by the investors, then they could justify a much larger investment, not to exceed $A+B+C$.

10.3 EFFECTIVENESS OF PUBLIC R&D AS A POLICY INSTRUMENT

The question for policymakers is clear: how to encourage innovation and technological change in transport and other sectors? Technological change itself does not exist in a vacuum but is influenced by other policies in place such as industry, economic and trade policy, in addition to measures such as carbon taxes or emissions trading, which put a price on greenhouse gas emissions. An investment leading to technological improvements can reduce the marginal cost of greenhouse gas abatement, thereby enabling a given reduction in emissions to be achieved at a lower cost to society (Parry, 2003). Thus the economic rationale for government support for R&D investment in greenhouse gas abatement is to compensate for the several forms of market failure, which causes there to be under-investment in R&D by private actors. Box 10.1 describes some forms of financial R&D support mechanisms in the private sector.

At a forum organized by Resources for the Future in Washington DC in 2001, on energy and environment, a session took place on R&D. John Wise, former Vice President for Research at Mobil Research and Development Corporation, and Gerry Taylor, Director of Natural Resource Studies at the Cato Institute, 'fundamentally agreed that the government role in funding research into new energy technologies was of limited value in terms of enhancing commercial productivity'. Overall, Wise said: 'the government serves the public best when it supports research into technologies that support environmental remediation; development of domestic sources; fragmented, low-tech industries such as homebuilding, and technologies that generate high risks for the developer, but high potential rewards to society'. Taylor said that, while there have been a handful of success stories, the government's overall track record on supporting energy R&D has been terrible. There are two fundamental reasons for this: incompetent programming, in the form of narrowly focused research initiatives, and political rather than economic motives influencing the funding process.

There is insufficient empirical evidence to permit estimation of a production function relating expenditure on R&D to innovations and GHG emission abatement. Moreover, the pace and direction of technology development is highly uncertain, and it is often a non-linear process. There is however an increasing trend in the US to perform ex-post analyses of the benefits and costs of government expenditure. One of the main challenges for the assessors has been to find a methodology to carry out the assessment of energy-related R&D.

Notwithstanding the virtual absence of evidence that would allow us to 'predict' a given quantity of innovation for a given investment in R&D, how can we advance the discussion of climate change-related R&D? The first point to note is that, if the climate change issue is to be addressed successfully, the world needs serious and continuing innovation, and R&D is an essential prerequisite for stimulating this phase of technology development; that is, the issue cannot be ignored. Instead of attempting to fill this production function gap directly, we can discuss the insights derived from

BOX 10.1   FINANCIAL AND FISCAL R&D SUPPORT MECHANISMS IN THE PRIVATE SECTOR

In the context of concern over the growing disparity between research and development (R&D) investment levels in the EU compared with the USA and Japan, R&D has been put at the heart of the EU development strategy. New targets for EU R&D investment have been established and an expert group has been formed to assess the issue. The task of raising industrial R&D investment levels is primarily the responsibility of industry itself. However, there is still a role for the public sector to play to stimulate private sector R&D investment levels. These levels are affected by a variety of framework conditions and policies governing business behaviour generally, and R&D and innovation activities in particular. There is a specific interest in financial and fiscal measures affecting the private sector's access to, and use of, finance for R&D. According to the expert group, these measures fall into three categories:

– Direct Financial R&D Measures involving the direct transfer of financial support for R&D from the public to the private sector via grants, conditional loans and so on;

– Indirect Fiscal R&D Measures (often shortened to Indirect or Fiscal measures) involving the public sector forsaking tax income from the private sector in exchange for approved R&D investment behaviour;

– Catalytic Financial R&D Measures in which the public sector takes actions that help R&D performers access external private sector sources of finance; which can then be used either to finance R&D directly or to generate profit, some of which is re-invested in R&D. Typical Catalytic Measures are:

(1) Risk Capital Measures, that is, measures taken by the public sector that catalyse the flow and use of risk capital for both R&D and innovation-related activities likely to increase R&D investment levels in the future;

(2) Loan and Equity Guarantee Measures, that is, measures whereby the public sector tries to encourage additional investment in R&D by offering to share part of the risk involved in the provision of support for R&D and innovation-related activities.

Source: DG Research Expert Group (2003).

both practice and theory yield with respect to the design and implementation of R&D programmes.

The R&D programme implemented by the US Department of Energy has been assessed by the National Research Council (NRC, 2001) and this analysis yields some lessons, which are presented in Box 10.2.

BOX 10.2   SUMMARY OF NRC REPORT

In 2000, the House Interior Appropriations Subcommittee of the US directed 'an evaluation of the benefits' that have ensued as a result of the Department of Energy's (DOE) energy efficiency and fossil energy programmes. The report was requested by Congress to identify general improvements that can be attributed to federal funding in these areas. In response to this the National Research Council published a report in 2001 that presented the results of this work (NRC, 2001).

From 1978 until 1999, the US federal government spent $91.5 billion (2000 dollars) on R&D, mostly through DOE programmes. This represents approximately one-third of total national public and private energy R&D funding. The two programme areas to be evaluated in this report – energy efficiency and fossil energy – have between them received $22.3 billion or 26 per cent of total DOE expenditure on energy R&D since 1978. In energy efficiency programmes, the transportation sector has always received the largest share of the budget: 42 per cent in 2000, and 43 per cent cumulatively between 1978 and 2000. Earlier (that is, in 1978), buildings and industry received 40 per cent and 18 per cent, respectively. This had changed to 25 per cent and 32 per cent, respectively, in 2000. The fossil energy programme has historically focused research on two Offices: the Office of Coal and Power Systems; and the Office of Natural Gas and Petroleum Technology. Between 1978 and 1981, 73 per cent of the budget was invested in technologies to produce liquid and gas fuel options from US energy resources: coal and oil shale. In 2000, however, only 30 per cent of the fossil energy R&D budget was devoted to coal conversion and utilization technologies.

The main task carried out by the assessors was to find a methodology to evaluate the benefits accrued by the programmes. One of the main challenges was to find a method that would represent both economic and non-economic benefits (and costs) of the programmes. This was important, as the nature of public funded research programmes is such that public benefits exist that are not lucrative for the private sector (for technologies not yet developed, for example). An evaluation framework was developed that considered the benefits and costs, both quantitative and qualitative, of the programmes. For each programme the committee selected a number of case studies that varied greatly in size but were representative of the programmes. These were then fitted into the evaluation matrices.

The conclusions of the assessment were that in general the DOE programmes had 'yielded significant benefits (economic, environmental, and national security-related), important technological options for potential application in a different (but possible) economic, political, and/or environmental setting, and important additions to the stock of engineering and scientific knowledge in a number of fields'. The committee judged the net realized benefits of the programmes to be in excess of the DOE investment.

However the committee also found many limitations to the benefits and potentials for improvement. They determined that DOE did not employ a consistent methodology to assess the programmes and that too often only the economic benefits were quantified and regularly overstated. The committee also ascertained that the organization and management of the programmes made a significant difference to the results of the programmes.

The energy efficiency programmes reviewed realized approximately $30 billion (1999 dollars) in benefits that mainly came from three modest building projects begun in the late 1970s and substantially exceeded the R&D investment of $7 billion (1999 dollars). The fossil energy programmes reviewed provided benefits in total of nearly $11 billion that exceeded overall the costs of $10.5 billion; however the period from 1978 to 1986 did not realize economic benefits.

The largest benefits were achieved by an order of magnitude in avoided energy costs in the buildings sector and avoided environmental costs from NO_x reductions achieved by a single programme in fossil energy.

The committee recommend that DOE develop and utilize an evaluation framework similar to that used here to assess regularly the benefits and costs of their programmes. DOE also needs to record consistently budget and cost-sharing data for all projects to enable better assessment and evaluation. The committee also comment that project failures do not mean overall programme failure. In fact a balanced portfolio of R&D programmes will generally contain some project failures, indeed one that does not could be viewed as overly conservative. Programme areas that did not live up to expectations were ones in which DOE tried to introduce a new technology but without the necessary incentives for adoption by the private sector.

A significant recommendation of the committee is that for short-term R&D programmes that are meant for rapid deployment, DOE should consider using some of the funds to develop appropriate economic incentives to enable market penetration of the technologies. The committee found that industry participation in R&D programmes is to be encouraged; however DOE must ensure that long-term as well as short-term goals are pursued.

Also in the USA, the Climate Change Technology Initiative (CCTI) is a programme run by the DOE that includes tax incentives for energy efficiency improvements and renewable technologies for buildings, light-duty vehicles and electricity generation. This programme encourages technology deployment, which is an important complement to R&D. The total budget for CCTI programmes in 2000 was $1.1 billion. The latest analysis reviewed and assessed the CCTI programmes sector by sector (US DoE, 2001). The report states that, historically, research and development programmes have helped develop technologies at lower cost than might otherwise occur. This statement is not, however, empirically demonstrated. Some quantitative analysis is undertaken for projects with specific programme goals. It is assumed that these goals are met and the impact on energy consumption and GHG emissions estimated. For example, if the PATH programme in efficiency improvements in houses is successful, an energy and emissions improvement of 1 per cent in 2010 and 2 per cent by 2020 will be achieved. (This does not appear to be very much if we consider that average annual energy intensity improvement globally is around 1 per cent, although it represents a 10 per cent acceleration in intensity improvements.) The Million Solar Roofs programme, another complementary technology deployment programme, is calculated to have considerably less impact on carbon emissions, even if the programme's goals are achieved. The Energy Information Administration of the DOE report that some advances have been made in reducing the cost of photovoltaic and wind technologies, although wind energy appears to have missed the target of achieving electricity generation costs of 2.5 cents per kWh by 2002. Much of the report focuses on technological advances that have been made in some sectors and a description of future targets.

Popp (2002) uses the number of patents as an indicator for the impact of energy prices on technological change. Patent data can serve as a proxy for

R&D expenditure, but there is not a direct correlation. Patent numbers can be expected to increase with R&D expenditure. The advantage of patent data over R&D expenditure data is that patents are more disaggregated and can provide a detailed record of innovation. Patent data can also be used to track the diffusion of an invention, as the inventors must apply for a patent in each country where they intend to market the product. Citations within a patent application also give an indication of the flows of knowledge among inventors. However there are significant limitations to patent data: patents vary considerably in their quality and value and so, while some patents are not worth anything, others are extremely valuable. Also most patents are the result of R&D but not all the results of R&D are patented, since it may not be in the interest of the firm to disclose in a patent application the results of a new discovery.

Popp (2002, 2003) shows that innovation responds quickly to incentives. Analysing the relationship between patenting activity and energy prices (for 11 energy technologies), Popp (2002, 2003, 2004) estimated a long-run energy R&D elasticity of 0.354, and a mean lag of 3.71 years. The elasticity is higher than estimated by other researchers, which Popp attributes to the highly aggregated data used in other studies. Another conclusion of this research is that not only does energy R&D respond quickly to energy prices but that there are diminishing returns over time. Relevant to the economic rationale given above is the fact that this work finds that the social returns to environmental research are high. Other researchers (Hall, 1996; Mansfield, 1996; Pakes, 1985) have also found that the social returns are higher (between 30 and 50 per cent) than the private returns (typically 7 per cent) to environmental research. Popp models empirical data and finds that environmental R&D investment crowds out other R&D investment, that is, there is an opportunity cost associated with environmental R&D that could be important.

Sagar and van der Zwaan (2005) examine public investment in energy R&D in OECD countries and compare it with the energy intensity improvement in the same countries. They find that there is little correlation between the variables. This is explained by the aggregate nature of energy R&D expenditure data and the differences in the type of spending are not visible from the data. For example, Japan spends 75 per cent of energy R&D on nuclear power, which accounts for less than 15 per cent of the country's energy supply. Therefore the authors suggest that energy R&D funding has to be specific and must be focused on, for example, energy efficiency if a benefit is desired in that area. There is also a missing link that must be considered, which is the effort required for deployment programmes. The authors find that publicly funded R&D will not be enough to induce technological change; identification of market barriers to the implementation of new technologies and a programme of deployment are necessary in order to achieve adoption of technological change. The relationship between early R&D and deployment programmes is not well understood and the two need to be balanced in order to maximize gains from innovation.

This is also discussed by Griliches (1992) and he has collected estimates from the literature of returns to R&D and R&D spillovers, which are given in Table 10.2.

Table 10.2   Selected estimates of returns to R&D and R&D spillovers

I. Agriculture	Rates of return to public R&D (%)
Griliches (1958) hybrid corn	35–40
hybrid sorghum	20
Peterson (1967) poultry	21–25
Schmitz-Seckler (1970)	37–46
tomato harvester	
Griliches (1964) aggregate	35–40
Evenson (1968) aggregate	41–50
Knutson–Tweeten (1979) aggregate	28–47
Huffman–Evenson (1993) crops	45–62
livestock	11–83
aggregate	43–67

II. Manufacturing	Rates of return to R&D (%)	
Case studies	Within (private: R&D)	From outside (spillovers)
Mansfield et al. (1968)	25	56
I–O weighted		
Terleckyj (1974) total	28	48
private	29	78
Sveikauskas (1981)	10–23	50
Goto/Suzuki (1989)	26	80
R&D weighted (patent flows)		
Griliches–Lichtenberg (1984)	46–69	11–62
Mohnen–Lepine (1988)	56	28
Proximity (technological distance)		
Jaffe (1988)		30% of within
Cost functions		
Bernstein–Nadiri (1988, 1989)		20% of within
differs by industry	9–27	10–60
Bernstein–Nadiri (1991)	14–28	Median: 56% of within

Source: Griliches (1992).

Another study by Sanyal (2001) has shown that the threat of future regulations in the electricity industry in the US has caused plants to increase environmental R&D spending. Deregulation and the resulting increased competition between plants has caused firms in the industry to transfer financial contributions from pooled electricity sector R&D programmes to individual company environmental R&D activities.

A discussion on the role of technology as a policy to mitigate GHG emissions is found in a short series of articles in *Weathervane*. Kopp (1998) discusses the suitable calculation of costs of investing in R&D specifically with the goal of abating GHG emissions. Specifically, Kopp (1998) questions the findings of the Clinton Administration's Interagency Analytic Team (IAT), which found in 1997 that a 40 per cent increase in the pace of technical change, giving rise to energy-efficiency improvements, would lead to a 65 per cent drop in the cost of GHG abatement in 2020. Kopp (1998) questions the credibility of this estimate and highlights the lack of cost information, pointing out also that technical change is achieved by R&D investment as well as learning by doing. In addition, the opportunity cost of investing R&D funds for GHG abatement, instead of other R&D activities, is a factor that was ignored in the IAT analysis. This is particularly important considering the potential for R&D-funded technologies to crowd out other technologies. Calculating the costs saved by R&D investment is difficult because of the uncertainty in the timing of GHG abatement activities and the nature of the policies that will be used to promote these activities.

In an attempt to review government support of R&D and its effectiveness, Luiten and Blok (2004) examine the case of innovation in the global paper industry. They examine the story of government research institutes attracting public funds, even when the prospects of the technology deteriorated. They show that, in this case, 25 years of R&D and over 15 years' government R&D support have not resulted in a proven technology. As a result of this analysis they make several recommendations that governments should adhere to when supporting R&D in energy-efficient technologies:

- The goals and expectations of government intervention should be made explicit in advance, so that they can be evaluated ex post. This requires insight into actors, technology networks, the technology, its claimed performance characteristics, and into the materialization of the technology over time. Such information may ultimately lead to the conclusion that government R&D support (in this case for a public research institute) is superfluous.
- The timing of intervention is significant – whereas the emergence of a technology network may require support, continued support for

more than ten years should be based on a critical evaluation in terms of the results achieved by the technology network.

- Long-term R&D support may be necessary in some cases. However, governments should have the courage to stop financial support if perspectives deteriorate.
- Monitoring of the R&D programme is very important although it can be difficult to obtain independent technology assessment since the experts who are capable of doing so are often involved in the network.

The International Energy Agency has a unique overview of energy systems around the world. Their conclusions (see Box 10.3) support the Goulder and Schneider hypothesis that progress at the requisite level requires both a supply (for example, subsidies) and a demand (such as, higher fuel prices via taxes or otherwise) response, and that government should concentrate on ensuring that long-term research is pursued.

BOX 10.3   THE INTERNATIONAL ENERGY AGENCY AND ENERGY R&D: A NORMATIVE VIEW

Governments must ensure adequate long-term R&D, particularly in the light of industry's decreasing investment in research activities, and avoid the tendency for co-operation with industry to push the government R&D portfolio toward short-term, lower-risk projects. Measures to internalize the costs of environmental externalities would help stimulate industry to do more of its own long-term R&D.

Technological advances are needed not only in incremental improvements, which are the most usual in industry, but also 'great leaps forward' are required. This will mean that governments must continue to play the role of the patient investor and wait to reap the rewards of this investment in later years.

Stimulation of private R&D requires both the push of public R&D and the pull of deployment programmes that can sustain the technologies until they are cost-efficient on the market. (IEA, 2000, p. 39)

10.4   MODELLING R&D IN CLIMATE CHANGE POLICY

Technological change as a function of R&D investment is modelled in a range of energy-economic models (Buonanno et al., 2003; Buchner et al., 2002), including the ERIS model used in Part II of this book (Turton, 2005; Barreto and Kypreos, 2004a). Goulder and Schneider (1999) develop a policy simulation model which concludes that achieving a 10 per cent reduction in carbon dioxide emissions is 'ten times more costly when technology subsidies are employed alone, as compared with the situation where technology subsidies are combined with policies that raise the price of carbon; the latter including carbon taxes and emissions trading'. Their findings derive from the fact that R&D subsidies address the spillover or 'appropriability' problem (variable 'B' in the earlier discussion) but do not confront the external cost problem (variable 'C': see earlier). By using a tax or emissions trading to bring the prices of fuel closer to their social cost, the costs of achieving a given target can be substantially reduced. Note that, in deriving this result, Goulder and Schneider operate under the same production function constraints[4] as others working in the field, and so their specific quantification should be treated with a degree of scepticism, but the direction of their argument is robust and useful.

Other work has been done attempting to quantify the costs and benefits of R&D expenditure in the USA. Davis and Owens (2003) have applied the method of real options to evaluate the optimal level of renewable electric R&D expenditures. They focus on the US government's renewable electric (RE) R&D programme that has been running since 1974 and received $13.5 billion (1992 dollars) up to 2000. Over this period approximately 90 per cent of funding was distributed to six main RE technologies: concentrating solar power, photovoltaics, geothermal energy, electric storage systems, wind and bioenergy.

Davis and Owens (2003) find that the discounted cash flow approach results in a net present value of −$53.5 billion for continued expenditure in renewable energy R&D. They also examined the alternative of postponing renewable energy deployment while continuing with cost-reducing R&D thus providing a sort of insurance policy should the price of fossil electricity increase significantly. This approach leads to a present value estimate of future expected cost savings from eventual installation of RE generation capacity of $30.6 billion dollars, net of current RE R&D expenditure and accounting for the current RE/conventional energy electricity price ratio of 1.29.

Davis and Owens' (2003) analysis also estimated the optimal annual RE R&D budget as a function of net present value of the RE technologies net

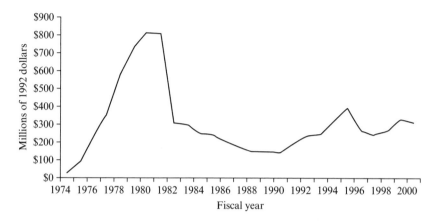

Source: FY73–FY90 Sisson Congressional Research Service article, FY90–FY00 Presidential budget requests, and DOE budget highlight documents in Davis and Owens (2003). Reproduced from Davis and Owens (2003) with permission from publisher (Elsevier).

Figure 10.2 Renewable energy R&D program funding (FY 1974–FY 2000)

of R&D expenses. It is clear that the amount of R&D funding in RE technologies over the duration of the RE programme has been very inconsistent, as shown in Figure 10.2. In 2001, annual expenditure was $300 million (1992 dollars).

Davis and Owens assumed that at the current rate of annual spending ($300 million), RE costs will decline by 1 per cent annually. They assume also that with increased R&D spending this rate will increase, although they cap this annual rate of decline at 4 per cent. At this maximum rate, an expenditure of $1.2 billion/year in R&D in RE is optimal and will lead to a net benefit of $50 billion (2000 dollars).[5] The authors emphasize that these numerical results are a function of the input values and it is clear that the assumptions of the relationship between R&D expenditure and cost decrease require further analysis. In sum, however, it appears that this could be a valid method to assess R&D expenditure and it is a good attempt to quantify the benefits and costs of expenditure using empirical data.

The size of the savings depends very strongly on when GHG abatement is carried out. The options are to continue to invest in R&D in GHG technologies or wait until the technologies are ready for cost-effective deployment. However this ignores the fact that a significant fraction of technology cost reductions are achieved through 'learning by doing', which means that the technologies must be introduced to the market to gain the experience required to lower the cost (Miketa and Schrattenholzer, 2004; Turton, 2005). It seems that the best approach will be to use a mix of options including both deployment and waiting. Kopp (1998) suggests that the introduction of GHG R&D-related incentives or the announcement of carbon taxes from a concrete point in time would induce private R&D expenditure and accelerate technological change. Market incentives such as carbon taxes and tradable permit schemes would encourage inventive activity more than technology-specific mandates and subsidies, since it is difficult to foresee which specific technologies are likely to be the most cost-effective options over the longer term.

10.5   TRANSPORT R&D

There is considerable private and public R&D carried out in the passenger car sector in all major car-producing regions of the world. The nature of passenger car research is extremely competitive and therefore collaborations among companies or with government tend to be in precompetitive research. There is very little ex post evaluation of the return on investment of passenger car research mainly owing to the secrecy surrounding costs in this area. Europe, the US and Japan all have significant public–private R&D programmes to reduce greenhouse gas emissions from passenger cars.

In January 2003, President Bush launched the $1.2 billion FreedomCAR and Fuel Initiative. This programme already existed in the form of the FreedomCAR and Vehicle Technologies Programme, although the new initiative provides further support. The goal of FreedomCAR is to develop emission- and petroleum-free cars and light trucks. FreedomCAR 'focuses on the high-risk research needed to develop the necessary technologies, such as fuel cells and advanced hybrid propulsion systems, to provide a full range of affordable cars and light trucks that are free of foreign oil and harmful emissions' – and that do not sacrifice freedom of mobility and freedom of vehicle choice.

The mission of the US Department of Energy, Office of Energy Efficiency and Renewable Energy, is 'to strengthen America's energy security, environmental quality, and economic vitality in public–private partnerships that (a) enhance energy efficiency and productivity; (b) bring clean, reliable, and affordable energy technologies to the marketplace; and (c) make a difference in the everyday lives of US Americans by enhancing their energy choices and their quality of life'.[6] The target is to make fuel cells accessible to large numbers of US Americans by 2020.

In the EU, basic research has been mainly carried out at national level, since it is conducted predominantly in universities, which are nationally funded. In recent years the desire to foster knowledge-based economies has

forced member states to re-examine this strategy. In 2000, a European
Research Area was set up to support a more coherent research policy in
Europe. Research Framework Programmes operate as instruments with the
objectives:

> To stimulate, organise and exploit all forms of cooperation in research, from col-
> laboration in joint projects and networks to the coordination of national
> research programmes, competition at the European level as well as the joint
> implementation of large technology initiatives and the common development of
> infrastructures of European dimension and interest. (CEC, 2005d)

For example the 6th Framework programme, running between 2002 and
2006, received 28 000 research proposals involving 150 000 institutions in 50
countries. On average, 20 per cent of the proposals were funded (CEC,
2004d). One thematic priority of the Framework Programmes is sustainable development, global change and ecosystems, under which sustainable
transport is funded. Research on 'sustainable surface transport' has been
allocated €670 million in funding over the period of the programme (out of
nearly €18 billion in total), which appears low compared with the US
FreedomCAR and Fuel Initiative. The sustainable surface transport work
programme is planned to achieve research objectives that implement the
policies set out in the Commission White Paper on European Transport
Policy, 'European transport policy for 2010: time to decide'. There are four
main objectives:

> Objective 1: new technologies and concepts for all surface transport
> modes (road, rail and waterborne),
> Objective 2: advanced design and production techniques,
> Objective 3: rebalancing and integrating different transport modes,
> Objective 4: increasing road, rail and waterborne safety and avoiding
> traffic congestion.

As the mode of transport responsible for most of the sector's greenhouse
gas emissions, road transport has attracted a lot of public R&D attention.
For example, there are European projects under way, such as the CIVITAS
initiative, which 'helps cities to achieve a more sustainable, clean and energy
efficient urban transport system by implementing and evaluating an ambitious, integrated set of technology and policy based measures', and
ECTOS, which is a demonstration project operating hydrogen fuel cell
buses in Reykjavik. In Iceland, there is considerable interest in fuel cells,
since 55 TWh per year of electrical energy can be harnessed economically
from geothermal and hydroelectric sources, at electricity costs of only
$0.02/kWh. Hydrogen produced from this source becomes increasingly

attractive with increases in the price of oil (Jonsson, 2003). The goal of the EU Framework Programme 'sustainable surface transport' research is to assist in achieving a hydrogen economy within a few decades. Some of these programmes comprise investment in deployment and diffusion rather than basic R&D, which are important complements to R&D.

Fuel cells also play a part in the Japanese strategy to reduce greenhouse gases from passenger cars. The Ministry of Land, Infrastructure and Transportation has stated that the development and diffusion of fuel cells will contribute to curbing emissions of carbon dioxide in the transportation and public welfare sectors. Therefore they are encouraged, through measures such as setting up a fuel cell project team, as well as promoting development of fuel cell vehicles and their introduction in governmental fleet. The Toyota Motor Show in October 2003 featured fuel cell vehicles from Toyota Motor Co., Nissan Motor Co., Honda Motor Co., Mitsubishi Motor Co. and Suzuki Motor Co. Honda has delivered three fuel cell vehicles to government offices and plans a limited market release of about 30 vehicles over the next two or three years in Japan and the US. Toyota has delivered to date six fuel cell hybrid vehicles in the US and Japan.

10.6   SUMMARY

- Technological innovation is likely to be a key requirement to reducing greenhouse gas emissions from passenger cars. It is partially driven by R&D investment.
- The 'public good' nature of R&D investment means that private firm R&D alone will not be sufficient to maximize net social benefits and therefore additional public R&D support is necessary (either directly or to stimulate additional private sector R&D).
- Although most countries undertake R&D investment as a policy measure to mitigate greenhouse gas emissions, there is very little ex post empirical analysis to estimate the rate of return on this investment.
- Technological developments, particularly invention and innovation, are highly uncertain processes. Despite this important caveat, R&D investment models can provide some insights into the amount of investment required to achieve technological improvements.
- Innovations are taking place in the energy efficiency of passenger cars, by improving the efficiency of conventional technology, such as petrol and diesel combustion, or developing new alternative technology that consumes less fuel and therefore produces much lower CO_2 emissions.

- Improvements in technology may not be sufficient to reduce CO_2 emissions to the level required. An appropriate hedging strategy should also include other policy interventions.
- A complementary deployment policy is necessary to R&D investment in order to ensure that technologies make the transition from innovation to market diffusion.

NOTES

1. Recall also that the analysis presented in Chapters 5 and 6 attempts to include the potential impact of technology learning on deployment of advanced vehicle and other technologies. See Section 4.2 for more details on the representation of learning in the ERIS model.
2. The assumption 'that the benefit to the marginal adopter from acquisition decreases as the number of previous adopters increases' (Karshenas and Stoneman, 1993).
3. The assumption 'that the return to a firm from adopting new technology depends on its position in the order of adoption, with high-order adopters achieving a greater return than low-order adopters' (Karshenas and Stoneman, 1993).
4. They follow Romer (1986) and assume 'diminishing returns to each factor including knowledge in the production function and reserving the linear knowledge–output relationship for *exogenous* spillover knowledge'.
5. This assumes linearity, which may be somewhat unrealistic.
6. Available at http://www.eere.energy.gov/hydrogenfuel/.

PART IV

Roadmap to a sustainable transport system

11. Future technology developments in transport

Future technology choice is one of the important elements in the realization of a sustainable transport system over the long term. However, there are a number of challenges to overcome before the advantages of new and emerging technologies can be fully exploited. To address these challenges policymakers are utilizing a range of measures, described in Part III of this book, that aim to shift today's transport systems towards sustainability.

The question of how and in what form sustainable development may ultimately manifest or materialize in the transport sector was explored in Chapter 5, where we described one configuration of a possible future long-term global sustainable transport system. From this scenario we can extract a number of key developments in vehicle and fuel production technologies needed for the emergence of a sustainable transport system. The analysis in Chapter 6 helped show which of the developments in the sustainable transport scenario presented in Chapter 5 are unlikely to emerge without some form of public support or intervention.

Sustainable development has been defined in Chapter 1 to include sustainable goals of economic growth, increasing equity between world regions, a reduction of global environmental stress, in particular carbon emissions, and maintaining secure energy supplies. The sustainable development scenario from Chapter 5 provides a dynamic picture of the technologies that may be required to shape sustainable transport. It illustrates the potential to achieve through technical innovation close to zero greenhouse gas emissions in 2100.

On this basis, this chapter summarizes the main long-term technology transitions identified in the scenario analysis in Chapter 5, and some of the implications for policy support. It is important to reiterate that the longer-term technology choices and energy system developments identified in Chapter 5 (such as in Figure 5.3) can be significantly influenced by near-term policies, which is why we focused in Part III on a range of short- to medium-term policy instruments. This is because, as discussed in Chapter 1, energy and transport systems relying on long-lived infrastructure can change only slowly, and so policy and investment choices today will have a significant bearing on the shape of transport and energy systems in decades to come. Moreover, the large-scale deployment and diffusion of technologies that are currently in the early stage of development or commercialization will also take time, and so long-term sustainability goals can only be realized if nearer-term policies provide sufficient support to those technologies most compatible with sustainable development.

We now turn to the main technology transitions in Chapter 5 and examine the specific technology developments needed to achieve sustainable automobility.

11.1   PASSENGER VEHICLE TECHNOLOGY DEVELOPMENTS

On the basis of the analysis of past trends in Chapter 1 it appears very likely that the private motor vehicle will continue to be an important technology throughout the 21st century. In order to achieve close to zero greenhouse gas emissions from transport by 2100, a transition from conventional petroleum internal combustion engines (ICEs) is required and the scenario in Chapter 5 identifies fuel cell vehicles as a possible replacement that can achieve sustainable development objectives, such as low greenhouse gas emissions.

However, the technology development and deployment path described by the sustainable transport scenario presented in Chapter 5 includes important roles for a number of bridging, or transition, technologies. The first significant technology development to occur in the transport sector under this scenario is the rapid adoption of hybrid-electric ICE technologies in the first half of the 21st century, reaching almost 10 per cent of travel by 2020, increasing to above 20 per cent by 2030 and peaking at almost 60 per cent in 2050. This hybrid technology configuration does not represent a radical departure from current ICE technology, and supplements existing vehicles systems and engineering requirements. These vehicles also continue to rely initially on the current fuel distribution infrastructure, although natural gas begins to replace petroleum as the main fuel for ICE and hybrid vehicles during the first half of the 21st century. This occurs because of the lower greenhouse gas emissions from natural gas, combined with depletion of cheap sources of conventional oil. By 2030, around 10 per cent of vehicles globally run on natural gas in the sustainable transport scenario, peaking at over 40 per cent in 2050.

The experience with manufacturing and assembling HEVs on a large scale leads to a rapid decrease in the incremental costs of hybrid vehicles, related mainly to the battery and system control, which increases their attractiveness. Improved and cheaper hybrid technology also helps with the longer-term introduction of fuel cell vehicles, where hybrid systems reduce the fuel cell power requirements, and hence the size and cost of the fuel cell system.

Experience with fuel cell vehicles in the scenario presented in Chapter 5 leads to a decrease in production costs for fuel cell technology overall also, although barriers remain because of the relative technical immaturity and higher cost of this technology (compared to HEVs), combined with the need to develop alternative fuel production and distribution systems. The limited availability of appropriate fuels and fuel distribution infrastructure is a significant impediment to the deployment of fuel cell vehicles relying on hydrogen and alcohols. Consequently, in the sustainable transport scenario described in Chapter 5, the fuel cell technology that is initially adopted on the largest scale is the one that can use existing fuel distribution infrastructure – the petroleum FCV. Late in the first half of the 21st century, petroleum FCVs are the leading passenger FCV technology, although they account for only a small share of the transport market. As mentioned above, this early adoption of petroleum FCV technologies facilitates experience with producing FCV systems on a large scale, leading to a rapid decrease in the costs of fuel cell system components, benefiting all FCV technologies (and, to a limited extent, stationary fuel cell technologies). It also allows the costs of the ultimate transition to hydrogen fuel cells to be spread over a longer period, so consumers and society are not confronted simultaneously with both the initially high costs of FCVs and the cost of establishing a new fuel production and distribution infrastructure.

Eventually, the drawbacks of petroleum fuel cell vehicles, including lower efficiency due to the need to reform fuel on-board, and carbon emissions, constrain their large-scale uptake, and they disappear from the market early in the second half of the century when other fuels become widely available. However, already by this stage fuel cell vehicles dominate the transport market under this scenario, and this dominance increases as the century progresses. By 2100, fuel cell vehicles account for close to 80 per cent of total travel, leaving only limited markets where alcohol- and gas-based ICE–HEV technologies continue to be attractive because of regional circumstances, possibly including limited availability of hydrogen.

As alluded to above, the fuel cell technologies that emerge to dominate automobile transport later in the century are fuelled almost entirely by either hydrogen or alcohols. H_2 and alcohol FCVs are ideal technologies for pursuing sustainable development, since both fuels can be produced from renewable resources, and pollution from these vehicles is also very low. Under the sustainable transport scenario described in Chapter 5, almost all world regions adopt one or the other of these technologies for most of their car transport requirements. This regional variability is illustrated in

Figure 5.4, and is partly determined partly by regional resource endowments. It is important to note that alcohol fuel cell vehicles remain attractive in some regions despite the lower end-use efficiency (due to on-board reforming) compared to hydrogen fuel cell vehicles.

It should be briefly mentioned that other technologies are also assumed to be adopted under the sustainable transport scenario, including lightweight materials, reduced rolling resistance tyres, better aerodynamics and incremental improvements in all drivetrain technologies, to name a few. These improve the fuel efficiency of all the engine configurations described above.

In broad global terms, technological development in passenger transport under this sustainable development scenario manifests as a transition from ICEs to ICE–HEVs to FCVs, with the last transition being the most critical for the emergence of a sustainable transport system. However, the introduction of technologies and energy carriers that are not compatible with the dominating technological regime can be very difficult (Kemp, 1997a; 1997b). Accordingly, given the current status of fuel cell technologies, where there exist technical barriers to commercial success, there is still a need for support for research and development (R&D) to reduce the costs of realizing a sustainable transport system.

The vehicle technology transition described above occurs hand-in-hand with a shift in transport fuels, initially from petroleum to gas to alcohols and hydrogen, with petroleum playing a critical role in the transition to hydrogen and alcohol FCVs. The necessary developments in fuel production for realizing the sustainable transport scenario presented in Chapter 5 are described below.

11.2 FUEL PRODUCTION FOR SUSTAINABLE TRANSPORT

The passenger car technology roadmap described above is incomplete without an accompanying fuel production technology roadmap. The developments in the global secondary-fuel production and distribution system under the sustainable transport scenario described in Chapter 5 are in many ways as important for realizing a sustainable and low-carbon transport and energy system as the adoption of new vehicle technologies. This is because the portfolio of vehicle technologies needed to realize sustainable greenhouse gas emissions can only be deployed if complementary fuel production technologies and systems are also in place.

One important fuel production feature of the sustainable transport scenario presented in Chapter 5 is the continuing importance of petroleum fuels. This occurs partly because of inertia in fuel production and distribution

Table 11.1   *Breakdown of transportation technologies by share of total transport energy demand*

Year	FCV H$_2$	FCV alcohol	FCV petroleum	ICE and aviation turbine H$_2$	ICE alcohol	ICE and pipeline compression systems CNG	ICE and aviation turbine petroleum	Steam engine coal
2000					0.43%	3%	97%	0.30%
2050	5%	3%	3%		4%	23%	62%	
2100	37%	5%	0%	16%	16%	4%	23%	

Note: rows may not add to 100 per cent owing to rounding errors.

systems (particularly the time required to establish equivalent systems for alternative fuels) but also because of limited substitution possibilities in some transport sectors, particularly in jet aircraft. Consequently, oil refinery output remains above the level in 2000 throughout the century, although it peaks in around 2040.

Table 11.1 presents the estimated progression of different fuel shares and transport technologies across all modes of transport between 2000 and 2100. While there is still a significant amount of petroleum used in 2100, it is mainly used for aircraft operation rather than passenger cars.

Under the scenario outlined in Chapter 5, the first significant development in the fuel mix in transport is an increasingly important role for natural gas. In many world regions the production and distribution infrastructure for this fuel is well developed, and most of the barriers to greater use of this natural gas in transport relate to the availability of vehicles able to use this fuel.

Chronologically, one of the next important features to emerge in fuel production under the sustainable transport scenario is the expansion of biomass-to-alcohol production, from comparatively very low levels today. This was shown in Figure 5.5. Alcohol fuels are initially attractive because they can be handled relatively easily and transported using existing infrastructure. However, the large-scale mobilization of biomass poses a number of significant challenges, which also apply to hydrogen production from biomass. These challenges relate particularly to finding sufficient productive land to devote to fuel production, while satisfying increasing human needs for food and fibre, and at very least *maintaining* environmental amenity. The scale of biomass production is best illustrated by considering that the resource potential identified by Rogner (1997; 2000) (and used here) was based on the availability of an additional 1.3 billion hectares of land globally.[1] Clearly, biomass production on a scale of this order of magnitude must address other aspects of sustainable development, including effective water and soil management, nutrient recycling and preservation of organic matter (Reijnders, 2005).

In addition to the necessary significant transformation to land management systems, and utilization of all organic waste streams, sustainable biomass production faces other challenges. Harvesting and transporting biomass to fuel synthesis plants represents a significant logistical challenge, considering the scale of biomass-based fuel production envisaged in the sustainable development scenario in Chapter 5. On the other hand, this may promote smaller-scale decentralized alcohol and hydrogen synthesis close to the feedstock source. Such decentralization, however, may merely shift logistical difficulties further down the production chain. On the other hand, there may also be benefits compared to today's relatively centralized oil industry because fuel production and demand centres may be proximate (compared to today's oil industry which relies on long-distance transport), and the fuel production system will no longer necessarily depend on a small number of large critical infrastructures (such as pipelines, shipping terminals and refineries) but instead on a less vulnerable network of energy producers.

Further developments in fuel production are partly illustrated in Figure 5.5, which shows the increasing importance of alcohol and hydrogen fuels required for the transition to sustainable technologies in transport. One can envisage that towards the end of the century biorefineries will exist on a scale similar to that of oil refineries today, producing a combination of alcohols, hydrogen and other petrochemical products, such as lubricants, bioplastics and other chemicals.

The challenges of mobilizing biomass feedstock on a large scale constrain somewhat the expansion of alcohol (and hydrogen) production in the sustainable transport scenario presented in Chapter 5. However, by the end of the first half of the 21st century most of these are overcome, and from then onwards alcohol production from biomass grows rapidly. Alcohols can also be thought of as a transition fuel that can achieve sustainability objectives before hydrogen distribution infrastructure is established. In the scenario in Chapter 5, these additional difficulties with distributing and handling hydrogen delay the large-scale production from biomass of this fuel until closer to 2080, although after this time the higher end-use efficiency of hydrogen fuel cell vehicles leads to a shift from alcohol to hydrogen production.

Looking more closely at hydrogen production, the preferred synthesis route remains steam methane reforming of natural gas for much of the 21st century (recalling that hydrogen can be produced from a range of feedstocks, including coal, gas and biomass, and via electrolysis of water). However, feedstock availability is not a major barrier with hydrogen production and utilization in transport compared to the need to create an extensive fuel distribution network. Once this network is established, however, the hydrogen can be produced from a variety of fossil and non-fossil primary-energy sources, with biomass becoming particularly attractive later in the century, and to a lesser extent hydrogen production from electrolysis of water. Importantly, the feedstock preference varies according to resource availability in different world regions, which illustrates also that using hydrogen can bring concrete energy security benefits as part of a transition to a sustainable energy system (Barreto et al., 2003).

Accordingly, above we have identified a number of key phases in the development of fuel production and distribution, comprising the following:

a. initially, additional use of gas in transport;
b. development of an extensive biomass feedstock production and processing system, while still satisfying human needs for food and fibre without expanding agricultural production in an unsustainable way;[2] and
c. the need to develop the storage and distribution infrastructure for hydrogen, and to a lesser extent alcohol fuels.

In the following chapter we discuss some of the implications of these developments, particularly the last two, which represent a major deviation from current trends in energy system development.

To summarize, the major new technologies necessary to realize the sustainable transport system described in Chapter 5 include hybrid vehicle technologies and fuel cell systems (including reformers), along with alcohol and hydrogen fuel production and distribution systems and infrastructure. This highlights the potential importance of innovation, in terms both of technology and of policy support, in a transition to sustainability. Given the slow rates at which energy and transport infrastructure develops, and the need for a major transformation of the energy system indicated in this study, this analysis provides further support for the notion that early and consistent action is necessary to achieve sustainable mobility.

However, in connection to ERIS's 'social planner' view, we should underline that a technological strategy such as the one described above is not the *only* technological strategy suited to achieve sustainable development. A number of other possible sustainable-development scenarios are described in, for example, Riahi et al. (2001) and Miketa and Schrattenholzer (2004), relying on other technological options.[3] Moreover, the scenario presented here explores a future world where efforts to reduce travel demand are no more or less successful than historical efforts. If governments and other actors are to be more successful in developing the institutions and incentives to change consumer preferences in terms of vehicle characteristics and travel behaviour, comparatively less effort will be needed in terms of adoption of advanced vehicle and fuel technologies to realize a more sustainable transport system.

NOTES

1. Which is similar to other estimates, such as in Fischer and Schrattenholzer (2001).
2. Sustainable agriculture was not explicitly mentioned as one of the sustainability criteria introduced in Box 1.1 for assessing E3 scenarios, but it is still an essential feature of sustainable development.
3. One example is the IIASA–WEC–A3 scenario relying on natural gas and nuclear energy.

12. Implications for policymaking

Over the last 30 years transport, in particular road transport, has been responsible for an increasing share of energy consumption and associated greenhouse gas emissions. The scenario described in Chapter 6 illustrates how this trend can be expected to continue if no intervention is made to address externalities in market operation, leading to an unsustainable transport system. A sustainable transport system, on the other hand, is more consistent with the scenario presented in Chapter 5, in which greenhouse gas emissions from transport in 2100 are roughly equal to or less than greenhouse gas emissions in 2000.

One of the challenges to realizing a sustainable transport system incorporated in the analysis presented earlier in Chapters 5 and 6 is that achieving other goals of sustainable development, such as economic development and more income equality between world regions, is likely to stimulate today's developing regions to follow a similar path of development to that followed in today's developed regions, leading to high levels of demand for private mobility. This presents not only challenges, but also opportunities for sustainable development. The previous chapter has summarized a number of well understood, technically viable alternative motor vehicle technologies at or near market standard that have the potential to alleviate some of the environmental impacts concomitant with the increase in road transport envisaged in the scenarios presented in earlier chapters.

However, as discussed briefly in Chapter 11, the introduction of technologies and energy carriers that are not compatible with the dominating technological regime can be very difficult (Kemp, 1997a; 1997b). This potential challenge relates to many of the technologies identified as important to realizing longer-term sustainable development, including hybrid-electric systems, and natural gas and alcohol fuels, but perhaps the most significant challenges relate more to fuel cell and hydrogen deployment. These technologies represent a significant departure from today's petroleum-based transport system requiring the development, essentially from scratch, of a complete technology chain including fuel production, distribution and retailing, in addition to overcoming technical barriers in the end-use fuel cell systems. Given the current status of fuel cell technologies, achieving commercialization still requires additional support for research and development (R&D) to reduce the costs.

The scale of the barriers associated with deploying hydrogen fuel cell vehicles, potentially the technology–fuel combination most compatible with longer-term sustainable development, identifies an important target for government intervention. As seen in Chapter 6, current market drivers alone are unlikely to stimulate the technology transition required for large-scale deployment of fuel cells.

To understand the implications for policymakers, and to begin to identify potential interventions, it is helpful to look at some of the elements of (and barriers to) a sustainable transport system separately. Two important elements discussed in Chapter 11 include the development of an extensive biomass production and processing system and hydrogen infrastructure. Developing these upstream elements of possible future transport system is likely to require a long-term overall strategic vision and substantial investment, and face long lead times before becoming profitable. This highlights the need for innovative approaches to investment, including public–private partnerships (for example, see PCAST, 1999), and the role for governments in providing the strategic framework in which private sector expertise can be exploited to realize long-term social goals, while ensuring other aspects of sustainability are addressed. Policy measures could include public financial incentives, efficiency standards and regulations, procurement programmes, technology R&D support, voluntary agreements and other measures and instruments discussed in Chapters 7–10.

Critically, the rate at and extent to which transport system development can be redirected towards sustainability depends substantially on the suite of policies implemented by governments around the world. The objective of this chapter is to assess the implications for policymaking of the technology transitions identified as important for achieving a sustainable transport system in the 21st century.

12.1   COMPARING TWO SCENARIOS

The two main scenarios described earlier in this book, in Chapters 5 and 6, provide a useful point of comparison from which to elucidate important policy objectives. To recap, the scenarios developed with the ERIS model describe (1) a future in which sustainable development is pursued explicitly; and (2) a 'no policy' scenario in which market forces alone determine future energy system development. These scenarios are otherwise identical, both being based on the B2 storyline from the IPCC Special Report on Emissions Scenarios (Nakićenović and Swart, 2000), which follows the median population and economic growth from a large number of scenario studies. In other words, both scenarios include the same assumptions regarding social and economic drivers, which generate the same demand for mobility and final energy.

The main difference in the assumptions used to generate the two sets of scenario results is that we assume that two aspects of sustainability, in particular greenhouse gas emission abatement and strategic management of resource depletion,[1] are pursued vigorously in the sustainable development scenario, but ignored in the 'no policy' scenario. In the latter scenario, this means that key current policy drivers of energy system development are excluded, including current and future climate change mitigation policies, efforts to promote energy security and some aspects of technology development (such as R&D).

It is helpful to compare some of the energy system development trends in the sustainable development scenario (Chapter 5) with those occurring in the scenario which excludes any policy or societal support for sustainability, presented in Chapter 6. Perhaps the best way to illustrate the main differences between these two scenarios is to compare two comprehensive measures of the environmental sustainability of automobile transport (the average efficiency and well-to-wheels emissions per kilometre of travel) in both scenarios. Figure 12.1 brings together results presented earlier in this book, and illustrates the importance of both higher efficiency and switching to low-carbon fuels in reducing greenhouse gas emissions in the sustainable transport scenario.

From our perspective, the divergence in greenhouse gas emissions in 2100 between the 'no policy' and sustainable, development scenarios reinforces the need for public intervention.

The divergence illustrated in Figure 12.1 occurs for a number of reasons, some of which we have already mentioned briefly. Initially, the scenarios diverge in terms of the rate and scale of adoption of HEV technologies, with reliance on conventional ICE vehicles continuing for much longer under the no-policy scenario. However, even in the absence of efforts to realize a more sustainable transport system, HEVs eventually become very attractive because of increasing fuel costs (resulting from depletion of cheap oil resources) and the resulting experience with manufacturing HEVs on a large-scale leads to decreasing costs and widespread penetration into the passenger transport market.

This is not the case with fuel cell vehicles, and without a desire to achieve sustainable development this automobile technology remains largely uncompetitive until towards the very end of the 21st century (see Figure 6.2). This is in contrast to the developments in the sustainable transport scenario in Chapter 5, where rapid adoption of fuel cell vehicles is desirable in order to exploit their high levels of fuel efficiency.

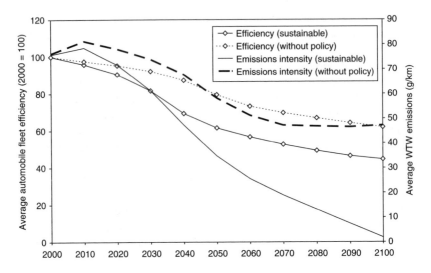

Figure 12.1   Comparison of efficiency and emissions intensity of car transport, sustainable transport and without-policy scenarios

Another important area of divergence, which accounts for a significant proportion of the divergence in well-to-wheels emissions presented in Figure 12.1 occurs in upstream fuel production. Without active pursuit of sustainable development, large-scale production of alcohol and hydrogen fuels fails to develop, with these fuels accounting for only a minor share of transport energy demand under the scenario presented in Chapter 6, and this is illustrated in Figure 12.2. Accordingly, as mentioned in Chapter 11, the technology developments associated with mobilizing these alternative fuels are as important as the vehicle technology transition in explaining the divergence in the two scenarios discussed here.

Some important indicators for the 'no policy' and sustainable transport scenarios are compared in Table 12.1. For instance, Table 12.1 shows that around 50 EJ less final energy is required to supply the same travel demand under the sustainable scenario. This is related to the superior energy efficiency in the sustainable scenario, which is reflected in the lower fuel consumption rate. As reported in Chapters 5 and 6, if the average tank-to-wheels fuel consumption values are converted to petrol-equivalent values, then the 'no policy' fuel consumption in 2100 is 6.2 l/100km, while the sustainable scenario fuel consumption rate would be 4.5 l/100km. This, along with a shift to low-emissions alcohol and hydrogen fuels, results in vastly different amounts of well-to-wheels greenhouse gas emissions from automobile transport in 2100 in the two scenarios:

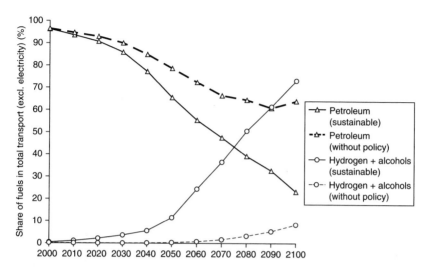

Figure 12.2   Comparison of shares of petroleum, alcohols and hydrogen, sustainable transport and without-policy scenarios

Table 12.1   Comparison of baseline (no-policy) and sustainable scenarios in 2100

Characteristic	2000	Baseline 2100	Sustainable 2100
Total transport energy demand (EJ)	80	290	240
Share of H_2 and alcohol fuels in transport (%)	0.4	8.4	73.2
Automobile travel demand (trillion km)	9	36.5	36.5
Average automobile fuel consumption rates (l/100km)	10.0	6.2	4.5
Total automobile well-to-wheels carbon emissions (Mt C)	700	1720	70

around 1700 Mt C in the no-policy scenario and less than 100 Mt C in the sustainable scenario.

12.2   BARRIERS ASSOCIATED WITH DEPLOYMENT OF ADVANCED PASSENGER CAR TECHNOLOGIES

The above discussion describes the key technology and fuel differences between the sustainable and the no-policy scenarios. This comparison has helped us identify the technologies required to realize a sustainable transport system, and potential targets for public support and government policy intervention. This is critical because there remain many technical and socio-economic barriers before this kind of technology deployment can occur.

The vehicle technology costs presented in Box 4.1 provide an insight into the considerable additional costs facing manufacturers and ultimately consumers for advanced conventional and new vehicle technologies, particularly during the early phases of technology introduction before economies of scale and the benefits of learning are realized. Similarly, the switch from petroleum to alternative fuels will incur costs for fuel refiners and distributors, although the depletion of cheap petroleum fuels means that the relative additional costs may be smaller. Partly for these reasons, even the sustainable transport system presented in Chapter 5 is, in 2050, still dominated by petroleum fuels, and largely conventional vehicle technologies. The fact that petroleum still plays such a large role 50 years into a scenario of sustainable development is largely indicative of the inertia in transport systems.

Long-term capital investments in new technologies and infrastructure are necessary to overcome the supply-side inertia in fuel production and delivery systems, requiring appropriate policy support. Importantly, the inertia in the transport sector means that the benefits of such strategic investments and technology support will not be fully realized for many decades, and these long timeframes further necessitate government involvement given potential risks.

There are important implications for the enduring role and, for a time, dominance of petroleum as a fuel for passenger cars well into the 21st century. As pressure increases on vehicle manufacturers to improve fuel efficiency in cars, the switch to diesel technology, already begun in Europe, may become more significant in advance of widespread sales of hybrid and other advanced conventional technologies. Kavalov and Peteves (2004) estimate that the feasible reserves for an increase in world diesel fraction from oil refining are between 3 and 4 per cent of the total oil refining yield. As the demand for diesel rises, production of this fuel will become more energy- and greenhouse gas-intensive, raising well-to-tank emissions. In addition, the limited flexibility to increase diesel production may create problems for the security of its supply. Production prices of diesel are forecast to rise above petrol production prices and the higher demand will create a scarcity of diesel in the market, further driving its price to increase (Kavalov and Peteves, 2004). The increasing price of diesel will contribute to the switch to alternative fuels and vehicle technology and perhaps even to petrol in the short term.

Investment in R&D partly drives environmental technological change. There are several forms of market failure at work that impede the investment in R&D necessary to drive sustainable development of passenger car transport. There is the fundamental issue of negative externalities associated with pollution; that is, if vehicle manufacturers are not affected by GHG emissions, they face few incentives to improve vehicle emission performance. Moreover, the benefits of emission abatement technologies are largely public, accruing to everyone (including future generations) and these benefits are not easily converted to returns on investment for firms (Chupka, 1997).

Jaffe et al. (2005) describe two market failures, which cause a double underinvestment in technology to reduce pollution. There are positive externalities associated with investment in R&D and the development of advanced technologies. For example, the 'public good' nature of R&D means that innovative firms cannot keep all the benefits of the innovation to themselves and therefore there are spillovers from undertaking R&D which cannot be captured by those who undertake the research. The firms therefore tend to engage in less R&D than the amount that would maximize net social benefits (Goulder, 2002).

The second externality reflects the uncertainty associated with high-risk investments such as investment in innovation. The asymmetry in information between the developer of the technology and potential investors makes it difficult for a firm to raise capital for an untried technology and more costly since investors may demand a risk premium on their investment. This effect discourages firms from investing in new vehicle and fuel technologies.

Additionally, many forms of energy used currently do not adequately reflect the external costs they impose, with regard to the greenhouse gas emissions and other externalities, although as fuel prices increase the prices may begin to match some of the external costs of energy. Nevertheless there is little benefit gained to the firm that produces products which use less energy in their operation and production. The additional costs incurred in a more advanced vehicle and reflected in the price are generally viewed in a negative light by consumers. Although some or all of the additional cost may be recovered in fuel savings over the lifetime of the vehicle, consumers often do not compare prices of vehicles taking fuel costs over the vehicle life into consideration. There often may not be adequate information and incentives available to consumers highlighting this issue. Therefore the higher cost of advanced vehicle technologies relative to conventional technologies represents an important barrier to deployment of clean technologies. Nonetheless, some firms may still face some indirect market incentives to pursue sustainable technologies, particularly where they can secure a marketing edge by appearing to be 'green'. However, such incentives are limited and in general in the absence of public policy there will be less investment in R&D for sustainable technology, and less deployment of such technologies, than is needed for efficient environmental and economic outcomes.

12.3   HOW CAN POLICIES RESOLVE THIS?

The sustainable transport scenario modelled here presents the vehicle and fuel technology systems required to achieve very low greenhouse gas emissions from passenger cars in 2100. In the scenario in Chapter 5, this is achieved primarily through technological advance, in both vehicles and fuel production over the next 100 years. However, the section above shows that there are many barriers obstructing the path to sustainable transport. Under our no-policy scenario, carbon emissions rise to around 1700 Mt C by 2100, owing to the slower introduction of new technologies, especially fuel cell vehicles, and the continued use of petroleum fuel.

As long as barriers exist to achieving a sustainable transport scenario, government policies are needed to overcome them. Previous chapters (7–10) have described supply- and demand-side policies, or sticks and carrots, which are in use worldwide to abate greenhouse gas emissions in transport and other sectors and they are summarized in Table 12.2. These are currently applied to specific features of passenger car transport where barriers exist to achieving the abatement of greenhouse gas emissions.

The focus of the scenario on replacing vehicle technologies and fuels with low carbon passenger car systems implies that the development and deployment of these technologies at low cost must be encouraged. The rate of deployment of new technologies is partly dependent on governments' commitment to sustainable transport as reflected in their policies. Policies supporting the supply of low carbon-emitting passenger cars to the market are required. This can be achieved by providing incentives to manufacturers to supply such products and also to consumers to create a demand for

Table 12.2   Supply-side and demand-side measures to achieve low carbon vehicle and fuel technology market deployment

Measure	Target
R&D incentives	Development of advanced technology vehicles and fuels
Fuel economy regulations	Require vehicle manufacturers to produce vehicles with high fuel economy
Voluntary agreements to reduce average CO_2 emissions	Require vehicle manufacturers to produce vehicles with low CO_2 emissions
Alternative fuels quotas	Introduction of alternative fuels to market, develop alternative fuel infrastructure
Tax breaks for advanced fuels and vehicle (AFVs) technologies	Incentive for consumers to purchase AFVs and alternative fuels, that is, create demand
Convert all fixed vehicle charges to distance-based taxes and charges	Reduce vehicle travel demand, counteract 'rebound effect' of purchase of efficient vehicles
Convert variable charges to CO_2-differentiated charges	Encourage purchase of AFVs

them. It is a common concern among vehicle manufacturers that, after making significant investments in low carbon technologies, there will not be a market demand for them. In general, economic instruments have been shown to provide more dynamic incentives than command and control measures for lower cost abatement through technological change (Requate, 2005).

One method to support the development of low-carbon technologies is through government support of private and public R&D. As described in Chapter 11, public support of R&D is necessary, particularly for technologies that are furthest from market deployment. Pre-competitive research represents a potential target for public R&D because the higher risk, and the limited ability of private firms to appropriate the benefits, mean under-investment is likely for technologies in this phase of development. There are signs that this has been recognized by governments and there are examples worldwide of public financial support for research groups and industry–public partnerships at a national level. Internationally, Japanese and US governments have signed a joint statement of intent to

pursue pre-competitive R&D in fuel cell and hydrogen technologies. The countries will bring together appropriate officials and technical experts to participate

4

4.

in workshops and seminars, as well as exchange experts and share information on current policies, technological programs, and developments in fuel cells and hydrogen production, storage and transport technologies. (Fuel Cells Bulletin, 2004).

In addition, an International Partnership for the Hydrogen Economy was established in 2003 by 14 countries, including the US and also the European Commission. Programmes such as these enable manufacturers to carry out R&D both in a private capacity to obtain a competitive edge in advanced technologies and within a public framework on pre-competitive research topics with public and industry support.

Another method of encouraging the supply of low-carbon vehicles is for governments simply to introduce regulations that command the sale of such vehicles. The CAFE regulation in the US is an example of such a scheme. However, there are some drawbacks associated with government deciding the level of fleet fuel economy or any other emissions standards. The negotiation process will almost certainly be subject to lobbying and therefore the regulation may not be sufficiently stringent to achieve optimal outcomes. Inefficiencies exist in many regulations, which allow no flexibility within a sector to comply with the regulation and so all firms must meet the same standard, regardless of whether it is costly for them to do so or not. Without equalization of marginal abatement costs within a sector, a regulation does not achieve abatement at least cost. Although in practice there are some examples of the use of regulation to achieve greenhouse gas abatement, it is becoming increasingly less popular as a policy instrument in environmental management policy as a result of these aspects.

An offshoot of regulation is the area of negotiated voluntary agreements (VAs), where for instance automobile manufacturers agree to reduce greenhouse gas emissions from the cars they produce. The main example of this is seen in the EU, where manufacturers have committed themselves to reducing CO_2 emissions from passenger cars by 25 per cent between 1995 and 2008. In the implementation of a voluntary agreement, there is not a huge difference from a regulation, especially if the agreement is binding. The disadvantages attributed to regulations above are valid for many voluntary agreements. The main advantage to policymakers is that it may be easier to implement a voluntary agreement than a regulation, which may require legislation. From the firm's perspective, there may be more flexibility in meeting the targets in a VA, which have a higher chance of being sectoral rather than firm-specific compared to simple regulation. However, during the target negotiation process, there is usually an asymmetry of information, in that firms have a much better idea of the level of greenhouse gas abatement potential, and the costs associated, than policymakers. This can lead to imbalance in the negotiation of targets, and the establishment of less than optimal standards.

Environmental regulations, or the threat of them, can stimulate R&D in GHG abatement technologies. If a firm realizes that the regulation of fuel consumption or greenhouse gas emissions is imminent, it may undertake additional R&D in developing abatement technologies in advance of the regulation in order to lower its marginal cost of abatement when the time comes. If it has undertaken and developed an abatement technology in advance of its competitors, it may even lobby for the introduction of stricter regulations or a VA to give it the competitive edge.

The European and Japanese automobile manufacturers' position papers on achieving a more stringent CO_2 emissions target of 120 g/km for passenger cars in Europe all state that it would be impossible to achieve deployment of advanced vehicle technologies without government fiscal incentives to encourage consumers to purchase these technologies. This may reflect strategic behaviour by manufacturers, but there is a genuine concern that, without demand in the marketplace for low carbon technologies, manufacturers will be unable to pass on to consumers all the costs of development and production of low-carbon vehicles. Indeed, much of the transport economics literature focuses on transport demand management (TDM), which uses price signals to reduce travel demand and indirectly create a demand for low carbon technologies.

Greene and Plotkin (2001) modelled energy scenarios for the US transport sector and estimate that, under existing policies, energy consumption and greenhouse gas emissions from transport will increase by approximately 45 per cent between 1997 and 2020. When they included in their model policies such as support for R&D in low carbon technologies, biofuels commercialization programmes and tax credits for hybrid vehicles, energy consumption and greenhouse gas emissions were still estimated to increase by approximately one-third by 2020. Only when they modelled a voluntary agreement or a regulation to increase fuel economy and all vehicle costs were switched to distance-based charges was growth in transport energy and greenhouse gas emissions curtailed, with a rise of 16 per cent of the former and 12 per cent of the latter, respectively, by 2020 (which also indicates some decoupling of energy demand and emissions).

This serves as a good example of the portfolio of policies that will be needed to introduce advanced low-carbon technologies to the market globally. Many types of travel demand instruments are described in Chapter 8. Most have the common goal of trying to internalize the external costs of transport using price signals to consumers. This also underscores the 'polluter pays principle'. The conversion of fixed costs such as annual vehicle circulation taxes or insurance charges to variable charges represents more holistic policymaking. By differentiating the charges by CO_2 emissions, motorists are encouraged to purchase a low-carbon vehicle and simultaneously to reduce the distance travelled. A reduction in distances travelled is beneficial to the reduction of other externalities caused by passenger cars: congestion, noise, local air pollutants and accidents, as well as greenhouse gas emissions. This is important since these other externalities cause significant damages, in some regions more than others. Indeed, Mayeres and Proost (2001) argue that greenhouse gas emissions may not be the most important transport-related issue for us to deal with in the future.

12.4 SUMMARY

- There is a wide difference in the amount of greenhouse gas emissions produced under the 'no policy' and sustainable scenarios.
- Policies are needed to support the development of new passenger car technologies and to create market demand for them.
- An overview of the portfolio of policy measure categories that will be needed and the direct transport issue they deal with is given in Table 12.2.

NOTE

1. Modelled explicitly as a requirement that global resource-to-production ratios of oil and natural gas be maintained above 30 years throughout the century.

13. Sustainable automobile transportation: synthesis of key conclusions

We own and drive cars for many reasons. Our car is a form of attire; it makes a statement about who we are and how much money we have. It expresses our self-image, or how we want to be viewed by the world. It also can be a symbol of freedom – a way of escaping from place and people, and a means out of constraint and into opportunity. It is also a means of transport, of getting from home to work, and from work to social interaction, with the time of departure decided by us. Some resist all these blandishments and never own or drive a car, and this itself makes a statement about us to the world. But for most, car ownership or access to the use of a car is a high priority, to be indulged as soon as circumstance and funds allow. As economies grow and associated per capita income rises, numbers of cars purchased and driven rise also.

And so 'freedom of the road' is embraced by most as a 'good thing', yielding many benefits individually and collectively.

But there are costs, and the cost litany seems to grow over time. These include death and maiming as a result of car-related accidents; emission of air pollutants, including nitrogen oxides, particulates and volatile organic compounds, which under certain conditions can make existence very unpleasant and in extreme circumstances threaten life itself; congestion, as too many cars compete for a given road space, resulting in wasted fuel and time, and increasing stress; and increasing dependence on imports of oil and gas from parts of the world that are increasingly unstable, with associated vulnerability to interruptions or other shocks associated with military and security issues. In addition, transport is recognized as the main area of growth in emissions of greenhouse gases everywhere.

This book is devoted to exploring how to address this last challenge, to answer the question: how can we stabilize and reduce the emissions of greenhouse gases from cars, while at the same time meeting the rising needs for mobility of a growing and more affluent population? The challenge is daunting, and means changing what we drive, and how we behave. The key message of this book is that this transition is indeed possible, and need not be painful. Although the focus is on managing greenhouse gas emissions, doing so will also contribute to mitigating most of the other costs associated with cars. If we reduce fossil fuel consumption we reduce dependence on imports from insecure parts of the world, reduce emissions of air pollutants and of greenhouse gases. If we drive more slowly, we will reduce the number of accidents and associated deaths and injuries, and fuel consumption and greenhouse gas emissions will fall. But there can be tradeoffs: a heavier and larger car may be safer, but it can use more fuel and emit more greenhouse gases than lighter models, and some technology choices can reduce greenhouse gas emissions but may result in increases in nitrogen oxide emissions.

As we address the challenge of greenhouse gas emissions from cars, it is important to be aware that we are not starting from a clean slate. We have already taken a variety of measures that contribute to a transition to a low carbon sector. For example, the European automobile industry invests approximately €20 billion annually in R&D, which represents 20 per cent of total European manufacturing R&D, while Japanese and American automobile companies' investments in R&D represent 13 per cent and 15 per cent, respectively, of the national R&D expenditure in manufacturing in those countries. Much of the investment has been driven by environmental concerns, for example in powertrain technology or light-weight materials (CEC, 2004d). This investment has yielded major gains in fuel efficiency, and created a knowledge base that may allow the industry to move from the internal combustion engine to fuel cell technology.

Further, our governments have imposed taxes on cars at time of registration, annually (called 'circulation taxes' in Europe) and on fuel in the form of excise duties (where the tax is based on the quantity of fuel, rather than the value). Although these taxes developed in Europe after the Second World War as a means of rationing scarcity and raising funds for government, they have serendipitously encouraged an auto fleet that is relatively fuel-efficient compared to jurisdictions that have not imposed such taxes, and this has yielded a dividend in the form of reduced greenhouse gases. For example, the petrol excise duty imposed in the UK and Germany is the equivalent of a carbon tax worth approximately €275 and €286/ton CO_2 emissions, respectively.[1] In 2004, revenue from taxes and duties on fuels and lubricants in EU15 comprised €233 billion (ACEA, 2006). And this experiential base is very important and useful as we look forward and explore options to achieve further progress in regard to greenhouse gas emissions.

In the first part of our book, we set the stage by examining each region of the world and its characteristics and trends as regards energy use, car numbers and use, and greenhouse gas emissions. A key message is that, while the OECD countries have been the main source of automobile greenhouse gas emissions over the past 30 years, the future is likely to see Asia become a dominant source, as its share of emissions (13.8 per cent in 2000) approaches a level more in line with its share of global population (53.5 per cent in 2000) over the next century. We then examine possible global energy–economy–environment (E3) scenarios that simultaneously achieve economic, environmental and social objectives, developed on the basis of assumptions concerning growth in gross domestic product, population in each region, assuming a degree of economic convergence and decarbonization of technology, associated with the development and implementation of carbon-efficient technologies in the 21st century. This 'thought experiment' yields futures that do achieve reduced pressure from passenger cars in regard to greenhouse gas emissions. But the deliverability of these futures depends on the feasibility of developing much more carbon-efficient technologies, and implementing policies that ensure that consumers demand them. These two preoccupations comprise the second and third parts of our book.

We begin by examining the evolution of engine technologies, and what is technically feasible and likely to be available, and then address the policy mix that is likely to stimulate adoption of these technologies by consumers.

Turning first to engine technologies, we examine the internal combustion engine and the various fuel options for this technology, then discuss the introduction of electric motors and the development of hybrid engines, and finally examine the prospects for a move to fuel cell technologies. For close to a century, the internal combustion engine (ICE) has been the dominant means of propulsion, powered almost exclusively by refined oil (diesel or petrol). The ICE has been continuously improved, so that, over time, more performance has been squeezed out of each litre of oil, the most important advance in recent years being the improvement in fuel injection which has allowed efficient diesel engines to become the most dominant type of passenger car propulsion in many countries in Europe. However, compressed natural gas is also used by about half a million vehicles. Use of the latter is limited by difficulties of gas storage, which must be in cylinders either compressed as CNG or liquefied natural gas (LNG). Gas-powered vehicles produce significantly fewer harmful emissions than petrol or diesel, with the possible exception of NO_x emissions, which can be higher. Despite the dominance of oil and gas, there are three alternative fuels now in widespread use: methanol, ethanol and biodiesel. Alcohol fuels, typically methanol and ethanol, are proven alternatives to gasoline and diesel. Most of the methanol is produced by steam reforming of natural gas to produce a mixture of CO and hydrogen, called 'synthesis gas', but it can also be produced (currently at higher cost) from coal and biomass. It is viewed as a possible transition fuel to a hydrogen economy because it can readily be used to produce hydrogen. Ethanol is less corrosive and toxic, and is produced commercially in a number of countries, usually by fermenting starch crops such as corn, barley, wheat and sugar cane. Biodiesel is synthesized from waste oil or directly from oil crops and can be used as a direct substitute for conventional diesel.

Battery electric vehicles have been developed and are in limited use as an alternative to the internal combustion engine. Their attractiveness to consumers depends on the cost and performance of energy storage batteries. So far, their driving range – with a maximum of around 200 kilometres – has limited their appeal. However, if the driving range problem can be solved, and if the electricity used to charge them were to be derived from low or zero-carbon sources, their adoption would transform the greenhouse gas emission performance of the car sector. One way of escaping the tyranny of recharging is to generate the electricity on board using another energy carrier. Fuel cell vehicles generate their own electric power on board through an electrochemical process using hydrogen fuel (pure hydrogen or hydrogen-rich fuel such as methanol, natural gas or even petrol) and oxygen from the air. Although prototypes exist, difficulties of durability, dependability, catalyst poisoning, hydrogen storage on board, its distribution and the costs of obtaining the fuel (steam reforming from natural gas, coal, biomass, electrolysis of water) all combine to make the option very expensive.

As an intermediate stage, between internal combustion and electric motors powered by fuel cells, hybrid electric vehicles have emerged as a possible transition to the post-internal combustion engine age. They include some combination of: 'stop and go' technology, whereby the internal combustion engine is switched off when the vehicle is stationary and an electric motor is used to restart the vehicle; regenerative braking, whereby some of the energy formerly dissipated in the form of heat on the break pads is captured and stored; direct powering of the drive shaft by the electric motor which increases power output with a smaller internal combustion engine; and fully independent operation of the vehicle by the battery, usually at low speeds. A number of models are on the commercial market combining some or all of these features. The potential exists to integrate hydrogen fuel cells into the hybrid engine, thereby further enhancing fuel efficiency and environmental performance generally at lower cost. The extent to which real change is achieved depends on overall 'well to wheel' efficiency, and the extent to which policy and consumer decisions support the transition. As regards the latter, history provides cautionary lessons. In the US, although average car efficiency increased by 21 per cent over the 1980 to 2003 period, average private vehicle efficiency only rose by 8 per cent, as many consumers shifted their preferences in favour of light trucks, which by 2003 comprised over 50 per cent of new car sales, a trend that is also evident in parts of Europe.

Thus we can envisage the technical feasibility of a substantial decarbonization of our car fleet, but only if policy supports the switch.

The energy systems model ERIS (Energy Research and Investment Strategies) is a 'bottom up' model which describes the global energy and transport system by modelling energy demands and technologies. It selects technologies from a given menu while maintaining engineering consistency which describes possible combinations of technologies ('energy chains') from resource extraction through energy conversion, distribution and end use, constrained by resource endowments and supply infrastructures. It incorporates the impact of experience with a new technology on the cost of that technology, such that the capital cost of a technology is a decreasing function of cumulative installed capacity. A scenario is identified whereby petroleum as a share of total transport fuel use falls from 97 per cent in 2000 to 61 and 23 per cent in 2050 and 2100, respectively, with natural gas use rising to 23 per cent in 2050, and fuel cells becoming the dominant source of energy by 2100, but with the mix varying by region. There is a commensurate stabilization and then reduction in global carbon emissions from automobile transport, which peak in around 2030, and fall well below 2000 levels by 2100. The various stages in this relatively benign outcome are plausibly identified, although it is important to recognize that the future is always a surprise, and therefore there will be new and perhaps revolutionary developments over this period that will transform outcomes in unexpected ways.

When we turn our attention to the policies that can engender the shift, as we noted earlier, we recognize that a number of countries have already introduced a variety of policies which either by design or otherwise encourage the delivery and use of more energy-efficient and therefore more carbon-efficient cars, and this experience provides an important base from which to learn about instrument design and likely effectiveness. These interventions positively affect some combination of fuel efficiency, and the availability and viability of alternative fuels and technologies. They may also manage traffic demand so as to reduce congestion and greenhouse gas and other emissions.

In terms of fuel efficiency, Japan has introduced its 'top runner' fuel efficiency targets, the US has mandatory Corporate Average Fuel Efficiency (CAFE) standards and in China fuel efficiency standards are prescribed by weight class. The State of California has led in the regulation of clean vehicle technology, with the introduction of the zero emission vehicle (ZEV) programme in 1990.

Turning to policy measures related to accelerating the introduction of alternative fuels, the European Union has set indicative (that is, non-mandatory) targets for the minimum proportions of biofuels and other renewable fuels sold on the market, and member states are authorized to exempt such fuels from excise duty. The US provides a tax credit of 14.3 cents per litre of bioethanol, whereas Brazil leads the world with its ethanol programme, which has achieved production costs comparable to those of petrol. As regards regulation of greenhouse gas emissions from cars, the California Air Resources Board (CARB) has proposed mandatory CO_2 emission standards (expressed as fleet average grams per mile) to commence in 2009. However, this proposal has been challenged by the Federal Government, and the court outcome is unknown at this time.

These technical and fuel measures are complemented by demand-side instruments, such as the taxes and charges in use in most jurisdictions, applied at some or all of the following stages: on the car at time of acquisition (Registration tax) and thereafter periodically (Circulation tax); on fuel, usually an excise duty; and for use, in the form of congestion, road user, parking and other charges. Japan, the US and a number of other countries have reduced the registration tax for fuel-efficient vehicles and hybrid vehicles; the UK has reconfigured its annual circulation tax to reflect carbon efficiency. The UK, Germany and Finland apply some of the highest excise duties in the world on fuel, and this is reflected in what motorists have to pay, which in turn influences consumption and carbon emissions. Road pricing and congestion charging are emerging as important new instruments for improving traffic flow and reducing demand, and thereby *inter alia* improving fuel efficiency and reducing carbon emissions. An important factor in determining the responsiveness of road users to these taxes and charges is the availability, convenience and cost of alternatives, notably collective transport. The success of the London congestion charge has been positively influenced by the parallel investment of much of the revenues in collective transport. Other relevant policies include information flows, with the EU now implementing the carbon rating of vehicles at point of sale, and a negotiated agreement with the industry that sets targets for average CO_2 efficiency per car of 140 g per km, to be achieved by 2008, with implementation of legislation to achieve a more stringent target of 120 g per km by 2012.

A policy instrument that supports all of the above is research and development (R&D). Private companies invest in R&D in order to give themselves a competitive edge. Given the global commitment to address climate change, and the allied benefits in so doing of reducing dependence on imported oil, there is a great 'first mover advantage' commercial prize to be won by the company that succeeds in creating competitive vehicles that are attractive to consumers and that also succeed in reducing greenhouse gas emissions. There is a public interest in supporting such research because, in addition to the commercial advantage that accrues to the relevant firms in the car industry, there is clear societal gain in reducing greenhouse gas emissions, reducing other air pollutants and reducing dependence on oil imports. And so we see the need for substantial private and public investment in R&D, and this is reflected in the major automobile centres of Europe, Japan and the US, where there are large private and public investments in R&D. Experience tells us that, because of the long-term nature of the problem, and the magnitude of the investment required, support must be sustained over decades, and that it is more likely to succeed if it is complemented by demand reflected in higher fuel and/or carbon prices that create a direct pay-off in savings for gains in fuel efficiency and reductions in emissions.

13.1 SOME CONCLUSIONS

We believe that the evidence supports the proposition that it is both possible and perhaps even likely that our planetary community will develop and then adopt a mix of technologies that can dramatically reduce the carbon intensity of our cars. Necessity is the mother of invention: our actions will be stimulated by a mix of rising oil prices, and occasional supply interruptions, apprehensions about our future, intense competition between auto manufacturers to capture the 'carbon free prize', a lot of 'learning by doing' both in regard to technologies and also in regard to our policies. The fact that the biggest future markets, China and India, are not major oil producers further increases the likelihood that major technology transitions will take place.

Over the past 20 to 30 years, a lot of intellectual and financial energy has been devoted to meeting this challenge, to the point that there is now available a cluster of competing technologies which we have documented, and others which are still so embryonic that they are not yet in the public domain. There has been an equal richness in the array of policy instruments that have recently come to the fore. The European Union has created an emissions trading scheme for CO_2 which applies at present to power generation and heavy industry, but which can be extended to other sectors. There are over 11 000 installations in the scheme across the EU25. Since the scheme's inception, trading has produced average price per tonne of CO_2 in the order of €15–20; for the first time, European energy consumers are faced with a signal that begins overtly to indicate that the capacity of the planet to absorb greenhouse gases is scarce. While the trading market is limited in scope and scale, and does not yet include the automobile sector – in part because excise duties already applied to petrol and diesel are a form of carbon tax – it does symbolize an intent to address the climate change challenge, and it comprises a template that is likely to be adopted in time by other jurisdictions in the planetary community. The intent of California overtly to address greenhouse gas emissions in the auto industry by regulation,[2] the use of voluntary agreements in Europe and Japan backed by an array of other instruments, the evolution of taxes and charges on cars and fuel to more closely reflect their performance as regards greenhouse gas emissions, all point towards a mutual re-enforcing of policy and technology. The fact that different countries are adopting differing emphases, with the US focusing on subsidizing technology, while Europe depends more on creating market signals, spreads the risk. We know also that our scenarios, and our marshalling of policy instruments are incomplete, and that our optimism may be misplaced. However, the balance of probabilities points to a view that the future will not be like the past, and that the profusion and sometimes the confusion of technologies and policies we have identified will result in a move away from fossil fuel dependence and rising greenhouse gas emissions from the passenger car sector.

NOTES

1. Excise duty from EU Oil Bulletin 01/07/2006, http://ec.europa.eu/energy/oil/bulletin/2006/duties-taxes-2006-07.pdf.
2. And, recently, through the courts (Office of the Attorney General, 2006).

References

AAMA (1996), *World Vehicle Facts & Figures*, American Automobile Manufacturers Association, ISBN 0317050809.

AAMA (1997), *World Motor Vehicle data*, American Automobile Manufacturers Association, ISSN 0085-8307.

ACEA (2004), *ACEA's Statement on the potential for additional CO_2 reduction, with a view to moving further towards the Community's objective of 120g CO_2/ km by 2012*.

ACEA (2006), ACEA Tax Guide 2006, available at http://www.acea.be/ASB20/axidownloads 20s.nsf/Category2ACEA/CED7D957932102C5C 125714D002D4DF4/$File/2006ACEATaxGuide~Introduction.pdf.

ACEA(2007), 'ACEA 1998 commitment' [online], Brussels, available at http://www.acea.be/acea_1998_commitment, accessed 2007.

ADAC e.V. (2004), Summary Report Part 1: 'Evaluation of Member State reports according to Article 9 of Directive 1999/94/EC', 'Study on the effectiveness of Directive 1999/94/EC relating to the availability of consumer information on fuel economy and CO_2 emissions in respect of the marketing of new passenger cars', To the European Commission, Directorate-General for Environment, Contract No.: 07010401/2004/377013/MAR/C1.

ADL (2002), *Guidance for Transportation Technologies: Fuel Choice for Fuel Cell Vehicles*, Final report; Phase II Final Deliverable to DOE, Arthur D. Little Inc., 6 February.

AFDC (Alternative Fuels Data Center) (2003), 'Alternative fuels, information and comparisons', U.S. Department of Energy, http://www.afdc.doe.gov/altfuels.html, October.

Airbus (2003), *Liquid Hydrogen Fuelled Aircraft – System Analysis*, Final Technical Report, Airbus Deustchland Gmbh, 24 September.

Alberini, A. and K. Segerson (2002), 'Assessing voluntary programs to improve environmental quality', *Environmental and Resource Economics*, **22**(1–2), 157–84.

Albrecht, J. (2000), 'The diffusion of cleaner vehicles in CO_2 emission trading designs', *Transportation Research Part D: Transport and Environment*, **5**(5), 385–401.

Albrecht, J. (2001), 'Tradable CO_2 permits for cars and trucks', *Journal of Cleaner Production*, **9**(2), 179–89.

Alexander, M. (1997), 'The rebound effect in energy conservation', PhD dissertation, available at www.leprechaun.co.uk/econ.html.

Argote, L. and D. Epple (1990), 'Learning curves in manufacturing', *Science*, **247**, 920–24.

Arnott, R. and J. Rowse (1999), 'Modeling parking', *Journal of Urban Economics*, **45**(1), 97–124.

Ausubel, J.H., C. Marchetti and P.S. Meyer (1998), 'Toward green mobility: the evolution of transport', *European Review*, **6**(2), 137–56.

Azar, C., K. Lindgren and B.A. Andersson (2003), 'Global energy scenarios meeting stringent CO_2 constraints – cost-effective fuel choices in the transportation sector', *Energy Policy*, **31**, 961–76.

Banerjee, A. and B.D. Solomon (2003), 'Eco-labeling for energy efficiency and sustainability: a meta evaluation of US programs', *Energy Policy*, **31**, 109–23.

Baranzini, A., P. Thalmann and C. Gonseth (2004), 'Swiss climate policy: combining VAs with other instruments under the menace of a CO_2 tax', in A. Baranzini and P. Thalmann (eds), *Voluntary Approaches in Climate Policy*, Cheltenham, UK and Northampton, MA, USA: Edward Elgar.

Barreto, L. and S. Kypreos (2000), 'A post-Kyoto analysis with the ERIS Model prototype', *International Journal of Global Energy Issues*, **14**(1/2/3/4), 262–80.

Barreto, L. and S. Kypreos (2004a), 'Endogenizing R&D and market experience in the "bottom-up" energy-systems ERIS model', **24**(8), 615–29.

Barreto, L. and S. Kypreos (2004b), 'Emissions trading and technology deployment in an energy-systems "bottom-up" model with technology learning', *European Journal of Operational Research*, **158**(1), 243–61.

Barreto, L. and H. Turton (2005), *Impact Assessment of Energy-Related Policy Instruments on Climate Change and Security of Energy Supply*, IR-05-002, International Institute for Applied Systems Analysis, Laxenburg, Austria.

Barreto, L., A. Makihira and K. Riahi (2003), 'The hydrogen economy in the 21st century: a sustainable development scenario', *International Journal of Hydrogen Energy*, **28**(3), 267–84.

Baumol, W.J. and W.E. Oates (1988), *The Theory of Environmental Policy*, Cambridge, UK: Cambridge University Press.

Bergmann, H., H. Diaz-Bone, U. Hartmann, U. Höpfner, M. Stronzik and S. Weinreich (2001), *Flexible Instrumente der Klimapolitik im Verkehrsbereich*, Final report to the Ministry of the Environment and Transport of Baden-Württemberg, Germany.

Bernstein, J.I. and M.I. Nadiri (1988), 'Interindustry R&D spillovers, rates of return, and production in high-tech industries', *American Economic Review Papers and Proceedings*, **78**(21), 429–34.

Bernstein, J.I. and M.I. Nadiri (1989), 'Research and development and intra-industry spillovers: an empirical application of dynamic duality', *Review of Economic Studies,* **56**, 249–69.

Bernstein, J.I. and M.I. Nadiri (1991), 'Product demand, cost of production, spillovers, and the social rate of return to R&D', NBER WP 3625.

Bevilacqua Knight Inc. (2001), *Bringing Fuel Cell Vehicles to Market: Scenarios and Challenges with Fuel Alternatives*, Consultant Study Report prepared for California Fuel Cell Partnership (CaFCP), California.

Boardman, B., N. Banks, H.R. Kirby, S. Keay-Bright and S.G. Stradling (2000), *Choosing Cleaner Cars: The Role of Labels and Guides. Final Report on Vehicle Environmental Rating Schemes*, TRI Record 00/10/02, Transport Research Institute, Napier University, Scotland.

Bonsall, P. (2000), 'Legislating for modal shift: background to the UK's new transport act', *Transport Policy,* **7**, 179–84.

Brau, R. and C. Carraro (1999), 'Voluntary approaches, market structure and competition. Concerted action on voluntary approaches (CAVA)', *Working Paper Series 99/08*, Paris.

Brau, R. and C. Carraro (2004), 'The economic analysis of voluntary approaches to environmental protection. A survey', *CRENoS working paper 04/20*.

Buchner, B., C. Carraro and I. Cersosimo (2002), 'Review: economic consequences of the US withdrawal from the Kyoto/Bonn protocol', *Climate Policy,* **2**, 273–92.

Buonanno, P., C. Carraro and M. Galeotti (2003), 'Endogenous induced technical change and the costs of Kyoto', *Resource and Energy Economics*, **25**(1), 11–34.

Button, K. and E. Verhoef (1998), *Road Pricing, Traffic Congestion and the Environment: Issues of Efficiency and Social Feasibility*, Cheltenham, UK and Northampton, MA, USA: Edward Elgar.

Calthrop, E., S. Proost and K. Van Dender (2000), 'Parking policies and road pricing', (Carfax) *Urban Studies*, **37**(1), 63–76.

Cameron, M. (1991), *Transportation Efficiency: Tackling Southern California's Air Pollution and Congestion*, Environmental Defense Fund and Regional Institute of Southern California, USA.

CARB (California Air Resources Board) (2003a), CARB website, http://www.arb.ca.gov/msprog/zevprog/2001rule/2001rule.htm.

CARB (2003b), Fact Sheet 2003 Zero Emission Vehicle Program Changes [online], http://www.arb.ca.gov/msprog/zevprog/factsheets/2003 zevchanges.pdf, accessed February 2006.

CARB (2004), *Report to the Legislature and the Governor on Regulations to Control Greenhouse Gas Emissions from Motor Vehicles*, California Air Resources Board, California, USA.

CARB (2005), *DriveClean.ca.gov: A zero or near-zero emission vehicle guide*, California Air Resources Board, USA.

Carlson, E.J., J.H. Thijssen, S. Lasher, S. Sriramulu, G.C. Stevens and N. Garland (2002), *Cost Modeling of PEM Fuel Cell Systems for Automobiles*, Future Car Congress 2002, Session: Fuel Cell & Vehicle System Analysis I (FCC16).

Council of the European Union (CEC) (2000), *Monitoring of ACEA/JAMA/KAMA's Commitment on CO_2 Emission Reductions from Passenger Cars (1995–1999)*, Joint Report of the European Manufacturers Association and the Commission Services, Brussels, 10.07.2000.

CEC (2001), *Monitoring of ACEA/JAMA/KAMA's Commitment on CO_2 Emission Reductions from Passenger Cars (2000)*, Commission Staff Working Paper, SEC(2001) 1722, Brussels, 8.11.2001.

CEC (2002a), *Monitoring of ACEA/JAMA/KAMA's Commitment on CO_2 Emission Reductions from Passenger Cars (2001)*, Commission Staff Working Paper, SEC(2002) 1338, Brussels, 9.12.2002.

CEC (2002b), *Taxation of Passengers Cars in the European Union – Options for Action at National and Community Levels*, Communication from the Commission to the Council and the European Parliament, COM(2002) 31 Final, Brussels.

CEC (2004a), Website of DG Environment, http://www.europa.eu.int/comm/environment/co2/co2_database.htm.

CEC (2004b), *Monitoring of ACEA/JAMA/KAMA's Commitment on CO_2 Emission Reductions from Passenger Cars (2002)*, Commission Staff Working Paper, SEC(2004) 140, Brussels, 11.2.2004.

CEC (2004c), *Science and Technology, the Key to Europe's Future – Guidelines for Future European Union Policy to Support Research*, Communication from the Commission, COM(2004) 353 final, Brussels.

CEC (2004d), *European Competitiveness Report*, Commission staff working document SEC(2004)1397.

CEC (2005a), *Stakeholder Consultation – EURO 5 Emissions Limits for Light Duty Vehicles*, http://www.europa.eu.int/comm/enterprise/automotive/pagesbackground/pollutant_emission/stakeholder_consultation/call_for_consultation.htm.

CEC (2005b), *Reducing the Climate Change Impact of Aviation*, Communication from the Commission to the Council, the European Parliament, the European Economic and Social Committee and the Committee of the Regions, COM(2005) 459 final.

CEC (2005c), *Monitoring of ACEA/JAMA/KAMA's Commitment on CO_2 Emission Reductions from Passenger Cars (2003)*, Commission Staff Working Paper, SEC(2005) 826, Brussels, 22.6.2005.

CEC (2005d), *Proposal for a Decision of the European Parliament and of the Council and the European Council Concerning the Seventh Framework Programme of the European Community for Research, Technological Development and Demonstration Activities (2007 to 2013)*, COM(2005) 119 final.

CEC (2006a), *Communication from the Commission : An EU Strategy for Biofuels*, Brussels, COM(2006) 34 final.

CEC (2006b), *Monitoring of ACEA/JAMA/KAMA's Commitment on CO_2 Emission Reductions from Passenger Cars (2004)*, Commission Staff Working Paper, SEC(2006) 1078, Brussels, 24.8.2006.

CEC (2007), *Communication from the Commission to the Council and the European Parliament Results of the review of the Community Strategy to reduce CO_2 emissions from passenger cars and light – commercial vehicles*, Brussels, COM/2007/0019 final.

Chupka, M. (1997), *Government Must Lead the Way in Technology and Diffusion: Will Technology Save the Day?*, Weathervane, November, Resources for the Future, Washington, DC.

Clark, R., J. Evans and I. Virrels (2002), *An Evaluation of Shell GTL Diesel – the Environmental Benefits*, Presentation at 8th Diesel Engine Emissions Reduction Workshop, 25–29 August, San Diego.

Convery, F.J., L. Redmond, L. Dunne and L. Ryan (2003a), 'Assessing the European Union emissions trading directive', *Economia Agraria y Recursos Naturales*, **6**(3), 65–81.

Convery, F., L. Dunne, L. Redmond and L. Ryan (2003b), 'Achieving behavioural change – policy instruments and the management of climate change', prepared for International Collaboration Projects on Sustainable Societies Meeting, Tokyo, 27 February–1 March.

COWI (2002), *Fiscal Measures to Reduce CO_2 Emissions from New Passenger Cars*, study contract for the EU Commission, DG Environment, Brussels.

Cullinane, K. (1993), 'An aggregate dynamic model of the parking compliance decision', *International Journal of Transport Economics*, **XX**(1), 27–50.

Dales, J.H. (1968), *Pollution, Property and prices: An Essay in Policy Making and Economics*, Toronto: University of Toronto press.

Davis, G.A. and B. Owens (2003), 'Optimizing the level of renewable electric R&D expenditures using real options analysis', *Energy Policy*, **31**, 1589–1608.

Davis, S.C. and S.W. Diegel (2004), *Transportation Energy Data Book: Edition 24*, Oak Ridge National Laboratory, ORNL-6973, Tennessee, USA.

Dawson, N.L. and K. Segerson (2003), 'Participation in industry-wide voluntary approaches: short run vs. long-run equilibrium', in A. de Zeuw and J. List (eds), *Recent Advances in Environmental Economics*, Cheltenham, UK and Northampton, MA, USA: Edward Elgar.

De Muizon, G. and M. Glachant (2004), 'The UK climate change levy agreements: combining negotiated agreements with tax and emissions trading', in A. Baranzini and P. Thalmann (eds), *Voluntary Approaches in Climate Policy*, Cheltenham, UK and Northampton, MA, USA: Edward Elgar.

DeCicco, J.M. and M. Ross (1993), *An Updated Assessment of the Near-Term Potential for Improving Automotive Fuel Economy*, Washington, DC: American Council for an Energy-Efficient Economy.

DeCicco, J., F. An and M. Ross (2001), *Technical Options for Improving the Fuel Economy of US Cars and Light Trucks by 2010–2015*, Washington, DC: American Council for an Energy-Efficient Economy.

Doyle, T.A. (1998), *Technology Status of Hydrogen Road Vehicles*, IEA Agreement on the Production and Utilization of Hydrogen, IEA/H2/TR1-98, available at <http://www.eere.energy.gov/hydrogenandfuelcells/hydrogen/iea/pdfs/tech_status.pdf>, accessed (1 December 2003).

Dresner, S., T. Jackson and N. Gilbert (2006), 'History and social responses to environmental tax reform in the United Kingdom', *Energy Policy*, **34**(8), 930–39.

ECCJ (Energy Conservation Centre Japan) (2005), *Manual Top Runner Program, revised* [online], http://www.eccj.or.jp/top_runner/index_contents_e.html, accessed May 2006.

ECMT (European Conference of Ministers of Transport) (2000), 'Monitoring of CO_2 Emissions from New Cars, Updated with Data to 1999', ECMT, Paris; available at <http://www.oecd.org/cem/topics/env/CO2Cars.pdf>, accessed (1 December 2003).

ECMT (2003a), 'Comparing existing transport taxes and charges with an optimal pricing benchmark', *Efficiency Transport Taxes and Charges 2003*, CEMT/CS(2003)4.

ECMT (2003b), 'Reforming transport taxes and charges', Group on Fiscal and Financial Aspects of Transport, CEMT/CS/FIFI(2003)1/REV1.

EEA (European Environment Agency) (1998), 'Towards a transport and environment reporting mechanism (TERM) for the EU. Part 1: TERM concept and process', European Environmental Agency in Cooperation with Eurostat, Copenhagen.

EEA (1999), 'Environment in the European Union at the turn of the century', Environmental assessment report No. 2, European Environment Agency, Copenhagen.

EEA (2002), 'Occupancy rates of passenger vehicles, Indicator fact sheet, TERM 2002 29', European Environment Agency, available at http://themes.eea.eu.int/Sectors_and_activities/transport/indicators/

technology/TERM29%2C2002/TERM_2002_29_EU_Occupancy_
rates_of_passenger_vehicles.pdf, accessed March 2005.

EERE (Energy Efficiency and Renewable Energy) (2005), *Hydrogen, Fuel Cells and Infrastructure Technology Program*, US Department of Energy <http://www.eere.energy.gov/hydrogenandfuelcells/> (14 February).

Ehrlich, P.R. and J.P. Holdren (1971), 'Impact of population growth', *Science*, **171**, 1212–17.

EIA (Energy Information Administration) (1999), 'Transportation sector', Module of the *World Energy Projection System*, Office of Integrated Analysis and Forecasting, Energy Information Administration, US Department of Energy, Washington, DC, USA.

EIA (2002), *International Energy Outlook 2002*, Office of Integrated Analysis and Forecasting, Energy Information Administration, US Department of Energy, Washington, DC, USA, March.

EIA (2003a), *Annual Energy Outlook 2003, with Projections to 2025*, US Department of Energy, DOE/EIA-0383(2003), Washington, DC.

EIA (2003b), *Annual Survey of Alternative Fuel Vehicles Suppliers and Users*, Form EIA-886, available at 'Alternatives to traditional transportation fuels 2002 (Table 14)', <http://www.eia.doe.gov/cneaf/alternate/page/ datatables/atf14-20_02.html> (1 December).

Etheridge, D.M., L.P. Steele, R.L. Langenfelds, R.J. Francey, J.-M. Barnola and V.I. Morgan (1998), 'Historical CO_2 records from the Law Dome DE08, DE08-2, and DSS ice cores', in *Trends: A Compendium of Data on Global Change*, Carbon Dioxide Information Analysis Center, Oak Ridge National Laboratory, US Department of Energy, Oak Ridge, Tennessee, USA.

EurObserver (2005), *Biofuels Barometer* [online], Directorate-General for Energy and Transport, Renewable Energy Publications, available at http://www.energies-renouvelables.org/observ-er/stat_baro/observ/baro167b.pdf, accessed January 2006.

European Bioenergy Networks (2003),'Liquid biofuels network activity report', Final Report, Contract no. 4.1030./s/01-1000/2001, France, accessed April 2003.

European Parliament (2003), *Directive 2003/87/EC of the European Parliament and of the Council of 13 October 2003 establishing a scheme for greenhouse gas emission allowance trading within the Community and amending Council Directive 96/61/EC*, Brussels.

Evenson, R. (1968), 'The contribution of agricultural research and extension to agricultural production', Unpublished Ph.D. thesis, University of Chicago.

Ewringmann, D., H. Bergmann, R. Bertenrath, R. Betz, F. Dünnebeil, U. Lambrecht, K. Rogge and W. Schade (2005), *Emissions Trading in the*

Transport Sector – Feasible Approach for an Upstream Model, Research Project commissioned by the German Federal Environmental Agency (UBA) UFOPLAN Scheme No. 202 14 198.

Faucon, R. and D. Leport (2002), *Fuel Requirements for Present and Future Vehicles*, report by Renault, Powertrain Division, Fuels Affairs, France.

FHA (Federal Highway Administration) (1996), *Highway statistics summary to 1995*, Office of Highway Information Management, US Federal Highway Administration.

Fischer, G. and Schrattenholzer, L. (2001), 'Global bioenergy potentials through 2050', *Biomass and Bioenergy*, **20**(3), 151–9; reprinted as RR-01-009, International Institute for Applied Systems Analysis, Laxenburg, Austria.

Fuel Cells Bulletin (2004), 'US Japan to collaborate on fuel cells, hydrogen R&D', 2004 (2), February, 1.

Fulton, L., T. Howes and J. Hardy (2004), *Biofuels for Transport: An International Perspective*, Paris: International Energy Agency.

GBG (Green Budget Germany) (2004), *Ecotax GBG-Memorandum 2004* [online], Munich, available at www.eco-tax.info (June 2006).

Gini, C. (1921), 'Measurement of inequality of income', *Economic Journal*, **31**, 124–5.

Glaister, S. (2001), 'UK Transport Policy 1997–2001', paper delivered to the Beesley Lectures on Regulation, The Royal Society of Arts, 2 September 2001; http://www.cts.cv.ic.ac.uk/staff/wp21-glaister.pdf.

Goh, M. (2002), 'Congestion management and electronic road pricing in Singapore', *Journal of Transport Geography*, **10**, 29–38.

Goldemberg, J., S.T. Coelho, P.M. Nastari and O. Lucon (2004), 'Ethanol learning curve – the Brazilian experience', *Biomass and Bioenergy*, **26**(3), 301–4.

Goodwin, P., J. Dargay and M. Hanly (2004), 'Elasticities of road traffic and fuel consumption with respect to price and income: a review', *Transport Reviews*, **24**(3), pp. 275–92.

Goto, A. and K. Suzuki (1989), 'R&D capital, rate of return on R&D investment and spillover of R&D in Japanese manufacturing industries', *Review of Economics and Statistics*, **LXXI**(41), 555–64.

Goulder, L.H. (2002), 'US climate-change policy: the Bush Administration's plan and beyond', Policy Brief, Stanford Institute for Economic Policy Research, California, USA.

Goulder, L.H. and S.H. Schneider (1999), 'Induced technological change and the attractiveness of CO_2 abatement policies', *Resource and Energy Economics*, **21**, 211–53.

Government of Canada (2005), 'Moving forward on climate change: a plan for honouring our Kyoto commitment', Project Green, http://www.climatechange.gc.ca/english/.

Greene, D. and A. Schafer (2003), 'Reducing greenhouse gas emissions from U.S. transportation', *Report for Pew Centre on Global Climate Change*, Virginia, USA.

Greene, D.L. and S.E. Plotkin (2001), 'Energy futures for the U.S. transportation sector', *Energy Policy*, **29**(14), 1255–70.

Griliches, Z. (1958), 'Research cost and social returns: hybrid corn and related innovations', *Journal of Political Economy*, **LXVI**, 419–31.

Griliches, Z. (1964), 'Research expenditures, education, and the aggregate agricultural production function', *American Economic Review*, **LIV**(6), 961–74.

Griliches, Z. (1992), 'The search for R&D spillovers', *Scandinavian Journal of Economics*, **94**, S29–47.

Griliches, Z. and F. Lichtenberg (1984), 'Interindustry technology flows and productivity growth: a reexamination', *Review of Economics and Statistics*, **LXVI**(2), 324–9.

Hakim, D. (2005), 'Battle lines set as New York acts to cut emissions', *New York Times*, 26 November.

Hall, B. (1996), 'The private and social returns to research and development: what have we learned?', in Bruce L.R. Smith and Claude E. Barfield (eds), *Technology, R&D, and the Economy*, Washington, DC: The Brookings Institution and the American Enterprise Institute.

Hamelinck, C. and A.P.C. Faaij (2001), 'Future prospects for production of methanol and hydrogen from biomass', Report NWS-E-2001-49, Copernicus Institute, Utrecht University.

Hamelinck, C., A.P.C. Faaij, H. den Uil and H. Boerrigter (2003), 'Production of FT transportation fuels from biomass; technical options, process analysis and optimisation, and development potential', Report NWS-E-2003-08, Copernicus Institute, Utrecht University, Utrecht, Netherlands.

Hamilton, C. and H. Turton (2002), 'Determinants of emissions growth in OECD countries', *Energy Policy*, **30**, 63–71.

Hammar, H., Å. Löfgren and T. Sterner (2004), 'Political economy obstacles to fuel taxation', *Energy Journal*, **3** (July).

Hanly, N., J. Shogren and B. White (2001), *Introduction to Environmental Economics*, Bath: Bath Press Ltd.

Heins, B. and L. Luettge (2002), 'The chemical industry in Germany: recent developments of the 1987 chemical industries social partners' agreement on environmental protection', in P.t. Brink (ed.), *Voluntary Environmental Agreements: Process, Practice and Future Use*, Sheffield: Greenleaf Publishing Limited.

Henke, J.M., G. Klepper and N. Schmitz (2003), 'Tax exemption for biofuels in Germany: is bio-ethanol really an option for climate policy?', paper presented at the *International Energy Workshop* jointly organised by the Energy Modelling Forum (EMF), International Energy Agency (IEA) and International Institute for Applied Systems Analysis (IIASA) at IIASA, Laxenburg, Austria, 24–26 June.

Herring, H. (1998), *Does Energy Efficiency Save energy: The Implications of Accepting the khazzom–Brookes Postulate*, EERU, Open University, available at http://technology.open.ac.uk/eeru/staff/horace/kbpotl.htm.

Higgins, G. (1992), 'Parking taxes: effectiveness, legality, and implementation, some general considerations', *Transportation*, **19**(3), 221–30.

Higley, C.J., F. Convery and F. Leveque (2001), 'Voluntary approaches: an Introduction', paper presented at CAVA, *International Policy Workshop on the Use of Voluntary Approaches*, 1 February, Brussels.

HM Revenue and Customs (2006), *Company cars*, available at http://www.hmrc.gov.uk/cars/ (June).

Honda (2005), 'Honda reaches 100,000-unit mark in cumulative global hybrid vehicle sales', Press Release, 24 May, http://world.honda.com/news/2005/c050524.html.

Howarth, R.B., B.M. Haddad and B. Paton (2004), 'Energy efficiency and greenhouse gas emissions: correcting market failures using public voluntary agreements', in A. Branzini and P. Thalmann (eds), *Voluntary Approaches in Climate Policy*, Cheltenham, UK and Northampton, MA, USA: Edward Elgar.

Huffman, W.E. and R.E. Evenson (1993), *Science for Agriculture: A Long term Perspective*, Iowa State University Press.

IBRD (2004), *World Development Indicators 2004*, International Bank for Reconstruction and Development, The World Bank, Washington, DC, USA.

ICF Consulting (2006), 'Including Aviation into the EU ETS: Impact on EU allowance prices', Final Report for the UK Department of Environment, Food and Rural Affairs and Department of Transport, available at http://www.defra.gov.uk/Environment/climatechange/trading/eu/pdf/including-aviation-icf.pdf (February).

IEA (International Energy Agency) (1997), *Energy Technologies for the 21st Century*, Paris: International Energy Agency.

IEA (2000), 'World energy outlook 2000', in *Strategies to Reduce Greenhouse Gas Emissions from Road Transport: Analytical Methods*, Paris: International Energy Agency, OECD.

IEA (2001), *Towards a Sustainable Energy Future*, Paris: International Energy Agency.

IEA (2003a), *Energy Balances of OECD countries*, Paris: International Energy Agency.

IEA (2003b), *Energy Balances of non-OECD countries*, Paris: International Energy Agency.

IEA (2003c), *Energy Statistics of OECD countries*, Paris: International Energy Agency.

IEA (2003d), *Energy Statistics of non-OECD countries*, Paris: International Energy Agency.

IEA (2003e), Unpublished data, personal communication with Alan Meier.

IEA (2004a), *World Energy Outlook 2004*, Paris: International Energy Agency.

IEA (2004b), 'Green taxation and subsidies for automobiles', Paris: Climate Change Database, available at http://www.lea.org/textbase/pamsdb/detail.aspx?mode=cc&id=966, accessed June 2006.

Immerzeel-Brand, E. (2002), 'Assessing the performance of negotiated environmental agreements in the Netherlands', in P.t. Brink (ed.), *Voluntary Environmental Agreements: Process, Practice and Future Use*, Sheffield: Greenleaf Publishing.

Imura, H. (1999), 'The use of unilateral agreements in Japan – voluntary action plans of industries against global warming', Working Party on Economic and Environmental Policy Integration, Report No. ENV/EPOC/GEEI(98)26/FINALOECD, Paris.

IPCC (Intergovernmental Panel on Climate Change) (1996), *Climate Change 1995: The Science of Climate Change*, Table 4, Cambridge, UK: Cambridge University Press.

IPCC (2001a), *Climate Change 2001: The Scientific Basis*, Contribution of Working Group I to the Third Assessment Report of the Intergovernmental Panel on Climate Change, Cambridge, UK: Cambridge University Press.

IPCC (2001b), *Climate Change 2001: Mitigation*, Contribution of Working Group III to the Third Assessment Report of the Intergovernmental Panel on Climate Change, Cambridge, UK: Cambridge University Press.

IRF (International Road Federation) (2000), *World Road Statistics: Data 1994–98*, Geneva: International Road Federation.

Jaffe, A. (1988), 'Demand and supply influences in R&D intensity and productivity growth', *Review Of Economics and Statistics*, **LXX**(3), 431–7.

Jaffe, A.B., R.G. Newell and R.N. Stavins (2005), 'A tale of two market failures: technology and environmental policy', *Ecological Economics*, **54**, 164–74.

JAMA (2004), 'JAMA Position on the Potential for Achieving the CO_2 Reduction Target of 120g/km in 2012'.

Japan for Sustainability website (2004), http://www.japanfs.org, accessed May 2006.

Jensen, P. (2003), *Potential Limitations of voluntary Commitments on CO₂ Emissions Reductions in Transport*, JRC; IPTS report.

Jonsson, H. (2003), 'Towards hydrogen economy in Iceland', presentation at *International Energy Workshop*, 24–26 June, Laxenburg, Austria.

Jungmeier, G., K. Koenighofer, M. Varela and C. Lago (2005), 'Economic and environmental performance of biofuels', WorkPackage 2, VIEWLS project, *Clear Views on Clean Fuels: Data, Potential Scenarios, Markets, and Trade of Biofuels*, EC Project NNE5-2001-00619.

Karmali, A. (2005), 'Emissions trading: aviation's next steps', *Environmental Finance*, December 2004–January 2005, London: Fulton Publishing.

Karshenas, M. and P. Stoneman (1993), 'Rank, stock, order, and epidemic effects in the diffusion of new process technologies: an empirical model', *RAND Journal of Economics*, **24**(4), 503–28.

Karshenas, M. and P. Stoneman (1995), 'Technological diffusion', *Handbook of the Economics and Innovation of Technological Change*, Oxford: Blackwell Publishers Ltd.

Kavalov, B. and S.B. Peteves (2004), *Impacts of increasing the automotive diesel consumption in the EU*, for the EU Commission, Report No. EUR 21378 EN, Luxembourg.

Keeling, C.D. and T.P. Whorf (2004), 'Atmospheric CO₂ records from sites in the SIO air sampling network', *Trends: A Compendium of Data on Global Change*, Carbon Dioxide Information Analysis Centre, Oak Ridge National Laboratory, U.S. Department of Energy, Oak Ridge, Tennessee.

Keith, D. and A. Farrell (2003), 'Rethinking hydrogen cars', *Science*, **301**, 315–16.

Kelly, J.A. (2003), 'Parking demand management as a policy tool', PhD thesis, UCD, Dublin, November.

Kelly, J.A. and J.P. Clinch (2003), 'Temporal variance of revealed preference on-street parking price elasticity', *Environmental Studies Research Series (ESRS)* Working Paper 04/02, Department of Environmental Studies, UCD, Dublin.

Kemp, R. (1997a), 'The transition from hydrocarbons: the issues for policy', in S. Faucheux, D. Pearce and J. Proops (eds), *Models of Sustainable Development*, Cheltenham, UK and Lyme, USA: Edward Elgar.

Kemp, R. (1997b), *Environmental Policy and Technical Change. A Comparison of the Technological Impact of Policy Instruments*, Edward Elgar, Cheltenham, UK and Lyme, USA: Edward Elagar.

Khanna, M. (2001), 'Non-mandatory approaches to environmental protection', *Journal of Economic Surveys*, **15**(3), 291–324.

Khanna, M. and L. Damon (1999), 'EPA's voluntary 33/50 program: impact on toxic releases and economic performance of firms', *Journal of Environmental Economics and Management*, **37**(1), 1–25.

Klaassen, G., A. Miketa, K. Riahi and L. Schrattenholzer (2002), 'Targeting technological progress towards sustainable development', *Energy and Environment*, **13**(4/5), 553–78.

Knutson, M. and L.G. Tweeten (1979), 'Toward an optimal rate of growth in agricultural production research and extension', *American Journal of Agricultural Economics*, **61**, 70–76.

Kohler, H. (2003), 'Proposal for European energy strategy for road traffic', *VDA Technical Congress*, Wolfsburg, 2–3 April.

Kopp, R.J. (1998), 'Climate policy and the economics of technical advance: drawing on inventive activity' [online], *RFF Climate Issue Brief #8*, January.

Kram, T., T. Morita, K. Riahi, R.A. Roehrl, S. Van Rooijen, A. Sankovski and B. De Vries (2000), 'Global and regional greenhouse gas emissions scenarios', *Technological Forecasting and Social Change*, **63**(2–3), 335–71.

Krarup, S. (2001), 'Can voluntary approaches be environmentally effective and economically efficient?', paper presented at CAVA, *International Policy Workshop on the Use of Voluntary Approaches*, 1 February, Brussels.

Kreutz, T.G., R.H. Williams, R.H. Socolow, P. Chiesa and G. Lozza (2003), 'Production of hydrogen and electricity from coal with CO_2 capture', *6th International Conference on Greenhouse Gas Control Technologies*, Kyoto, Japan.

Kypreos, S., L. Barreto, P. Capros and S. Messner (2000), 'ERIS: a model prototype with endogenous technological change', *International Journal of Global Energy Issues*, **14**(1/2/3/4), 374–97.

Landwehr, M. and C. Marie-Lilliu (2002), *Transport Projections in OECD Regions: Detailed Report* [online], International Energy Agency, http://www.iea.org/textbase/papers/2002/Transport.pdf.

Leggett, J., W.J. Pepper and R.J. Swart (1992), 'Emissions scenarios for IPCC: an update', in J.T. Houghton, B.A. Callander and S.K. Varney (eds), *Climate Change 1992: The Supplementary Report to the IPCC Scientific Assessment*, Cambridge: Cambridge University Press, pp. 69–95.

Letendre, S.E. and W. Kempton (2002), 'The V2G concept: a new model for power?', *Public Utilities Fortnightly*, 15 February, Virginia, USA.

Lightfoot, H.D. and C. Green (2002), 'Energy intensity decline implications for stabilization of atmospheric CO_2 content', *Report No. 2001-7*, October 2001, McGill Center for Climate and Global Change Research, Canada.

Lipman, T.E., J.L. Edwards and D.M. Kammen, (2004), 'Fuel cell system economics: comparing the costs of generating power with stationary and motor vehicle PEM fuel cell systems', *Energy Policy*, **32**, 101–25.

Lovins, B.A. and B.D. Williams (1999), 'A strategy for the hydrogen transition', *10th Annual U.S. Hydrogen Meeting*, National Hydrogen Association, 7–9 April, Virginia, USA.

Luiten, E. and K. Blok (2004), 'Stimulating R&D of industrial energy-efficient technology. Policy lessons – impulse technology', *Energy Policy*, **32**(9), 1087–1108.

Lyon, T.P. and J.W. Maxwell (2003), 'Self-regulation, taxation and public voluntary environmental agreements', *Journal of Public Economics*, **87**(7–8), 1453–86.

Mansfield, E. (1968), *Industrial Research and Technological Innovation*, New York: W.W. Norton.

Mansfield, E. (1996), 'Microeconomic policy and technological change', *Conference Series, [Proceedings]*, Federal Reserve Bank of Boston, June(40), 183–213.

Mansfield, E., J. Rapoport, A. Rambo, S. Wagner and G. Beardsley (1977), 'Social and private rates of return from industrial innovations', *The Quarterly Journal of Economics*, **91**(2), 221–40.

Manzini, P. and M. Mariotti (2003), 'A bargaining model of voluntary environmental agreements', *Journal of Public Economics*, **87**(12), 2725–36.

Marland, G., T.A. Boden and R.J. Andres (2003), 'Global, regional, and national CO_2 emissions', in *Trends: A Compendium of Data on Global Change*, Carbon Dioxide Information Analysis Centre, Oak Ridge National Laboratory, U.S. Department of Energy, Oak Ridge, Tennessee.

Marx, T.G. (2000), 'The role of technology in responding to concerns about global climate change', *The Kyoto Commitments: Can Nations Meet Them with the Help of Technology?*, ACCF Center for Policy Research, Washington, DC.

Matsuno, Y. (2001), 'Pollution control agreements in Japan: conditions for their success', paper presented at the *European Consortium for Political Research Paper Archive – Joint Sessions of Workshops*, Grenoble, France.

Maxwell, J.W., T.P. Lyon and S. Hackett (2000), 'Self-regulation and social welfare: the political economy of corporate environmentalism', *Journal of Law and Economics*, **43**(2), 583–617.

Mayeres, I. and S. Proost (2001), 'Should diesel cars in Europe be discouraged?', *Regional Science and Urban Economics*, **31**, 453–70.

Mazurek, J. (1998), *The Use of Unilateral Agreements in the United States: The Responsible Care Initiative*, prepared for the Working Party on Economic and Environmental Policy Integration, OECD report ENV/EPOC/GEEI(98)25/FINAL.

McDonald, A. and L. Schrattenholzer (2001), 'Learning rates for energy technologies', *Energy Policy*, **29**(4), 255–61.

Mehlin, M., A. Guehnermann and R. Aoki (2004a), *Preparation of the 2003 review of the commitment of car manufacturers to reduce CO₂ emissions from M1 vehicles*, Final Report of Phase 1 to the Directorate-General for Environment, DLR – German Aerospace Centre, Service Contract No. 3040/2002/343537/MAR/C1, Berlin, Germany.

Mehlin, M., C. Vance, A. Guehnermann and S. Buchheim (2004b), *Preparation of the 2003 review of the commitment of car manufacturers to reduce CO₂ emissions from M1 vehicles*, Final Report of Task A to the Directorate-General for Environment, DLR – German Aerospace Centre, Service Contract No. 070501/2004/377441/MAR/C1, Berlin, Germany.

Menanteau, P. (2003), 'Can negotiated agreements replace efficiency standards as an instrument for transforming the electrical appliance market?', *Energy Policy*, **31**(9), 827–35.

Menon, A. (2000), 'ERP in Singapore – a perspective one year on', *TEC*, **41**(2), 40–45.

Michaelis, L., D. Bleviss, J-P. Orfeuil, R. Pischinger, J. Crayston, O. Davidson, T. Kram, N. Nakićenović and L. Schipper (1996), 'Mitigation options in the transportation sector', in *Climate Change 1995: Impacts, Adaptation and Mitigation of Climate Change: Scientific–Technical Analyses*, Inter-governmental Panel on Climate Change, Cambridge: Cambridge University Press.

Miketa, A. and L. Schrattenholzer (2004), *Roadmap to deploying technologies for sustainable development*, IIASA Interim Report IR-04-074, Laxenburg, Austria.

Millock, K. (2000), 'The combined use of taxation and voluntary agreements for energy policy', *Nota di Lavoro 109.2000*, Fondazione Eni Enrico Mattei, Venice, Italy.

Millock, K. and F. Salanié (2000), 'Collective environmental agreements: an analysis of the problems of free-riding and collusion', *Fondazione Eni Enrico Mattei Working Paper 108.2000*, Venice, Italy.

Ministry of Environment (Japan) (2003), 中核的温暖化対策技術検討会，民生・運輸部門における中核的対策技術に関する中間報告 ('Meeting on core technology for global warming mitigation: Interim report on core technology for global warming mitigation in residential, commercial and transportation sectors'), Tokyo.

Mobility Car Sharing (2006), website available at http://www.mobility.ch/upload/docs/PDF/MM%20d%20Jahresabschluss%202005pdf.

Mohnen, P. and N. Lepine (1988), 'Payments for technology as a factor of production', University of Montreal, Department of Economics, Paper No. 8818.

Montero, J.P., D. Ellerman, P. Joskow, R. Schmalensee and E. Bailey (2000), *Markets for Clean Air: the US Acid Rain Program*, Cambridge: Cambridge University Press.

Moura, F. (2006), 'Driving energy system transformation with "Vehicle-to-Grid" power', Interim Report IR-06–025, International Institute for Applied Systems Analysis, Laxenburg, Austria.

MRI (Mitsubishi Research Institute) (2005), 'Japan's voluntary emissions trading scheme (J-VETS) [online]', available at http://www.et.chikyuk ankyo.com/english/ (October).

Musters, A.P.A. (1995), *The Rebound Effect: An Introduction*, Netherlands: Netherlands Energy Research Foundation.

Nakićenović, N. (1991), 'Diffusion of pervasive systems: a case of transport infrastructures', *Technological Forecasting and Social Change*, **39**, 181–200.

Nakićenović, N., P.V. Gilli and R. Kurz (1996), 'Regional and global exergy and energy efficiencies', *Energy – The International Journal*, **21**(3), 223–37.

Nakićenović, N. and Swart, R. (eds) (2000), *Special Report on Emissions Scenarios (SRES), A Special Report of Working Group III of the Intergovernmental Panel on Climate Change*, Cambridge: Cambridge University Press, UK.

National Academy of Sciences (2002), *Effectiveness and Impact of Corporate Average Fuel Economy (CAFE) Standard*, Washington, DC: Transportation Research Board.

Neftel, A., H. Friedli, E. Moor, H. Lötscher, H. Oeschger, U. Siegenthaler and B. Stauffer (1994), 'Historical CO_2 record from the Siple Station ice core', in *Trends: A Compendium of Data on Global Change*, Carbon Dioxide Information Analysis Center, Oak Ridge National Laboratory, U.S. Department of Energy, Oak Ridge, Tennessee.

Neij, L., P.D. Andersen, M. Durstewitz, P. Helby, M. Hoppe-Kilpper and P.E. Morthorst (2003), 'Experience curves: a tool for energy policy assessment', IMES/EESS Report Number 40, Department of Technology and Society, Environmental and Energy Systems Studies, Lund University, Sweden.

NHTSA (2005), 'Fuel economy website of the National Highway Traffic Safety Administration', http://www.nhtsa.dot.gov/cars/rules/cafe/New PassengerCarFleet.htm.

NRC (U.S. National Research Council) (1992), *Automotive Fuel Economy, How Far Should We Go?*, Committee on Fuel Economy of Automobiles and Light Trucks Energy Engineering Board, commission on Engineering and Technical Systems, National Academy Press, Washington, DC.

NRC (2001), 'Energy research at DOE: was it worth it?', Washington, DC: National Academy Press.

NRC (2003), 'Effectiveness and impact of corporate average fuel economy (CAFE) standards', Committee on the Effectiveness and Impact of Corporate Average Fuel Economy (CAFE) Standards and Board on Energy and Environmental Systems of the National Academies National Academy of Sciences, Washington, DC: National Academy Press.

Odell, P.R. (2004), *Why Carbon Fuels will Dominate the 21st Century's Global Energy Economy*, Brentwood: Multi-Science Publishing Co Ltd.

OECD (1999), *Voluntary Approaches for Environmental Policy: An Assessment*, Paris: OECD.

OECD (2002a), *Strategies to Reduce Greenhouse Gas Emissions from Road Transport: Analytical Methods*, Report IRTD No. E109210, OECD, Paris.

OECD (2002b), *Voluntary Approaches: Two Japanese Cases*, ENV/ EPOC/WPNEP(2002) 12/FINAL, OECD, Paris.

OECD (2003), *Voluntary Approaches for Environmental Policy: Effectiveness, Efficiency ad Usage in Policy Mixes*, OECD, Paris.

Öeko-Institut e.V (1998), *New Instruments for Sustainability – The New Contribution of Voluntary Agreements to Environmental Policy*, Final Report, Darmstadt, Germany.

Office of the Attorney General (2006), 'Attorney General Lockyer files lawsuit against "Big Six" automakers for global warming damages in California', News Release 06-082, 20 September 2006, http://ag.ca.gov/newsalerts/release.php?id=1338 (September).

Ogden, J.M., R.H. Williams and E.D. Larson (2004), 'Societal lifecycle costs of cars with alternative fuels/engines', *Energy Policy*, **32**, 1–27.

Ogushi, T. and S. Kure (2003), 'Carbon dioxide test emissions trading project in Japan', paper presented at the OECD Global Forum on Sustainable Development: Emissions Trading and Concerted Action on Tradable Emissions Permits (CATEP Country Foum held on 17–18 March, OECD Headquarters, Paris.

Olson, M. (1965), *The Logic of Collective Action*, Cambridge, MA: Harvard University Press.

OTA (Office of Technology Assessment) (1995), *Advanced Automotive Technology: Visions of a Super-Efficient Family Car*, OTA-ETI-638, Washington, DC.

Pakes, A. (1985), 'On patents, R&D, and the stock market rate of return', *Journal of Political Economy*, **93**(2), 390–409.

Parry, I.W.H. (2003), 'On the implications of technological innovation for environmental policy', *Environment and Development Economics*, **8**, 57–76.

Parsons, E. and W. Shelton (2002), 'Advanced fossil power systems comparison study', prepared for the National Energy Technology Laboratory (USA), December.

PCAST (1999), 'Powerful partnerships: the federal role in international co-operation on energy innovation', President's Committee of Advisors on Science and Technology, Panel on International Co-operation in Energy Research, Development, Demonstration and Deployment, Washington, USA.

Peterson, W.L. (1967), 'Return to poultry research in the United States', *Journal of Farm Economics*, **49**, 656–69.

Popp, D. (2002), 'Induced innovation and energy prices', *American Economic Review*, **92**(1), 160–80.

Popp, D. (2003), 'Lessons from patents: using patents to measure technological change in environmental models', *NBER Working Papers 9978*, National Bureau of Economic Research, Inc., USA.

Popp, D. (2004), 'ENTICE: endogenous technological change in the DICE model of global warming', *Journal of Environmental Economics and Management*, **48**(1), 742–68.

Redmond, L. and F. Convery (2005), 'The evolution of the European market in CO_2 allowances', *Conference presentation at the 14th Annual Conference of the European Association of Environmental and Resource Economists.* Bremen, Germany, available at http://www.webmeets.com/files/papers/EAERE/2005/216/Conference%20Paper%20for%20EAERE.pdf (September).

Reijnders, L. (2005), 'Conditions for the sustainability of biomass based fuel use', *Energy Policy*, **34**(7), 863–76.

Requate, T. (2005), 'Dynamic incentives by environmental policy instruments – a survey', *Ecological Economics*, **54**(2–3), 175–95.

Riahi, K. and R.A. Roehrl (2000), 'Greenhouse gas emissions in a dynamics-as-usual scenario of economic and energy development', *Technological Forecasting and Social Change*, **63**, 175–205.

Riahi, K., R.A. Roehrl, L. Schrattenholzer and A. Miketa (2001), *Technology Clusters in Sustainable Development Scenarios*, Progress Report of Environmental Issue Groups, International Forum of the Collaboration Projects in Spring 2001, Tokyo, Japan.

Rogner, H.H. (1997), 'An assessment of world hydrocarbon resources', *Annual Review of Energy and the Environment*, **22**, 217–62.

Rogner, H.H. (2000), 'Energy resources', in *World Energy Assessment: Energy and the Challenge of Sustainability*, Chapter 5, UNDP/WEC/UNDESA (United Nations Development Programme, World Energy Council, UN Department of Economic and Social Affairs), Washington/New York.

Romer, P.M. (1986), 'Increasing returns and long-run growth', *Journal of Political Economy*, **94**, 1002–37.

Ryan, L., S. Ferreira and F. Convery (2005), 'Stimulating the use of bio-fuels in the European Union: implications for climate change policy', *Energy Policy,* **34**(17), 3184–94.

Ryan, L., S. Ferreira and F. Convery (2006), 'Effectiveness of fiscal and other measures to manage greenhouse gas emissions from the automobile sector: evidence from Europe', *Planning and Environmental Policy Research Series (PEP) Working Paper 06/06*, Department of Planning and Environmental Policy, University College Dublin.

Sagar, A.D. and B. van der Zwaan (2005), 'Technological innovation in the energy sector: R&D, deployment, and learning-by-doing', *Energy Policy*, **34**(17), 2601–8.

Samuelson, P. (1954), 'The pure theory of public expenditures', *Review of Economics and Statistics*, **37**, 350–56.

Sandler, T. (1997), *Global Challenges – An Approach to Environmental Political and Economic Problems*, Cambridge: Cambridge University Press.

Sanyal, P. (2001), 'Powering a green progress: environmental research in the absence of regulatory oversight', Brandeis University working paper, by private communication.

SASOL (2005), *Technologies and Processes*, http://www.sasol.com/sasol_internet/frontend/navigation.jsp?navid=1600033&rootid=2 (October).

Sauer, A. and F. Wellington (2004), *Taking the High (Fuel Economy) Road*, World Resources Institute Report, November.

Schafer, A. (1995), *Trends in Global Motorized Mobility; The Past 30 Years and Implications for the Next Century*, WP-95-49, International Institute of Applied Systems Analysis, Laxenburg, Austria.

Schafer, A. (1998), 'The global demand for motorized mobility', *Transportation Research Part A*, **32**(6), 455–77.

Schafer, A. (2003), personal communication.

Schafer, A. and D.G. Victor (2000), 'The future mobility of the world population', *Transportation Research Part A*, **34**, 171–205.

Schafer, A., S. Kypreos, L. Barreto, H. Jacoby and P. Dietrich (1999), 'Automobile technology in a CO_2-constrained world', in B. Eliasson, P. Riemer and A. Wokaun (eds), *Greenhouse Gas Control Technologies*, Proceedings of the 4th International Conference on Greenhouse Gas Control Technologies, Interlaken, Switzerland, pp. 911–16.

Schmitz, A. and D. Seckler (1970), 'Mechanized agriculture and social welfare: the case of the tomato harvester', *American Journal of Agricultural Economics*, **52**, 567–77.

Schrattenholzer, L., A. Miketa, K. Riahi, R.A. Roehrl, M. Strubegger, G. Totschnig and B. Zhu (2004), *Achieving a Sustainable Global Energy*

System, Cheltenham, UK and Northampton, MA, USA: Edward Elgar Publishing.

Schumpeter, J.A. (1942), *Capitalism, Socialism, and Democracy*, New York: Harper and Brothers.

Seebregts, A., S. Bos, T. Kram and G. Schaeffer (2000), 'Endogenous learning and technology clustering: analysis with MARKAL model of the western European energy system', *International Journal of Global Energy Issues*, **14**(1/2/3/4), 289–319.

Segerson, K. and N.L. Dawson (2003), 'Voluntary agreements with industries: participation incentives with industry-wide targets', *Department of Economics Working Paper Series. Working Paper 2004-06*, University of Connecticut, USA.

SFA Pacific (2000), 'Gasification: worldwide use and acceptance', report prepared for the US Department of Energy, Office of Fossil Energy, National Energy Technology Laboratory and the Gasification Technologies Council (Contract DE-AMO1-98FE65271), SFA Pacific Inc., Mountain View, California.

Shapouri, H., J. Duffield and M. Wang (2002), 'The energy balance of corn ethanol: an update', *Agricultural Economic Report Number 813*, United States Department of Agriculture, Office of Energy Policy and New Uses, Washington, DC.

Simbeck, D.R. and E. Chang (2002), 'Hydrogen supply: cost estimate for hydrogen pathways – scoping analysis', SFA Pacific Inc., Mountain View, California.

Steiger, W. (2002), 'SunFuel-Strategie: Basis nachhaltiger Mobilitaet' (Sunfuel-strategy: a basis for sustainable mobility), paper presented at *World Renewable Energy Policy and Strategy Forum 'Renewable Energies – Agenda 1 of Agenda 21'*, Berlin, 13–15 June http://www.world-council-for-renewable-energy.org/conevents/Forum1en.html, accessed July 2005.

Sterner, T. (2003), *Policy Instruments for Environmental and Natural Resource Management*, Washington, DC: Resources for the Future Press.

Sveikauskas, L.(1981), 'Technological inputs and multifactor productivity growth', *Review of Economics and Statistics*, **63**(2), 275–82.

Ten Brink et al. (2005), 'Service contract to carry out economic analysis and business impact assessment of CO_2 emissions reduction measures in the automotive sector', European Commission Contract no. B4-3040/2003/366487/MAR/CZ, Brussels.

Terleckyj, N. (1974), *Effects of R&D on the Productivity Growth of Industries: An Exploratory Study*, National Planning Association, Washington, DC.

TfL (Transport for London) (2006), *Congestion Charging* [online], available at http://www.cclondon.com/index.shtml, accessed June 2006.

The White House (2005), *Statement from George W. Bush*, Climate Change Fact Sheet, [online] The White House website, available at http://www.whitehouse.gov/news/releases/2005/05/20050518-4.html (May).

Thomas, C.E., B.D. James, F.D. Lomaxm and I.F. Kuhn (2000), 'Fuel options for the fuel cell vehicle: hydrogen, methanol or gasoline?', *International Journal of Hydrogen Energy*, **25**, 551–67.

Toyota (2005), 'Toyota Worldwide Hybrid Sales Top 500,000 Units', *Press Release*, 25 November, http://www.toyota.co.jp/en/news/05/1125_2.html.

Tsuchiya, H. and O. Kobayashi (2002), 'Fuel cell cost study by learning curve', paper submitted to the *Annual Meeting of the International Energy Workshop*, Energy Modeling Forum/International Institute for Applied Systems Analysis, 18–20 June, Stanford University.

Turton, H. (2005), *Measuring the Impact of Energy Technology Investment on Long-term Sustainability*, Report to the EC-sponsored SAPIENTIA Project, Interim Report IR-05-038, International Institute for Applied Systems Analysis, Austria.

Turton, H. and L. Barreto (2004), *The Extended Energy-Systems ERIS Model: An Overview*, IR-04-10, International Institute for Applied Systems Analysis, Laxenburg, Austria.

Turton, H. and L. Barreto (2006), 'Long-term security of energy supply and climate change', *Energy Policy*, **34**, 2232–50.

Turton, H. and F. Moura (2006), 'Vehicle-to-grid systems for sustainable development: an integrated energy analysis', *Technological Forecasting and Social Change* (submitted).

Turton, H. and L. Barreto (2007), 'Automobile technology, hydrogen and climate change: a long-term modelling analysis', *International Journal of Alternative Propulsion*, **1**(4), 397–426.

U.S. DoE (2001), *Analysis of the Climate Change Technology Initiative: Fiscal Year 2001* [online], available at http://www.eia.doe.gov/oiaf/climate/, accessed June 2005.

U.S. DoE (Department of Energy) (2005), *Hybrid Vehicles Tax Incentives* [online], available at www.fueleconomy.gov/feg/tax_hybrid.shtml, accessed June 2005.

UK Department of Transport (2002), *Attitudes to Local Bus Services* [online], available at http://www.transtat.dft.gov.uk/tables/2002/fperson/busloc02.htm, accessed March 2005.

UK HM Revenue and Customs (2007),'Company cars–guidance for employees' [online], available at http://www.hmrc.gov.uk/helpsheets/ir203.pdf, accessed January 2007.

UN (United Nations) (1987), 'Our common future', *Report of the World Commission on Environment and Development*, also known as *Brundtland Report*, UN General Assembly 42nd Session, 4 August.

UN (1997), 'Overall review and appraisal of the implementation of Agenda 21', *Earth summit +5*, 21–23 June, New York.

UN (1998), *World Population Projections to 2150*, Population Department, United Nations Department of Economic and Social Affairs, New York.

UN (2004), *World Population to 2300*, Population Division, Department of Economic and Social Affairs, United Nations, New York.

UNDP (United Nations Development Programme) (2004), *Human Development Report 2004*, United Nations Development Programme, New York.

UNFCCC (United Nations Framework Convention for Climate Change) (2005), *Essential Background – Kyoto Protocol* [online], available at http://unfccc.int/essential_background/kyoto_protocol/items/2830.php, accessed June 2006.

US Department of Energy (USDOE) and US Environmental Protection Agency (USEPA) (2003a), *Fuel Economy Guide Model Year 2004*, http://www.fueleconomy.gov/feg/FEG2004.pdf, accessed 1 December 2003.

US Department of Energy (USDOE) and US Environmental Protection Agency (USEPA) (2003b), 'Fuel cell vehicles', <http://www.fuel economy.gov/feg/fuelcell.shtml>, accessed November 2003.

US EPA (2003), 'International analysis of methane and nitrous oxide abatement opportunities: report to energy modelling forum', Working Group 21, U.S. Environmental Protection Agency, June 2003, available at http://www.epa.gov/nonco2/econ-inv/pdfs/methodologych4.pdf and http://www.epa.gov/nonco2/econ-inv/appendices.html.

US EPA (2004), *Protecting the Environment Together: Energy Star and Other Voluntary Programs*, 2003 Annual Report, http://www.epa.gov/appdstar/pdf/cppd2003.pdf.

Verhoef, E. (1996), *The Economics of Regulating Road Transport*, Cheltenham, UK and Northampton, MA, USA: Edward Elgar.

Vine, E., P. du Pont and P. Waide (2001), 'Evaluating the impact of appliance efficiency labelling programs and standards: process, impact, and market transformation evaluations', *Energy*, **26**(11), 1041–59.

VTPI (Victoria Transport Policy Institute) (2006), *Transport Demand Management Encyclopedia* [online], available at http://www.vtpi.org/tdm/index.php, accessed June 2006.

Wachs, M. (2003), *Improving Efficiency and Equity in Transportation Finance*, The Brookings Institute, Washington, DC.

Wallstrom, M. (2004), *Community strategy to reduce CO_2 emissions from passenger cars*, Letter to the Chairman of the Committee on the Environment, European Policy, European Commission, Brussels.

Wang, M. (2001), 'Assessment of well-to-wheel energy use and greenhouse gas emissions of Fischer–Tropsch diesel', Centre for Transportation

Research Argonne National Laboratory Report, prepared for Office of Technology Utilization, Office of Transportation Technologies, U.S. Department of Energy, Washington, DC.

WBCSD (World Business Council for Sustainable Development) (2004), *Mobility 2030: Meeting the challenges to sustainability*, Full Report 2004, The Sustainable Mobility Project, World Business Council for Sustainable Development, Geneva, Switzerland.

Webb, K. (1999), 'Voluntary initiatives and the law', in R. Gibson (ed.), *Voluntary Initiatives: The New Politics of Corporate Greening*, Peterborough: Broadview Press, pp. 32–50.

Weiss, M.A., J.B. Heywood, A. Schafer and V.K. Natarajan (2003), 'Comparative assessment of fuel cell cars', MIT LFEE 2003-001 RP, Massachusetts Institute of Technology, Cambridge, MA.

Weiss, M., J.B. Heywood, E.M. Drake, A. Schafer and F. Au Yeung (2000), 'On the road in 2020: a life-cycle analysis of new automobile technologies', Energy Laboratory Report# MIT EL-00-003, Massachusetts Institute of Technology, Cambridge, Massachusetts.

Weitzman, M.L. (1974), 'Prices vs. quantities', *The Review of Economic Studies*, **41**(4), 477–91.

Williams, R.H., M. Bunn, S. Consonni, W. Gunter, S. Holloway, R. Moore and D. Simbeck (2000), 'Advanced energy supply technologies', in *World Energy Assessment: Energy and the Challenge of Sustainability*, Chapter 8, UNDP/WEC/UNDESA (United Nations Development Programme, World Energy Council, UN Department of Economic and Social Affairs), Washington/New York.

WWF (World Wildlife Fund) (2000), 'Will voluntary agreements at EU level deliver on environmental objectives?', paper at *UNEP Voluntary Initiatives Workshop*, September.

Yagishita, T. and S. Ueda (2003), 'Recent expansion of bioenergy utilization in Japan – subjects and countermeasures', paper presented at IEA Bioenergy Task 29 workshop 18–20 June, Streatley, United Kingdom.

Zahavi, Y. and A. Talvitie (1980), 'Regularities in travel time and money expenditures', *Transportation Research Record*, **750**, 13–19, National Research Council, Washington, DC.

Index

AAMA (American Automobile Manufacturers Association) 12, 33
abatement 110, 241
  comparison of impact from vehicle production and operation 141
  marginal costs of 143
  optimal emissions abatement level 110–11
  and voluntary agreements 184
abatement costs 134, 185
ACEA (European Automobile Manufacturers Association) 248
ADL (Arthur D. Little Inc. report to DOE) 60, 65
aerodynamics, improved 198
AFDC (Alternative Fuels Data Center) 40, 41, 42, 44, 47
Airbus 62
air transport 9, 73, 76
  commercial hydrogen aircraft 62
  energy demand 8, 231
  in ERIS model 58
  and EU Emissions Trading Scheme 137–8
Alberini, A. 183
Albrecht, J. 140, 141
alcohol fuel cell vehicles 79, 229
alcohol fuels 74, 90, 231
  from biomass 70, 232
alcohol or petroleum FVC with on-board reformer 47
alcohol vehicles with ICEs 41–3
Alexander, M. 117
alternative fuels 40–43, 113, 125–6
  excise duty exemption 161
  tax policies 160–61
aluminium, in car manufacture 142
American Council for an Energy-Efficient Economy 176

'Analytical Methods of Road Transport Sector Strategies to Reduce Greenhouse Gas Emissions', OECD 113
annual circulation tax 145–7, 150–54
anthropogenic climate change 2
Argote, L. 62
Arnott, R. 168
Asia
  GHG emissions 249
  two-wheeled vehicles 12
  see also Japan, China
atmospheric composition 2
Australia
  agreement with automobile industry 193
  excise duty exemption on biofuels 161
  National Average CO_2 Emissions (NACE) targets 193
Ausubel, J.H. 16
autonomous energy efficiency improvements (AEEIs) 83
auto-thermal reformers 65
average standard value system 119
  Japan 120
Azar, C. 16

Banerjee, J. 174
Baranzini, A. 191
Barreto, L. 1, 29, 30, 32, 57, 62, 65, 88, 89, 94, 143, 218, 233
barriers, to the deployment of advanced passenger car technology 240–42
battery electric vehicles 44–5, 250
Bergmann, H. 139
Bevilacqua Knight Inc. 46
biodiesel 42–3, 250
  Japan 127, 128
  USA 128